The *Summa musice* is a treatise on practical music from *c.* 1200. A manual for young singers who are learning Gregorian chant, it provides a compact but comprehensive introduction, in a mixture of prose and verse, to notation, performance and composition.

There are chapters on the history of Christian chant, on plainchant and on polyphony – the last being a precious account of unwritten and improvised traditions. The two authors of the treatise provide a revealing glimpse of what might be called the 'intellectual style' of medieval thought about music. Indeed, the *Summa musice* is an introduction to medieval culture: what educated people thought worth knowing about music; how they reasoned when they discussed musical questions.

This book provides an edition of the original Latin text, taken from the only surviving manuscript, together with an English translation, introduction and editorial commentary.

CAMBRIDGE MUSICAL TEXTS AND MONOGRAPHS
General Editors: Howard Mayer Brown, Peter le Huray, John Stevens

The series Cambridge Musical Texts and Monographs has as its
centres of interest the history of performance and the history of
instruments. It includes annotated translations of important
historical documents, authentic historical texts on music, and
monographs on various aspects of historical performance.

CAMBRIDGE MUSICAL TEXTS AND MONOGRAPHS

General Editors: Howard Mayer Brown, Peter le Huray, John Stevens

Summa musice

O decus. o lybie regnum. kartaginis urbem. O lacerandac fratris
opes. o punica regna. O duces frigios. o dulces aduenas. quos tanto tem
pore dispsos equore. iam hiemps septima iactauerat ob odium iunonis.
Scilla tabies. cyclopum sanies. sceleno pessima traduxerat ad solium
dydonis. Qui me crudelib; exercent odiis. arentis lybie post casum
frigie. quos regno naufragos excepam. me miseram. quid feci. que me
is emulis. ignotis populis. & genti barbare sydonios & tyrios subieci.
Achidolant. achidolant. iam uolant carbasa. iam nulla spes dydoni.
ue tyrus colonis. Plangite sydonii. quod more gladii. deperii. p amo
rem frigii predonis. Eneas hospes frigius. hyarbas hostis tyrius.
multo me temptant crimine. sed uario discrimine. nam sitientis
lybie. regina spreta linquitur. & thalamos lauinie troianus hospes
sequitur. Quid agam misera. dydo regnat altera. hai uiri nimium.
mors agit ee teta. Deserta sitis regio. me grauii cingit prelio. fra
tris me terret ferritas. & numadum crudelitas. insultant hoc puer
no. dydo se fecit helenam. regina nro gremio. troianum fouit ad
uenam. grauis odimo. furiosa ratio. si mala pseram p benefi tio.
Anna uides. que sit fides deceptoris pfidi. fide ficta. me relicta.
regna fugit punica. nil sorori. nisi mori. soror resta unica. Seuit
scilla. nec tranquilla se pmittunt equora. Soluit ratem. tempe
statem. nec exhorret uiguus. Dulcis soror. ut quid moror. aut qd
cessat gladius. Fulget sydus orionis. seuit hyemps aquilonis.
scilli regnat equore. tempestatis tempore. palinure n secure.
classem soluit littore.

O decus, O Libie regnum, the lament of Dido, whose music is mentioned in the
Summa musice and described as a setting that matches its text because it is 'low-
lying and ponderous' (lines 2136–9). Munich, Staatsbibliothek, MS Clm. 4598,
f. 61r–v (c. 1200, from the Tirol). The poem O decus, O Libie regnum is also
preserved among the Carmina Burana.

THE *SUMMA MUSICE*:
A THIRTEENTH-CENTURY
MANUAL FOR SINGERS

EDITED, WITH TRANSLATION AND INTRODUCTION

CHRISTOPHER PAGE

Sidney Sussex College, Cambridge

The right of the
University of Cambridge
to print and sell
all manner of books
was granted by
Henry VIII in 1534.
The University has printed
and published continuously
since 1584.

CAMBRIDGE UNIVERSITY PRESS
Cambridge
New York   Port Chester
Melbourne   Sydney

Published by the Press Syndicate of the University of Cambridge
The Pitt Building, Trumpington Street, Cambridge CB2 1RP
40 West 20th Street, New York, NY 10011–4211, USA
10 Stamford Road, Oakleigh, Melbourne 3166, Australia

First published 1991

Printed in Great Britain at the University Press, Cambridge

British Library cataloguing in publication data

Summa musice: a thirteenth-century manual for singers.–
   (Cambridge musical texts and monographs).
   1. Chants, history
   I. Page, Christopher
   782.3222

Library of Congress cataloguing in publication data

Summa musice. English & Latin.
   Summa musice: a thirteenth-century manual for singers /
   edited with translation and introduction by Christopher Page.
      p.   cm. — (Cambridge musical texts and monographs)
   Formerly misattributed to Johannes de Muris.
   Includes bibliographical references and index.
   ISBN 0-521-40420-7 (hardback)
      1. Music – Theory – 500 – 1400 – Early works to 1800.   2. Chants
(Plain, Gregorian, etc.) – Instruction and study – Early works to
1800.   3. Singing – Instruction and study – Early works to 1800.
I. Page, Christopher.   II. Muris, Johannes de. ca. 1300-ca. 1350.
III. Title.   IV. Series.
MT5.5.S913   1991
782.32′22 – dc20   91-8948

ISBN 0 521 40420 7

DL-T

For singers everywhere, but especially for:

Margaret Philpot
Rogers Covey-Crump
Leigh Nixon
John Mark Ainsley
Charles Daniels
Rufus Müller
Andrew Tusa

Contents

Preface

Geoffrey Chaucer, in *The Prioress's Tale*, relates how a young boy went to school to learn 'doctrine', that is 'to syngen and to rede'. Learning his Latin from the Psalms and prayers in the Primer, the boy hears the other children singing *Alma redemptoris mater* as they 'lerned hire antiphoner'. The kind of schooling which Chaucer describes in this Tale was the foundation of many productive clerical lives spent in the cloister, in the cathedral close or in the service of a magnate. To sing and to read: that was the 'doctrine' that promising young boys were taught in medieval Europe, and a man of clerical education never became so grand that he outgrew the simple compliment of the Old French poets: *il scet bien lire et chanter.*

The purpose of this book is to provide a new text and translation, briefly introduced and succinctly annotated, of a manual written *c.* 1200 for masters teaching boys to sing plainchant and to appreciate Latin eloquence. The work of two authors whose names have hitherto been obscured,[1] it is a practical manual which has been known since Gerbert's pioneering edition of 1784 as the *Summa musice.* It is remarkable for many things, not least for its highly unusual form comprising prose chapters followed by versified treatments of the same teaching using a wealth of

---

[1] Their names are Perseus and Petrus. In the unique manuscript of the treatise, the scribe attributes the *Summa musice* to 'Johannes de Muris, as I believe', but the words 'as I believe' (*ut credo*) were later deleted and Gerbert duly ignored them. As a result, he attributed the *Summa musice* to Johannes de Muris, with whose name it has long been associated. On the question of authorship see below.

figurative language. Among the many sections of special interest
are a chapter on polyphony and several chapters on composition.
There are practical hints for performers of chant, and the treatise
also refers to musical instruments in an unusually informative
manner, discussing the way in which they are tuned and
mentioning their use in the training of novices. Every subject is
approached in a practical fashion for the benefit of schoolboys, but
the work also reveals a profound awareness of the history of
Christian music from the first reed pipes of shepherds around the
beginning of the world, through the virtuosi of Antiquity such as
Orpheus and Amphion, to Fathers such as Gregory, and on to the
present. This historical perspective gives a rich and persuasive
context to the technical details discussed in the text, making the
Summa musice a vivid document of plainchant theory and practice
around 1200. With its quotations from Classical poets, its echoes of
Christian Latin authors such as Prudentius, and its use of
grammatical terminology side by side with newer terms and
concepts drawn from Aristotle, the Summa musice restates the right
of music to be regarded as a fundamental training for young minds
in a clerical world poised between the literary learning of the
twelfth century and the logical rigours of the thirteenth.

Despite its interest and importance, the Summa musice has
received little attention since Gerbert published an imperfect text
of it in 1784.[2] Riemann certainly read the treatise,[3] as did Peter
Wagner[4] and Heinrich Besseler.[5] Isolated passages from the Summa
musice have also been used in various textbooks and monographs,[6]
while a few extracts have been cited in studies of medieval

---

[2] Gerbert, Scriptores, III, pp. 190–248. Gerbert's text is discussed below in Chapter
    4.

[3] Riemann's remarks on the treatise, together with significant annotations by
    Haggh, can be read in the latter's translation of Riemann's study, History of
    Music Theory, pp. 201–3 (including a complete translation of Chapter XXIV,
    concerning polyphony) and p. 389.

[4] Einführung in die Gregorianischen Melodien, II, Neumenkunde, p. 172.

[5] 'Studien zur Musik des Mittelalters', II, p. 207.

[6] Including, for example, Fleischer, Die germanischen Neumen, pp. 50 and 57, n. 3;
    Floros, Universale Neumenkunde, II, p. 184; Hibberd, 'Musica Ficta and
    Instrumental Music', pp. 220f; Page, Voices and Instruments, pp. 117, 133, 211,
    216; and Warren, 'Punctus Organi and Cantus Coronatus', p. 130.

instruments.[7] The chapter on polyphony, with its description of several techniques which seem to lie somewhere between composition and improvisation, has attracted the attention of at least one ethnomusicologist.[8] Otherwise, the *Summa musice* seems to have been almost completely neglected, as may be judged by the fact that a recent authoritative survey of verse and prose in medieval Latin treatises on music before *c.* 1280 fails even to mention it.[9]

The text has not been re-edited since Gerbert, nor has there been an English translation of the treatise (nor a translation into any language as far as I am aware). Having now attempted both I can well understand why others may have been reluctant to undertake the task. In many places the text of the *Summa musice* presents severe problems; during the course of preparing this edition I found that a large number of highly contracted words in the manuscript (and many convoluted constructions in the Latin) threatened to retard progress indefinitely. Only at the last minute, for example, did I realise that *pmti* in the manuscript was to be expanded as *Predicamentis,* that is to say as a direct reference to the *Categories* of Aristotle. A search through the medieval Latin translations of the Philosopher eventually uncovered the passage in question.

Preparing the translation proved no easier labour, for in some places, and especially in the metrical sections, the *Summa musice* is brutally difficult. In offering a new edition with an English translation I have incurred many debts. Professor John Stevens read many sections of the introductory chapters and translation with characteristic care and attention. I am also grateful to Professor Howard Mayer Brown, who long ago gave me the advice that finally helped me obtain a microfilm of the manuscript which contains the *Summa musice* after my years of trying without success. Roy Gibson checked the entire translation; how he must have rejoiced to return to his chosen author, Ovid! I am responsible, of course, for any mistakes that remain. Professor Miles Burnyeat

---

[7]   Including, for example, Bachmann, *The Origins of Bowing,* pp. 80 and 107; and Page, 'The Medieval *Organistrum* and *Symphonia,* II, Terminology', pp. 75–6.

[8]   Gerson-Kiwi, 'Drone and *Dyaphonia Basilica*'.

[9]   Yudkin, *De musica mensurata.* This book was published too late for me to take full account of it.

clarified several airy allusions to Aristotle in the text of the treatise. Professors Barry Dobson and D. W. Lomax gave me their advice about the Spanish military order of St Iago. Dr John Caldwell, Dr David Chadd and Professor Jill Mann kindly gave their advice on certain knotty points. Duane Lakin-Thomas and Dr Ann Lewis gave me much practical help and advice, as did my wife, Régine.

Abbreviations

AH	*Analecta Hymnica medii aevi*, ed. G. M. Dreves, C. Blume and H. M. Bannister, 58 vols. (Leipzig, 1886–1922)
AM	*Antiphonale monasticum* (Tournai, 1934)
AR	*Antiphonale sacrosanctae Romanae Ecclesiae* (Paris, Tournai, Rome, 1949)
AS	*Antiphonale Sarisburiense*, ed. W. H. Frere (London, 1901–25)
BHL	Bibliotheca Hagiographica Latina
CB	Carmina Burana
CSM	Corpus Scriptorum de Musica
DMA	Divitiae Musicae Artis
GB	*Graduel de Bénévent avec prosaire et tropaire,* Paléographie musicale, 15 (Tournai, 1937–53)
GR	*Graduale sacrosanctae Romanae Ecclesiae de tempore et de sanctis* (Paris, Tournai, Rome, 1952)
GS	*Graduale Sarisburiense*, ed. W. H. Frere (London, 1894)
HGJ	*Hucbald, Guido and John on Music,* trans. W. Babb and ed. C. Palisca (New Haven, 1978)
LA	*Antiphonaire monastique (XII siècle): Le codex 601 de la Bibliothèque Capitulaire de Lucques,* Paléographie musicale, 9 (Tournai, 1906–9)
LR	*Liber responsorialis* (Solesmes, 1895)
LU	*Liber Usualis* (Tournai, 1961)
PM	Processionale monasticum (Solesmes, 1893, R 1949)
SYG	*Le Codex 903 de la Bibliothèque Nationale de Paris (XIe siècle): Graduel de Saint-Yrieix,* Paléographie musicale, 13 (Tournai, 1925–30)

VP   *Variae preces ex liturgia tum hodierna tum antiqua collectae*
      (Tournai, 1901, R 1939)
WA   *Antiphonaire monastique (XIIIe siècle): Le codex F.160 de la*
      bibliothèque de la cathedrale de Worcester, Paléographie
      musicale, 12 (Tournai, 1922–5)

Intervallic notation in the *Summa musice*

The *Summa musice* employs the standard gamut, dividing the letter series into three parts as follows (Latin, lines 803–10):

1

The Authorship of the Treatise

Like many writings of the Middle Ages, the *Summa musice* survives
in a 'late' manuscript copied by a scribe whose interest in the
material before him was partly that of a collector and antiquarian.
The treatise is known from one manuscript, now number 264/4 of
the Archiv des Benediktinerstiftes in St Paul in Lavantthal. A paper
manuscript, dating from the early years of the fifteenth century or
possibly from the very last years of the fourteenth,[1] it could be
French and may be Parisian.[2] Two scribes can be traced in it, the
copyist of the *Summa musice* being the main hand; unfortunately,
his work is inelegant and so highly contracted that it is very

---

[1] Michels, *Notitia artis musicae*, pp. 31–4, gives an inventory of the contents of the
manuscript and places the hands in the early fifteenth century, a judgement
with which I concur. The manuscript must date from after 1394, for ff.70–78
carry a copy of a letter from the University of Paris to the King of France, dated
to that year. For a convenient selection of close parallels, compare Paris, Bibl.
Univ. 216 (1388, no indication of provenance), Mazarine 3476 (1390, no
indication of provenance) and Arsenal 522 (a. 1395, Soissons), reproduced in
Samaran and Marichal, *Catalogue des manuscrits en écriture Latine*, I, plates LXb,
LXIa, LXVIIa. Compare Brown, *A Guide to Western Historical Scripts*, plate 39
(Erfurt, 1390). The kind of large textura which the scribe uses for the verse
passages of the treatise was increasingly restricted in the fifteenth century to
liturgical manuscripts of large format and to elementary schoolbooks (Bischoff,
Latin Palaeography, p. 134). The scribe's choice of script is therefore a
judgement upon the content and character of the treatise. There is also an
inventory and description of the manuscript in Koller, 'Aus dem Archive des
Benediktinerstiftes', pp. 41–5. Koller dates the manuscript to the fourteenth
century. Unfortunately the writing of the manuscript is now too faded for
photographic reproduction here.

[2] As suggested by Michels, *Notitia artis musicae*, p. 31. The evidence is weak,
however. The letter from the University of Paris mentioned in the previous

difficult to read in many places. Gerbert remarks upon these difficulties in the third volume of his *Scriptores* where he prints the text of the *Summa musice* and indeed of most of the other treatises in the codex. Little is known for certain about the history of the book prior to his time.[3]

Ulrich Michels has already provided a description and inventory of the manuscript.[4] In addition to the *Summa musice*, the book contains all or part of several treatises by Johannes de Muris, the remarkable *Tractatus de differentiis et gradibus cantorum* by Arnulf de St Ghislain, a fragment of the second chapter of Franco's *Ars cantus mensurabilis* and some minor pieces. One of these, on f.30v, incorporates a few metrical lines of the *Summa musice*.[5] Most of these materials reflect a fully developed taste for the apparatus of scholasticism with its formal *questiones* pursuing an ideal of thorough and dispassionate enquiry. Johannes de Muris was a master of this manner as applied to the theory of music, and the scribe attributes the *Summa musice* to him – quite wrongly, as we shall see, for the treatise is a work of a very different sort.

By *c.* 1400, when the manuscript was copied, it had already become impossible to name the author of the *Summa musice* with any certainty. The scribe closes his copy with the words 'Here ends the *Summa* of Master Johannes de Muris, as I believe' (*ut credo*). Another hand has deleted the words 'ut credo' and Gerbert duly ignored them; as a result the text passed into his monumental anthology of 1794 as *Ioannis de Muris Summa Musicae*. Most of the scholars who have ever cited the treatise have accepted this attribution to Johannes de Muris, and only in the later part of this century has it become customary to speak of the *Summa musice* as the work of an anonymous theorist.[6]

note, the appearance of a brief treatise on ff.29v–30 by one Ptolomeus de Paris (printed in Gerbert, *Scriptores*, III, pp. 284–5) and the scribe's obvious taste for the formalities and language of scholasticism, add little weight to the argument.

[3] Gerbert says that the manuscript had been recently sent to him from Paris (Gerbert, *Scriptores*, III, p. 189). Compare BN, fonds latin 7370.

[4] Michels, *Notitia artis musicae*, pp. 31–4.

[5] The notes are printed by Gerbert (*Scriptores*, III, p. 303). The passage quoted corresponds to lines 206–7 in the Latin text edited below, with a slight textual variant noted and discussed in the apparatus.

[6] For example, Haggh, *History of Music Theory*, p. 389; Michels, *Die Musiktraktate*, pp. 116–17 and Warren, 'Punctus Organi and Cantus Coronatus', p. 130.

Smits van Waesberghe, however, saw no reason to regard the work as anonymous. Leafing through the treatises in a British Library manuscript he noticed an allusion to a *Summa Iohannis*, and with a leap of faith that can only astound less agile minds he concluded that the *Summa* in question was none other than our treatise. From that moment on he regularly referred to it as the *Summa Iohannis*. [7]

All of this – from the scribe to Smits van Waesberghe – would seem to be mistaken, for the author of the *Summa musice* names himself three times. He first appears at 611–17:

It may also be asked why these syllables [*ut, re, mi, fa, sol, la*], rather than others, are the names of the six aforesaid degrees of the hexachord, that is to say: why are these letters put into the syllables? Some would reply that this arrangement is fortuitous and without any rational basis, but I do not believe that. PERSEUS says that some people, seeking some consolation for their incompetence, declare that the positions of the parts of speech are fortuitous...

Could Perseus be the author of the *Summa musice?* One thing is certain: he is not the Roman satirist of that name whose surviving works contain no such remark as the one cited here. More to the point, however, is that the name Perseus is introduced immediately after a personal intervention by the author:[8]

I do not believe that. PERSEUS says...

Perseus appears again at 1985–9:

7 Smits van Waesberghe, 'Some Music Treatises and their Interrelation', p. 107. This identification is accepted and repeated in the volumes of the series *Divitiae musicae artis* prepared under the auspices of Smits van Waesberghe (see DMA. A. II, pp. 39 and 64f; A.Xb, pp. 45–6 and 58).

8 It is not unusual for Latin authors of the twelfth and thirteenth centuries to speak in the first person and then to move abruptly (as it may seem to modern taste) into the third person by using their own name. Compare, for example, the *Integumentum Ovidii* of Johannes de Garlandia, where Johannes speaks in the first person and then moves immediately into the third (Ghisalberti, *Integumentum Ovidii*, p. 31).

Chant is performed badly through powerlessness by old men, by boys and by the infirm, and this is a venial thing because natural inability excuses such people, whence PERSEUS teaches that 'a fault arising from Nature is not to be mocked'.

We do not find the last words of this passage in the writings of the Classical Perseus.

A third and final reference to Perseus (2222–3) leaves little doubt that he is the author of the text and also demonstrates that the question of authorship in this treatise is resolved by a surprising answer. In the Metrum that accompanies Chapter XXII there is a reference to the way in which some composers of chant put a distinctive stamp upon their compositions. 'Sometimes', the text continues (and we must remember that this is a metrical section):

writers of poems also fix a special, gracious mark in books. PERSEUS and PETRUS are taught to observe this, for they adorn their verses with their tokens (*signa*).

This reads like an authorial 'signature' in which Perseus (and now someone called Petrus of whom we have heard nothing so far) draw attention to themselves by putting their own special *signa*, surely their names, into the poetry. The *Summa musice* would not be unique as a plainchant treatise of the thirteenth century by *two* authors,[9] and there seems no need for any Johannes, be he Johannes de Muris or another. The *Summa musice* was most probably written by Perseus and Petrus.

Of Petrus we can say nothing, for his name was shared by tens of thousands. With his colleague, however, we have better hope of success, for the name Perseus appears to have been extremely rare in the twelfth and thirteenth centuries.

Let us begin with the homeland of the *Summa musice*. Peter Wagner placed the text in Germany because of an apparent

---

[9] See the Mettenleiter Anonymous II – or rather *anonymi*, since the treatise appears to have been compiled by two monks of Hailsprunne in 1295. It is probably of no special significance that the *Summa musice* sometimes evokes a single author with first person pronouns ('I have frequently noticed...') and sometimes uses plural pronouns ('We are ready to end this book here').

reference to staffless neumes. In the event this is incorrect, for Wagner misconstrued the passage (see the Appendix for a discussion of the lines in question). More recently, Ulrich Michels has added a further consideration in his book on the treatises of Johannes de Muris, for there he observes that the *Summa musice* refers to the inhabitants of German territory as *Teutonici*, a usage which, in his view, marks the author of the treatise as German.[10] This is not a persuasive argument, however, for the word 'Teutonici' was used throughout Europe in the twelfth and thirteenth centuries.[11]

In the year 1949 the *Summa musice* made a sudden journey northwards to Liège when Smits van Waesberghe published an article on a set of music treatises supposedly emanating from a 'school' in the region of that city, the *Summa musice* among them.[12] Although his article represented a great advance in the classification and analysis of the treatises he considered, subsequent research has done little to strengthen his putative Liège school and something to weaken it. The principal text in Smits van Waesberghe's group is the *De musica* of John 'of Affligem' (*c.* 1100), to which the *Summa musice* owes a significant debt. Smits van Waesberghe placed it firmly in the tradition of his Liège school, and yet in recent years Palisca, Gushee and Huglo have argued strongly – to my mind irresistibly – that John was working 'between St Gall and Bamberg',[13] and the question naturally arises whether the *Summa musice* might have been written nearby.

There is some important evidence in the passage of the *Summa musice* concerning solmisation syllables. John says that *ut, re, mi, fa, sol* and *la* are used by the English, the French and the Germans but

[10] *Die Musiktraktate*, p. 17.

[11] I am most grateful to Anne-Marie Bautier of the Comité du Cange for consulting as yet unpublished materials from the *Novum glossarium* on my behalf and for giving me her opinion on this point.

[12] Smits van Waesberghe, 'Some Music Treatises and their Interrelation', p. 107.

[13] HGJ, pp. 87–100, provides an excellent discussion and summary of the evidence, to which should now be added the contrary views of Huglo, 'L'auteur du traité de musique dédié à Fulgence d'Affligem'. Huglo concedes that the diffusion of John's treatise, the authors whom John cites, the mnemonic chants that he employs, and certain other chants cited in his treatise and Tonary pertain indisputably to a Germanic tradition.

not by the Italians who employ different syllables, and 'those who wish to learn them may arrange to do so with these people'.[14] Perseus and Petrus go further, however, and in lines 577–81 they extend the list of nations as shown in italics:[15]

The French, the English, the Germans, the *Hungarians, the Slavs, the Danes* and others on this side of the Alps use these names for the hexachord degrees. The Italians, however, are said to use other degrees and names; inquire of them if you wish to know what they may be.

This list proves that Perseus and Petrus were not writing in Italy; it also suggests that the German Empire was their home. Denmark lay immediately to the north of the Empire; the kingdom of the Hungarians was situated to the south-east; the Slavs lay to the east (the Kingdom of Poland). All of these realms shared a common boundary with the German Empire of *c.* 1200 and defined its borders for virtually the whole of its northern, eastern, and south-eastern extent.

The authors' use of the word 'organistrum' (414, 1114 and 1216) also points to Germany; the term has become thoroughly naturalised in modern scholarship, but a survey of its use in medieval sources suggests that it was principally employed in areas of High and Low German speech.[16]

It may also be significant that the *Summa musice* cites the antiphon *O gloriosum lumen* (1506, 1561), a chant with a predominantly German distribution.[17]

A somewhat sharper focus may perhaps be provided by the reference at 2139 to a Latin song beginning *O decus, O Libie regnum.* This can be identified as a poem in the celebrated *Carmina Burana* collection, probably copied *c.* 1225–30, either in Bavaria or South

---

[14] Smits van Waesberghe, *Johannis...De musica*, p. 49; HGJ, pp. 103–4.

[15] For 'the Danes' the Latin text has *Dacis*. 'Dacia' was originally the name of a province of the Roman Empire north of the Danube, but it was habitually used during the Middle Ages as the Latin name for Denmark, or indeed for Scandinavia in general. 'The Scandinavians' would therefore also be an acceptable translation, and one that does not affect the argument being developed here. See *Dictionary of Medieval Latin from British Sources*, 'Dacus'.

[16] Page, 'The Medieval *Organistrum* and *Symphonia*, II, Terminology', p. 84.

[17] Huglo, 'L'auteur du traité de musique dédié à Fulgence d'Affligem', p. 16.

Tirol; Carinthia (where the manuscript of the treatise now lies) has also been suggested.[18]

We are led in the same direction by the authors' discussion of the intervallic notation of Hermannus Contractus (1148f). They took it from John 'of Affligem', no doubt, but their interest in this system suggests that they considered it to be of importance. As Palisca remarks, this notation 'was short-lived and geographically confined', and it points to southern Germany and Switzerland.[19]

There is one further reason for favouring Germany as the homeland of the *Summa musice*, and that is the identity of the mysterious Perseus. A search of *Gallia Christiana*, of published obit registers and other extensive lists has succeeded in producing only two individuals named Perseus, and *both* of them spent their lives in the same place within a few years of one another.

The place is Würzburg and the Cathedral of St Kilian. Würzburg, situated in Bavaria, would do well as a location for the *Summa musice*. Following Palisca and Huglo, we have been assuming that John 'of Affligem' wrote his *De musica*, a text to which the *Summa musice* is deeply indebted, in the area between St Gall and Bamberg; Würzburg is some forty-five miles west of Bamberg. A Bavarian provenance accords with the authors' mention of the Latin song *O decus, O Libie regnum* (2139); we have already seen that this elaborate *cantio* has been preserved in the *Carmina Burana* collection, either compiled in Bavaria or in a more southerly region where the Bavarian colouring of the vernacular was marked.

The archives of the cathedral of St Kilian, now in the Bayerischen Hauptstaatsarchiv in Munich, reveal two individuals named Perseus (sometimes written Persius), both of whom were deacons of the cathedral. The earlier of the two was already deacon in 1163, and by 1165 he is listed as 'Magister Persius summus decanus';[20] he died in 1182 or 1183.[21] The younger Perseus first

---

[18] Steer, '*Carmina Burana* in Südtirol', with a comprehensive review of previous opinions. The poem *O decus, O Libie regnum* is CB 100, preserved in other manuscripts of *c.* 1200 (including one with staffless neumes, see Frontispiece) all from what is now Austrian territory. See Hilka and Schumann, *Carmina Burana*, notes to CB 100.

[19] HGJ, p. 151, n. 7.

[20] Amrhein, *Reihenfolge*, p. 83.

[21] *Ibid.*

appears, in 1182, as Perseolus, 'little Perseus', no doubt to distinguish him from his senior namesake; by 1195 he is listed as a canon; in 1205 he is *Perseus maioris ecclesie Wirzeburc decanus* involved with the administration of the hospital for the poor facing the bishop's palace.[22] By 1206 he is *decanus* and by 1207 *maior decanus*. He died between 1215 and 1217.[23]

These dates, running from *c.* 1160 to 1215–17 are somewhat surprising, for since the days of Gerbert the *Summa musice* has generally been regarded as a product of the fourteenth century. Only Riemann, as far as I am aware, has suggested that the content of the treatise would accord with a twelfth-century date.[24] If one of the two deacons from Würzburg was indeed an author of the *Summa musice* then it would appear that Riemann was right, and that the text must be moved back in time as much as a century.

What are the objections to a date of *c.* 1160 to 1215? Above all there are the references to a certain Salomon (28 and 1157) who is mentioned in the company of famous theorists such as Odo and Guido. If this is Elias Salomon, whose *Scientia artis musice* was completed in 1274, then the older and the younger Perseus need concern us no further. However, the identification of the Salomon mentioned in the *Summa musice* with Elias Salomon has troubled several readers of the treatise, including Smits van Waesberghe who proposes an alternative candidate of the eleventh century, while Joseph Dyer, sharing these doubts, warns that the Salomon of the treatise may be the biblical King of Israel.[25] These objections

---

[22] *Monumenta Boica*, XXXVII, number 132 (1182), number 152 (1195) and number 167 (1205).

[23] *Monumenta Boica*, XXXVII, number 169 (1206), number 171 (1207) and numbers 189 and 195 (1215–18, when Perseus is replaced by Iringus).

[24] *Geschichte der Musiktheorie*, p. 237. Haggh, *History of Music Theory*, p. 202, renders Riemann's observation thus: 'one must not overlook the fact that the entire treatise deals only with *musica plana*...and that according to its contents it could definitely be dated in the twelfth century, since not a single word mentions the existence of mensural music, and the term "discantus" is not even used'.

[25] For Smits van Waesberghe's doubts see *DMA*. A. Xb, p. 58, and for those of Dyer, 'A Thirteenth-Century Choirmaster', pp. 86–7. There seems to be nothing to recommend Smits van Waesberghe's candidate (a bishop of Liège who died in 1048). Dyer's objection, that the *Summa musice* attributes a remark to a Salomon who is clearly the biblical King of Israel (at line 42), carries very little weight, since it is inconceivable that the authors of the *Summa musice*

are not persuasive ones, however, and there is a prima-facie case for identifying the Salomon of lines 28 and 1157 with Elias Salomon. Nonetheless, there is always the possibility that these references to a certain Salomon are interpolations. As we shall see, the *Summa musice* incorporates a number of interpolations ranging from short passages to an entire chapter. The name Salomon only appears in lists of theorists; such passages were perhaps particularly susceptible to revision by scribes who wished to bring the list up to date or who sought to insert the name of a theorist whose writings they knew.

A second objection to a date of *c.* 1200 rests on the final chapter, number XXV. In opposition to Riemann, who suggested that the content of the *Summa musice* poses no objection to a date in the 1100s, Heinrich Besseler pointed to this final chapter where there are several references to the Franciscans and the Dominicans.[26] The foundation of the Franciscan Order dates from 1209, while the founding chapter of the Dominicans was held in 1216; there is no possibility that a reference to these Orders could appear in a twelfth-century text.

The true import of chapter XXV is somewhat different, however, for it provides evidence that the *Summa musice* was indeed written during the early years of the thirteenth century. The point missed by Besseler, by Smits van Waesberghe and by other commentators, is that chapter XXV, which mentions the friars, is a later addition. Here are the headings of the last three chapters as they accompany those chapters in the manuscript:

XXIII   Que sint vicia in novo cantu cavenda
XXIV   De poliphonia
XXV   Integumentum musice

imagined King Solomon as having played a part, with Odo, Guido and Hermannus Contractus, in the development of staff notation (see line 1156). Clearly, we are dealing with at least two Salomons: a theorist (lines 28 and 1157) and the King of Israel (line 42). It is perhaps worth emphasising that the name Salomon was not a rare one in the twelfth and thirteenth centuries. When John 'of Affligem' imagines a group of singers arguing about the ways in which they have been taught by their various singing masters, 'Master Solomon' is one of the names that he employs (Smits van Waesberghe, *Johannis...De musica*, p. 134; HGJ, p. 147).

[26] 'Studien zur Musik des Mittelalters', II, p. 20, n. 2.

There are reasons for supposing that Chapter XXIV, concerning polyphony, was originally the final one. As they begin it, the authors clearly feel that the end is now in sight (2297–8):

Nunc autem huic operi finem proponentes imponere

while its Metrum ends at 2386 with an abrupt and valedictory announcement that 'we are ready to end this book here'. Furthermore – and I take this to be a revealing detail – Chapter XXV is not listed in the scribe's table of the chapters in the treatise. Since the scribe, who was working *c.* 1400, cannot possibly have composed Chapter XXV himself (for it contains a reference to the Templars, dissolved in 1312), we can only assume that he was copying from an exemplar whose list of chapters had not been revised from its original state to accommodate the added chapter, number XXV. If we subtract that chapter from the list given above we find that the final section is now the one devoted to polyphony, as in the treatise to which the *Summa musice* is so deeply indebted, the *De musica* by John 'of Affligem'.

When was Chapter XXV added to the *Summa musice*? The reference to the Templars establishes 1312 as a *terminus ad quem*, but there is evidence that the chapter is significantly older than that. The Templars are mentioned as the author presents a review of the nineteen grades of society corresponding to the nineteen degrees of the gamut. The following are the grades which he compares to the seven *graves* of the gamut, presented in ascending order of excellence (2525–30):

The laity living in charity...Itinerant pilgrims...the Order of Brothers with the Sword...the Templars...the Hospitallers...the Trinitarians...the Teutonic Knights...the Order of lepers.

The lepers, often spoken of in the Middle Ages as persons marked out for the special favour of God,[27] are placed in the supreme position, but otherwise this list is dominated by the monastic military orders all of which were involved in crusading activities on

---

[27] On this view of leprosy in the later Middle Ages see Le Grand, *Statuts d'Hôtels-Dieu et de Léproseries*, pp. xxvi–xxvii.

various frontiers. The Templars were founded to meet the needs of the Latin Kingdom of Jerusalem, while the Hospitallers began as a fraternity serving a hospice for poor and sick pilgrims in the Holy City. The Knights of the Teutonic Order, created in the Holy Land in the wake of the Third Crusade, 'became the spearhead of German penetration of the Baltic lands, making themselves in the process a major territorial power in eastern Europe'.[28] The Trinitarians were regular canons of a kind, whose principal objective was to release Christian captives from heathen hands.

This leaves one group unidentified. Who are the Brothers with the Sword? It is conceivable that they belong to the Spanish Order of St Iago, founded in the twelfth century and sometimes called the Order *de spata*, meaning 'of the sword';[29] but why should the author of this second-layer chapter have put *one* Spanish military order of monks into his list when there were several others, equally powerful and distinguished? Why no order of Calatrava or Alcántara? A more plausible interpretation, I suggest, is that the Brothers with the Sword are the knights universally known to modern historians as the Swordbrothers (in Middle High German of the thirteenth century, *schwertbruder*).[30] This Order was confirmed by Pope Innocent in 1204 and its task was to advance the Christian cause in the province of Livonia around Riga bay.

There is one crucial detail in the history of the Brothers with the Sword: their Order was dissolved in the year 1237.[31] On 12 May

---

[28] Lawrence, *Medieval Monasticism*, p. 175.

[29] I am most grateful to Professor R. B. Dobson, of Christ's College, Cambridge, and Professor D. W. Lomax, of the University of Birmingham, for advice concerning the Spanish orders.

[30] On the Order of the Brothers with the Sword, see von Bunge, *Der Orden der Schwertbrüder*; Benninghoven, *Der Orden der Schwertbrüder*; Christiansen, *The Northern Crusades*; and Urban, *The Baltic Crusade*. The principal contemporary source for the history of the Order is Henry of Livonia's chronicle; the text is edited in Bauer, *Heinrici Chronicon Livoniae*, and translated in Brundage, *The Chronicle of Henry of Livonia*. A second major source, compiled in the last years of the thirteenth century, is translated by Smith and Urban, *The Livonian Rhymed Chronicle*. For the term 'schwertbrüder' used in thirteenth-century vernacular chronicles see Hirsch and others, *Scriptores Rerum Prussicarum*, III, p. 540; IV, p. 73; and V, p. 73.

[31] On the dissolution of the Order see Benninghoven, *Der Orden der Schwertbrüder*, p. 369f. The last Swordbrother can be traced in Riga in 1259, by which time he was already seventy years old.

that year the Brothers were formally received into the Order of Teutonic knights, having first 'laid down their own emblems ... those who had been called the Swordbrothers ... exchanged their emblem for a cross'.[32] If this identification is correct, then it allows us to date the second-layer chapter of the *Summa musice*, number XXV, with some accuracy. It must have been composed before the dissolution of the Brotherhood of the Sword in May 1237, but the references to the Franciscan and Dominican friars could scarcely have been written much before 1225, even though the foundation of those Orders can be placed earlier.

This argument sheds new light upon the date of the *Summa musice* and the question of whether Perseus of Würzburg (junior or senior) could have been one of the two authors of the treatise. If a supplementary chapter was added to the end of the text between *c.* 1225 and 1237 then it is obvious that the *Summa musice* must have been in existence before that time, and this brings us to within a few years of the death of Perseus junior between 1215 and 1217. Now is the moment to remember Riemann's judgement that 'according to its contents [the *Summa musice*] could definitely be dated in the twelfth century'.[33] Perseus and Petrus seem to know nothing of any mensural notation (1124–5), and their discussion of polyphony in Chapter XXIV shows no trace of what might be crudely termed 'Notre Dame' terminology: no *motetus, conductus, copula* nor even *discantus*. They discuss the meanings of the term 'tenor' but show no awareness of any polyphonic sense of the word (1821–40). As for their use of Aristotle, all the references to the Philosopher that I have been able to identify in the *Summa musice* pertain to works available in Latin versions by 1200.

In conclusion, the evidence suggests that the *Summa musice* was composed, perhaps around 1200, by two authors named Perseus and Petrus, the latter unknown but the former perhaps to be identified with one of the two *decani* of that name at the cathedral of Würzburg.[34]

---

[32] The quotation is from the Livonian Rhymed Chronicle (Smith and Urban, *The Livonian Rhymed Chronicle*, p. 28).

[33] See n. 24 above.

[34] The surviving noted liturgical books from the cathedral of Würzburg are inventoried in Wegner, *Kirchenjahr, passim*, but there are no sources even roughly contemporary with the *Summa musice*.

2

The Scope and Character of the Treatise

The *Summa musice* is a practical manual for teaching boys to sing from plainchant notation. Like the *Disticha Catonis,* a famous collection of schoolroom maxims which is quoted almost verbatim in the first lines of the work, the *Summa musice* is a schoolbook.[1] We can also read it as a literary work designed to kindle a flame of devotion to Christian history and to the writings of the Ancients: Horace, Ovid, Virgil and more besides. The literary ambitions of the *Summa musice* are plain enough in the authors' decision to construct their treatise from passages of prose alternating with versified and highly figurative statements of the same information (of which more below), but it is also part of the literary nature of the *Summa musice* that it is such a *verbal* work. There is not a single table or diagram of the sort to be found in other treatises on music theory; there is only one musical example and the authors refer to their reluctance to mix musical notation and prose (1935–6).

Perseus and Petrus have also pruned away most of the thorny terms and topics of chant theory. They never use the Greek string-terminology which gives many treatises an alarming appearance

---

[1] On Cato as a basic treatise for the study of grammar and morals see the remarks of Alexander Nequam, approximately contemporary with the *Summa musice:* 'After the boy has learned his ABC and is imbued with other boyish rudiments, let him then learn Donatus and that useful compendium of morals which the common herd thinks is the work of Cato...'. Translation from Hunt, *The Schools and the Cloister,* p. 35. See also Lapidge, 'The Study of Latin Texts', p. 102 and p. 131, n. 34.

('proslambanomenos', 'hypate meson', and so on) nor the accepted terms for mathematical relations and proportions like 'sesquitertia' and 'superbipartiens'. They never broach the kind of speculative topics that pleased the fancy of some theorists (a comparison between neumes and the metrical feet of Classical prosody, for instance), and they avoid certain questions, such as the division of the semitone, which lead so many other theorists into technicalities. They even dispose of the monochord, so often thought of today as the essential tool of medieval music theory, with a few words of blunt good sense: 'not everyone owns a monochord, nor is one always readily available' (864–5).

This is not to say that the *Summa musice* is an easy read. Despite assurances in the text that the treatise is designed for the use of boys, the Latinity and literary style of the work are such that there are many passages of a highly compressed and difficult kind. In line after line of verse the *Summa musice* seems to be undoing its own stated purpose: to 'say small things to the small'.[2]

If we are troubled by that discrepancy, however, then we do well to remember that the subjection of richly literary texts such as Ovid's *Ars amatoria* and Horace's *Ars poetica* to the rudimentary skills and understanding of young boys is one of the most curious and recurrent aspects of medieval schooling.[3] We should also remember the role of the schoolmaster, the *magister*, who wields the rod in medieval depictions of schoolrooms and who would have directed his pupils in their study of the *Summa musice* with a firm hand.[4] The only one with a copy of the work, he would read the treatise aloud, probably sentence by sentence, and the pupils would be asked to construe the Latin, having written the dictated passage upon a slate. Like all medieval schooltexts, therefore, the *Summa musice* would have been experienced first (and perhaps foremost) by its young readers as a sustained exercise in Latin grammar. Since much of the *Summa musice* is composed in verse and expressed in highly figurative terms, this would be an exercise

---

[2] 'Parvis parva loquor' (line 49).

[3] On the classroom study of Horace and Ovid see Friis-Jensen, 'Horatius liricus et ethicus'; Botschuyver, *Scholia in Horatium*; Hexter, *Ovid and Medieval Schooling*; and Olsen, *L'étude des auteurs classiques*.

[4] For a medieval illustration of a schoolroom – and of a master who is not sparing the rod – see Smits van Waesberghe, *Musikerziehung*, plate facing p. 5.

in grammar in the fullest medieval sense of that word, implying not merely the study of accidence but also, for example, the careful analysis of figures of speech.[5] In accordance with the usual medieval explanation of the usefulness of verse in teaching – that verse is more memorable than prose – we may suspect that the rhyming hexameters of the *Summa musice* are composed to be learned by heart.[6] This is not to say, however, that they are intended to yield their meaning quickly. Many of them are riddling formulations of what has already been expressed in prose, designed to extend the pupils' Latinity and to enhance their ability to interpret the figurative language of poetry.[7]

If the students could not arrive at the meaning themselves then the *magister* would expound the verses. Some theorists explicitly call for this classroom technique. The author of the treatise which Coussemaker published under the title *Cuiusdam carthusiensis monachi Tractatus de musica plana* quotes some verses very similar to those in our treatise and adds that 'these verses should be expounded for the benefit of the young in the following way'.[8] A prose explanation follows.

Approached in this way the *Summa musice* might well occupy a great deal of schoolroom time, and it becomes easier to understand the character of the treatise when it is viewed in this

---

[5] A substantial number of figures of speech and grammatical or stylistic faults are named in the *Summa musice* (ellipsis, macrologia, nugatio, antonomasia and synecdoche, for example), and the concepts which some of them embody are adapted to create a vocabulary for describing the melodic characteristics of chant (2242, 2258, 2261–2). There could scarcely be a more vivid illustration of the medieval tendency to think of plainchant theory as a kind of applied Grammar.

[6] For the use of verse in the Middle Ages as an aid to the memorisation of teaching see Godman, *Alcuin: the Bishops, Kings and Saints of York*, pp. lxxviii–lxxix (on the *opus geminatum*, i.e. the tradition of works in two paired parts, one in verse and the other in prose, and the uses of verse). See below Chapter 3, n. 5.

[7] The more difficult lines in the Latin are given in footnotes to the translation. The precise meaning of some of them will probably never be known.

[8] Coussemaker, *Scriptorum*, II, p. 44. Such expositions could be given in the vernacular, to judge by a passage in the most long-lived of all medieval versified treatises, the grammatical treatise entitled *Doctrinale* (*c.* 1200) by Alexander de Villa Dei. Alexander invites the schoolmaster to expound difficult passages *laica lingua*.

light. Presenting a compact history of music from its invention to the present day, adorned with choice excerpts from Classical poets, from the Bible and from Aristotle, the *Summa musice* is not just an introduction to the performance of plainchant but is also, in a modest way, a glance down the contents page to the book of clerical culture.

However, in contemplating the greater purpose of the *Summa musice*, we should not forget that Perseus and Petrus are practical musicians who are proud to own that the aim of their art, whatever its devotional purpose, is principally to produce delight, a point they make with both clarity and candour (1496–7). They seem to admire at least one chant, indeed, precisely because its beauty arises from what is technically an irregularity.[9] The centre of that art is liturgical chant, and they are aware of its long history in which oral and written transmission have intertwined (389). They also know how to teach it; we can hear the sounds of the choirschool in their advice that a novice singer should look at each note in his music and continue to sing it until sure of the next, for that was how a singer could train his eye and ear to recognise the intervallic steps from one neume to another (1205–7). In the same way, it is surely practical experience that prompts them to advise singers with poor voices to play instruments with lettered keys such as the organistrum, organ and (here it finds a place) the monochord (1210–19).

The first half of the *Summa musice* relates how staff notation emerged after generations of evolution reaching back to the Flood. It is an exhilarating story told by two writers who share a deep relief and satisfaction that it is over. There is relief because obscurity has been dispelled by light, and there is satisfaction because, whatever the reverence due to Antiquity, the gradual progress of knowledge means that the youngest in time always have the clearest sight (185–6). It is from this position of strength that Perseus and Petrus offer a conspectus of music history.

What sense of the past do we find in the treatise? The Ancient World is shadowy indeed, evoked only by its mythical musicians, Orpheus and Amphion. The feeling for what we would now call Late Antiquity is weaker still; even Boethius is evoked only once as

---

9   This is the responsory *Letetur omne seculum*, discussed at lines 1491 and 1549.

a theorist (167), although his presence as a philosopher and poet is more strongly registered (236–40). The Gregorian legacy is the only one that Perseus and Petrus acknowledge; their 'Ancients' seem to be the anonymous singers of the early Middle Ages, perhaps 700–900, who inherited the Gregorian legacy and studied how they might fix it with notation. Perseus and Petrus have some sense of a contemporary tradition in secular music, at least with regard to instrumental practice, and it lacks the disdain which some other theorists express for what they regard as the uninformed and instinctive music of minstrels and the common people.[10]

This belief in what music truly is, and of what it is for, results in an apotheosis of the voice that colours the musical aesthetic of the twelfth and thirteenth centuries. According to Chapter V, the first thing which the ancient fathers of Christian music did was to examine the physiology of the larynx (472–5). This allowed them to colonise three principal areas of pitch for chant according to the capacity of the human voice, namely the *graves*, *acute* and *superacute*.

The supremacy of the human voice over all other instruments is made plain in the *Summa musice* (420–23), as in other music treatises of the Middle Ages.[11] In part, no doubt, its wellsprings lie in the special place of the voice in all human expression and transaction. It is also a belief in the unique power of the voice to embody the gift of reason which God had given Man to raise him above all other creatures (462f). The belief in the voice was also a matter of taste, however, for there is evidence that until *c.* 1300 the artistic horizons of instrumental and vocal music were differently placed and that the tessituras of musical instruments were often set relatively high, at least in comparison to male voices.[12] Until *c.* 1300, and perhaps long after, the great creative journey of medieval musicians and composers was essentially a vocal odyssey, just as the history of music, as it is written in the *Summa musice*, is a

---

[10] Compare, for example, the dismissive comments in the *Dialogus* (*c.* 1000), formerly attributed to Odo of Cluny (Gerbert, *Scriptores*, I, p. 256).

[11] Compare the remarks in the *Speculum musice* of Jacques de Liège (Bragard, *Jacobi Leodiensis Speculum musicae*, I, p. 54): 'Art imitates nature; there is no small musicality in voices which instruments can never match'.

[12] Page, *Voices and Instruments*, p. 138.

history of what the voice did best when turned to its supreme purpose.

The sense of history which Perseus and Petrus bring to their treatise is also a sense of melody. To know the history of music from 'around the beginning of the world' to the present was to appreciate the great tradition of chant. It stood approved by the greatest minds. As an anonymous theorist of *c.* 1000 explains: 'the kind of music that we are expounding here is proved to be perfect with a sweeter, truer and more natural harmony in the judgement of the most expert musicians and the most holy men'.[13]

The plainchant theorists of the Middle Ages were usually individuals of an academic cast of mind (as we would now term it) who had come to care deeply for the traditions of chant. A delight in the vocal melody of chant, a profound sense of the spirituality of its purpose and a fierce pride in their own musical learning often made them purists of an implacable sort. They could barely endure the knowledge that the chants in their books contained errors introduced by the faculty of the human mind which they admired least: spontaneous impulse, *motus animi.* They were textual critics of a kind, who thought in terms of tradition and emendation.[14] All the while, however, their passionate pedantry was inflamed by the enormous difficulties they faced in bringing the material which they loved under any kind of systematic control. The theorists of the tenth and eleventh centuries, in particular, were deeply conscious of the multifarious traditions created by the unreliability of staffless neumes and by the fallibility of human memory; the anonymous author of the *Dialogus,* composed *c.* 1000, believed that he had encountered a singer who knew the 'antiphoner of St Gregory' in an unusually pure form, and there he found that nearly everything was perfectly regular.[15] Such men were rare, at least in the judgement of the theorists.

It is in this spirit of passionate pedantry that Perseus and Petrus devote Chapters XIV–XX to the hierarchy of pitches in a mode, understood to be a stylistic profile for melody defined by the habitual use of certain melodic gestures (especially opening and closing gestures), by a certain tessitura and by the pull of various

[13] *Dialogus* (Gerbert, *Scriptores,* I, pp. 275–6).
[14] *Ibid.,* pp. 251 and 162.
[15] *Ibid.,* p. 251.

degrees in the scalar outline of the mode. The aim of these chapters is to produce singers who can identify the mode of any chant, but a great deal more is involved than a facile ability to file chants away into rigid categories. Modal identification in this context is the key to a complex set of controls and relationships within the corpus of the chant repertoire. An informed singer who can assign a chant to its mode – even if irregularities in the melody demand that the classification be a tentative one – will nonetheless have a sense of the melodic behaviour appropriate to it in terms of compass, tessitura and closing gesture, and he will be able to remove damage done by corruption and caprice. He will also know how to compose a chant properly. If the chant is one that is followed by recitation – as an antiphon is followed by a psalm – then a secure modal classification will enable the singer to match them correctly.

The *Summa musice* elaborates a complex hierarchy of pitches. The most important are the four modal finals *D*, *E*, *F* and *G*. Next come the affinities *a*, ♮ and *c*, all placed a fifth above their finals (save the highest final, *G*, which has no affinity) and used as substitutes for them in several contexts, but 'principally because of a necessity created by the semitone'.[16] These are followed by the initial notes permitted to chants in each mode, and then the lowest and highest acceptable notes. Taken together these points of definition establish the 'constitution' (*lex*) of the mode and its 'regular range' (*cursus*).

Perseus and Petrus now introduce the concept of tessitura. In Chapter XVII they explain that the distinction between the authentic and plagal form of a mode is not simply a matter of the extreme pitches which can be allowed in each case: it also depends upon how often a chant ascends or descends into a certain region of pitch.

It is in this context that Perseus and Petrus make (or at least pass on) a notable contribution. In Chapter XVIII they explain what they call the *claves discretivas*, the 'distinguishing notes'. These help a singer to classify a chant as either authentic or plagal by giving him a systematic (indeed a statistical) way of measuring its

[16] Chapter XV, *passim*. See Pesce, *The Affinities*.

tessitura. These distinguishing notes, all placed on the little finger of the Guidonian hand, are *F* for the Protus, *G* for the Deuterus, *a* for the Tritus and ♮ for the Tetrardus. Consider the example of the Protus: to the extent that a chant of the Protus has more notes above *F* than below, then to that extent it is authentic; to the extent that it has more notes below *F* than above, then to that extent is plagal. So it is for the other modes.

This system has been called mechanical,[17] but it is actually quite flexible. In proposing it, Perseus and Petrus implicitly acknowledge that a definitive classification of chants is often impossible precisely because many melodies resist mechanical methods of classification. One must therefore speak of modes which do not belong to either an authentic or a plagal category but nonetheless *tend* in a certain direction.

The issue of modal classification, which has dominated Chapters XIV–XVIII, is completed and finally diffused in Chapter XIX, one of the longest and most complex of the treatise. To sense the presence of a mode in any given chant, Perseus and Petrus now expand the concept of a modal function from the individual pitch to the formula: a group of pitches whose disposition, while highly variable, is nonetheless perceived as variation rather than essential difference.

They begin with the *tropus*, or 'turn'. The 'turn' is a brief melodic formula that establishes the modal affinity of a chant so decisively that it overrules all other, previous modal indications. No matter how the chant has been behaving up to that point, when the 'turn' appears one must yield to it and take the mode from there: 'cedere nos oportet'. A very clear example of the 'turn' is provided by the responsory *Gaude Maria* (1774), cited as a chant that begins and continues showing the characteristics of mode III, but which ends in mode VI; this chant opens with a rising fourth *G–c* characteristic of mode III, but comes to a close on *c*, the substitute final of the Tritus and an unmistakable signal of that mode (described at 1444–6). The clarity and decisiveness of such a 'turn' is its most important quality, and in the judgement of ears profoundly attuned to the idioms of chant it often introduced a change of modal quality so strongly felt that only a violent

[17] See *Grove 6*, 'Mode'.

language of twisting and bending could express the effect (*retorqueo, retorsio, conversio*).

The modal taxonomy of the twelfth and thirteenth centuries rests principally upon the ways in which chants come to a close, and since a 'turn' has the power to evoke a mode so decisively it must be principally regarded as a form of closure. A 'turn' can appear at the beginning of a chant, and then there will be no effect of 'twisting'; it can also appear in the middle, but it pertains 'chiefly to the region around the end' (1760). It is the very last melodic movement significant enough to be recognised as a phrase (1870).

Next, the authors explain what they mean by a *tenor*. The concept which they proceed to explain at 1821–49 is an inheritance from later eleventh- and twelfth-century theory. In short, it is that the reciting note of a Psalm Tone, which varies from mode to mode, exercises a control over all chants belonging to that mode.[18] In a sense this is no more than a rationalisation of what happens in practice. When an antiphon, for example, was followed by a psalm ending in the *Gloria patri* (followed in turn by a repetition of the antiphon), then the singer's sense of the pitch relationships within the antiphon would be filtered through the recitation note used for the psalm. When Perseus and Petrus speak of the *tenor* they mean both the reciting tone used for the psalm and the closing formula of the *Gloria patri*. Already in the *Micrologus* of Guido of Arezzo we find that the reciting notes of the psalm tones are regarded as the upper limit for the first note of a chant and for the last notes before a pause during the course of a chant, but in the *De musica* of John 'of Affligem' we find an author who mingles aspects of Psalm Tone and mode. The *Summa musice* adopts this doctrine, for Perseus and Petrus speak of the *tenor* as something 'holding a chant within the bounds of its mode'

---

[18] For a discussion of this doctrine see the article by Powers cited in the previous note. In a great deal of plainchant theory from the twelfth century on there is a clear sense that chants such as sequences, which never have to be dovetailed into any musical situation involving recitation, are thereby somehow irregular because they lie beyond the reach of a powerful and orthodox control. See, for example, Johannes, *Metrologus*, pp. 80–81, and *Commentarius Anonymus in Micrologum Guidonis Aretini*, pp. 127 and 145.

(1823–4). This is the concept found in John's treatise and aptly described by Powers:[19]

The addition of the tenor to the final and the initials further refines the hierarchy of single pitch modal functions, for it implies that one among the secondary strong points has a certain limiting power and governance over the others; it is the one which in fact is the upper limit of theoretical possibilities for a resting point, and it is to be established by reference to the Psalm-tone tenor.

The result is that the *Summa musice* describes a complex hierarchy of single pitches in a mode, those for the authentic Protus being shown in Example 1.

Example 1: The structural notes of the authentic protus according to the *Summa musice*

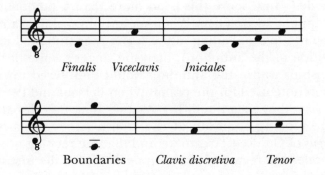

These controls may seem somewhat mechanical, and it is their fate to appear so when presented in schoolmasterly Latin. To singers of *c.* 1200, however, who had memorised and internalised vast amounts of chant, and who were profoundly familiar with the characteristic turns of related melodies, these means of distinguishing chants would surely have been recognised as the distillation of wisdom and experience.

The formal study of music is useful, say Perseus and Petrus, because a skilled musician can 'compose new and correctly formed

---

19 *Grove 6*, 'Mode'.

chant, can judge the same and can emend music that is not correctly formed' (224–5). Composition has pride of place in this list of skills, and the sections of the *Summa musice* which deal with composition and the 'expressive' properties of chant are among the most arresting in the treatise. To some extent, no doubt, the theorists who emphasise the importance of composition (for Perseus and Petrus are by no means alone in doing so) are responding to the great wave of liturgical composition whose principal monument is the corpus of rhymed offices composed between 1000 and 1300; several passages in the theorists tend to confirm this view.[20] Nonetheless, as early as *c.* 1100 John 'of Affligem' recognised that his readers might live in religious communities which did not need new compositions, and that any composers among them would therefore turn to non-liturgical Latin poetry.[21] Whatever the external circumstances, it is plain that the theorists' interest in new chant sprang from a distinctly theoretical preoccupation. These writers had gradually evolved a large body of theory which was complex, to be sure, but was nonetheless a kind of simplified drawing of chant, comprehensible (and deeply satisfying) because it was firm in outline. It was clear to anyone who investigated the matter that the drawing was very sketchy indeed. By discussing composition, however, the theorists surely hoped to inspire composers to follow it so that theory and practice would match down to the finest line.

For the most part this was a matter of modal control. The prescriptive counterpoint manuals of Western tradition, with their tables of 'good' and 'bad' practice, have their origin in the increasingly rigorous language which theorists of the eleventh and twelfth centuries used to define what a chant of any mode may do: how far it may rise, how low it may descend, what notes it should iterate, what notes it should rarely touch and so on.[22]

---

[20] See, for example, *Cuiusdam carthusiensis monachi Tractatus de musica plana* (Coussemaker, *Scriptorum*, II, p. 444): 'Moderni tamen in compositione cantuum ecclesie...imo volentes cantum historialem de aliquo sancto vel festo componere...'. The importance of composition is stressed by a number of plainchant theorists. See, for example, *Commentarius Anonymus in Micrologum Guidonis Aretini*, p. 99, and the Schneider Anonymous, p. 113.

[21] Smits van Waesberghe, *Johannis...De musica*, p. 116; HCJ, p. 137.

[22] For such precepts and instructions about good and bad compositional practice see especially the Seay Anonymous, pp. 28f.

Legislation of this kind is easy to formulate; it is not so simple to find a language which can describe the aesthetic and expressive effects of music. The search for such a language is not a major preoccupation of the *Summa musice*, nor perhaps of any medieval essay on music, but there is nonetheless an aesthetic terminology of a kind within the text, and one that deserves a closer look.[23]

On the lowest level of description, the *Summa musice* displays what is perhaps one of the most fundamental of all the associations which the mind is accustomed to make between sound and feeling, for Perseus and Petrus associate a lower tessitura with texts whose matter is sad (*tristis*) or arduous (*laboriosus*), and a higher tessitura with texts whose matter is joyful (*leta*). The relatively loose muscular movements which are required to sing lower pitches, and the slower vibrations of lower frequencies, naturally evoke the feelings which many languages convey with metaphors of weight: 'bent down with sadness', 'heavy with care' and so on. The complex metaphorical existence of a word like Latin 'gravis' ('low in pitch, of grave consequence') shows how tightly woven these patterns of associations can be.

It would be easy to regard the vocabulary and conceptual range of the *Summa musice* (and of other medieval treatises) as very narrow in this respect, and as one that does little more than acknowledge the instinctive associations that we have been describing. That would be unwise, however. The primary contrast between joy and sadness is the essential scheme of Christian feeling and the contrast can hardly be avoided when Mankind is set before a God who offers the prospect of infinite welcome or infinite rejection. 'Tristis es anima mea'; 'Letatus sum': Christian affective piety is strongest in the delights of love or in the pain of separation, and it is no surprise to learn that when medieval singers withdrew from the repertory of chant far enough to contemplate it in objective terms then they found the language of joy and sorrow immediately to hand and that they rarely looked futher.

Singers who had drawn a vast amount of chant into their memories would surely have been more conscious of formulaic structures that loosely united vast areas of the repertoire than of

[23] The essential starting-point for any consideration of the issues raised in the following pages is now Stevens, *Words and Music in the Middle Ages, passim.*

individual word/music relationships in specific chants. Indeed, the theorists hardly ever comment on such relationships; when they draw attention to a detail in a chant it is almost invariably a musical one and there is rarely any suggestion that the salience of the musical detail promotes a salience in the text at the corresponding point.

If the evidence of the plainchant treatises is any guide then we may suspect that the language most medieval singers instinctively chose to distinguish one chant – considered as both words and music – from another would have been founded upon generic or external contexts rather than upon internal particularities. It might be a biblical context, as when Perseus and Petrus speak of the antiphon *Doleo super te* where David laments the death of Jonathan (2138), or perhaps the liturgical context, as when they describe the joyfulness of chants during the time of Epiphany (2145f). Or it might be the context of genre, as when the authors say that all tracts should possess a lamenting quality (2140f). Most of the time, we may imagine, medieval singers were not stirred out of their habitual sense of ritual and duty to contemplate their chants in aesthetic or affective terms.

While it may be valid to insist on the essentially general terms in which medieval singers perceived the relationship of words and music in chant, there are clear signs in the *Summa musice* that singers sometimes drew distinctions in matters of words and music which are not only fine but also too fine for a modern listener who has not been immersed in chant since childhood. We have seen that Perseus and Petrus distinguish a category of chant whose textual material is *leta*, 'joyful'; their ruling is that texts of that kind should have melodies which range among the *acute*. They go on to say, however, that some texts are not only *leta* but also *iocosa*, 'jesting', or 'humorous', and that such words should have melodies with leaps in them (2143–9). They clearly expect the distinction between *leta materia* and *leta et iocosa materia* to be reflected in the music.

Here is one example of a text which they judge to be *leta*, or 'joyful' (2146):

Surrexit pastor bonus qui posuit animam suam pro ovibus suis et pro suo grege mori dignatus est.

The good shepherd arose [from the dead] who laid down his life for his sheep and was deemed worthy to die for his flock.

There is no difficulty in sharing the view that this text is joyful; it states the fundamental truth and mystery of Man's salvation. As for the setting, Perseus and Petrus recommend it as one that matches its joyful subject by moving frequently among the *acute*. They also praise it for the melodic repetition over the words 'pro ovibus', something which may be heard, they say, with delight; however, they do not suggest that this melodic felicity enhances the words 'pro ovibus', nor even that it projects the meaning of the text as a whole in any way (2255–6).

Here, for comparison, is a text which Petrus and Perseus cite as one whose matter is not only joyful but also *iocosa*: an antiphon employed for the feasts of St John the Evangelist and St John ad Portam Latinam (2149):

Propter insuperabilem evangelizandi constanciam exilio relegatus divine visionis et allocucionis meruit crebra consolacione relevari.

On account of the unstoppable constancy of his evangelising, sent away into exile he merited that he be raised up with the abundant consolation of divine vision and speaking.

The setting is one that Perseus and Petrus recommend because it matches the quality of its text with leaps (*cum saltu*, 2147). It is difficult indeed to discern what is *iocosa* in the text of this antiphon. Its simple assertion that an indefatigable preacher was rewarded might well be cause for joyfulness. Thus it is *leta*. At the same time, however, it cannot now be confidently judged as 'jesting', 'humorous', 'droll' or 'facetious', and there we nearly exhaust the usual dictionary definitions of *iocosa*. Furthermore, the melodic leaping which Perseus and Petrus praise is virtually confined to the opening movement of an otherwise conjunct melody, which may strengthen our suspicion that the melodic gestures which medieval singers regarded as 'expressive' in some way were often to be found at the beginnings of chants (though not only there), and that in drawing attention to these gestures the theorists are not necessarily revealing a conception of the whole chant, both words and music, in aesthetic or affective terms. As far as *iocosa* applied to this chant is concerned, we must be content to miss the distinction which Perseus and Petrus are making.

Their comments on the aesthetic properties of the modes provide an example of terminology which appears to be impressionistic but may have ascertainable substance. In Chapter XXII the authors describe how different people are pleased by different modes (2109–14):

it delights some to hear the fastidious and courtly wanderings of the first mode, others [to hear] the falling and dark profundities of the second. Some are more fortified by the austere and haughty dancing of the third; the sound of the fourth attracts some as if in a caressing and flattering way.

This passage, which continues until each one of the eight modes has been characterised, is one of the most colourful in the treatise; indeed, it is purple, and it is no surprise to find that our authors have borrowed it from a more characterful Latinist, John 'of Affligem'. Other theorists were also impressed by John's flights of rhetoric, and there are echoes of it throughout twelfth- and thirteenth-century theory.[24] What were the theorists impressed by? In large measure it must have been the rhetorical zest of John's passage, figurative at every turn. And what medieval author could resist an enumerated list of properties? Yet there may have been more to the theorists' admiration than a delight in verbal fancy. For example, the reference to the 'falling and dark profundities' of the second mode need not bewilder a singer who is familiar with figuration like this, common enough in mode II:

[24] See, for example, the Schneider Anonymous, p. 109, who is clearly much impressed by John's rhetoric.

Example 2: Opening of the introit *Ecce advenit* (II). Source: Tonary of John 'of Affligem'. See *Summa musice* 1499 and 1552.

Nor is the reference to the 'haughty dancing' of the third mode mysterious, given the frequency of movements like this in mode III:

Example 3: Opening of the responsory *Gaude Maria* (III, initially). Source: **WA** 271. See *Summa musice*, 1774.

Let us look more closely at one of the most perplexingly figurative phrases which Perseus and Petrus have borrowed from John: the 'courtly wanderings' (*curiales vagationes*) of mode I. We encounter the adjective 'curialis' elsewhere in the *Summa musice* where it is said that authentic modes characteristically descend to their final 'in a courtly and gradual fashion' (1684–5). Taken together, these references typify the generalising nature of medieval comments on the musical and aesthetic characteristics of plainchant, for here we find that an adjective which appeared to be a key term in characterising mode I is now applied to *all* the authentic modes. Nonetheless, this second instance of *curialiter* is revealing for Perseus and Petrus cite several chants which, in their judgement, descend 'in a courtly and gradual fashion'. Here are the closing figures of four chants which, according to their account, end in this way:

Example 4: Closing gestures of the antiphons (a) *Circumdantes circumdederunt me*, (b) *Nisi ego abiero*, (c) *Reges Tharsis*, and (d) *Volo pater*. All mode I.

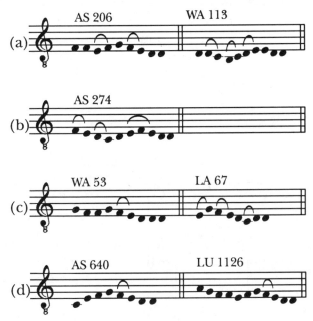

These examples suggest that a mode I chant moves 'in a courtly and gradual fashion' when it descends to its final in a conjunct fashion, never falling to the final through any greater distance than a tone. Indeed, it seems that the adverb 'paulatim', 'in a gradual fashion', is the equivalent of the modern 'conjunct' or 'stepwise', and is just as familiar a concept in this context as *saltus*, 'leap', which the authors employ elsewhere. But why should such melodic movement be called 'courtly'? Since 'curialiter' is an essentially impressionistic term in this context (which is what makes it interesting) it may be impossible to give more than an impressionistic answer to that question. Could it be, however, as Norbert Elias has emphasised, that courtly demeanour requires an appearance of calm, restraint and the concealment of abrupt or impatient impulses,[25] and that this is why the melodic movements above could be described as 'courtly'?

[25] *The Court Society, passim.*

Perseus and Petrus proceed to explain that just as an authentic chant moves in a courtly way, so a plagal chant tends rather to close 'by falling or tumbling' (1689). It is here, more than in any other passage of the treatise, that we sense the almost microscopic focus of terms which, at first sight, seem too impressionistic to allow any clarity of view. The authors cite the communion *Tu puer propheta* (mode II) as an example of a plagal chant which moves to its close by 'falling or tumbling':

Example 5: Closing gesture of the communion *Tu puer propheta*. Sources: **SYG**, 199; **GS**, m; **LU** 1502.

The only difference between this ending and the mode I closures listed above would seem to be that the interval of a minor third (*F* to *D*), inserted near the end of the chant, represents a departure from conjunct motion. That seems to be enough to establish a modal affiliation to ears trained during long hours to be especially sensitive to the close of chant. As Perseus and Petrus explain, 'a plagal chant inclines to its end more by falling and tumbling, as through a minor third or some greater interval' (1682–92).

The *Summa musice* appears to be the earliest medieval source to employ the term 'polyphony' (2295, 2299 and 2301) and the chapter which Perseus and Petrus devote to that art is one of the most curious parts of the entire treatise.

The authors describe five different polyphonic techniques, but with the exception of the term 'organum' there is no overlap with so-called 'Notre Dame' terminology. In place of 'discantus', 'motetus', 'conductus', 'copula' and the rest, Perseus and Petrus use terms which are neatly and consistently Greek in origin: 'diaphonia', 'triphonia' and 'tetraphonia'. As their names imply, these are techniques using two, three and four parts respectively. Within this scheme there is a distinction between techniques using a drone, called *basilica*, and techniques without a drone, invariably employing contrary motion, called *organica*. Since the descriptions of these techniques are often somewhat impenetrable (some of the details being only mentioned in the figurative language of the Metra) it will be well to summarise the information here.[26]

DIAPHONIA BASILICA: one singer holds a note continuously while another, beginning a fifth or an octave above, sings a *cantus*, now ascending, now descending, always agreeing in his pauses with the one who holds the foundation for him. This would result in a melody over a drone. Although it appears to be so simple, this is the only technique where the *Summa musice* does not mention the possibility of there being more singers than there are lines. The implication is that this was a technique for two singers only and it may therefore have been an improvised practice, or at least one in which the singer performing what the authors call *cantus* was given considerable freedom (perhaps in the matter of ornamentation) in performance. It should be emphasised that this is not a description of 'Parisian' organum purum under another name, for the lowest voice does not change in pitch at any time (2308–13; 2367–8).

DIAPHONIA ORGANICA: a two-part technique using contrary motion: 'one ascends, the other descends and vice versa'. They must come together when they pause, either on a unison, a fifth or an octave. The authors do not say whether the two parts move note against note, but a general comment at the close of the chapter has the revealing remark that in *organica* it often happens that 'the lower part has few notes and the upper part many; in those cases the few are to be protracted and the many sung rapidly' (2355–9). Although singular verbs are used ('one ascends, the other descends') this technique is a 'melodia duorum vel plurimum canentium' (2314–15) and can therefore involve more than two singers; it is also described as difficult: the instrument of the voice 'has to work hard' when performing it (2319). The text does not say whether one of the voices is derived from chant, and indeed

---

[26] These descriptions have attracted very little attention hitherto, although substantial extracts in translation (made from Gerbert's text) are offered in Haggh, *History of Music Theory*, pp. 202–3. See also Gerson-Kiwi 'Drone and *Dyaphonia Basilica*'. Their interest lies particularly in that they do not appear to relate in any direct manner to the central French tradition of polyphony (as observed by Besseler, 'Studien zur Musik des Mittelalters, II', p. 207), and that some of the techniques seem to be poised between improvisation and composition.

the polyphonic techniques in question would seem to be akin to the remains of twelfth-century organum associated with St Martial. The possibility that Perseus and Petrus envisage two (or even more) voices on the top line suggests that this technique is no longer improvisatory (or no longer purely so) and has proceeded to the ensemble execution of written compositions (2314–19; 2369–70).

TRIPHONIA BASILICA: a single note is sung by one or more individuals as a foundation. Beginning a fifth above the foundation note, one singer (or it may be several) performs a *cantus*; beginning an octave above the foundation, one singer (or again it may be several) performs the same chant. The result is a series of parallel fourths over a drone. There are no further specifications except that all the singers may end in unison with the foundation (2320–27; 2373–4).

TRIPHONIA ORGANICA: two independent lines are sung in contrary motion over a foundation sung in *notis pausatis,* presumably protracted notes but not all of the same pitch (i.e. this is not a drone but a relatively slow-moving lowest part). The middle part should begin a fifth, or perhaps a fourth, above the foundation, and the top part should begin an octave above the foundation. Any of the lines may have more than one singer, and the voices should all pause together either at the fifth or the octave. A final remark seems to allow for a more active lowest part and what is presumably note-against-note counterpoint in three parts (2328–38; 2375–6).

TETRAPHONIA: doubling of a *cantus* at the fifth, octave and twelfth, resulting in one kind of organum described in the *Musica enchiriadis* and in the *Scientia artis musice* of Elias Salomon (2339–45; 2377–84).

3

Sources and metrics

The authors of the *Summa musice* name all of their main sources except the most important: the *De musica* by John 'of Affligem'. As an introduction to the rudiments of chant, to the modes, to the rights and wrongs of chant composition, and finally as a brief compendium of polyphonic practice, the *Summa musice* owes a significant debt to John's treatise. As the list of sources given below will reveal, this indebtedness sometimes extends to the structure and even to the diction and syntax of some passages. These are relatively few in number, however, for even when they are following John, Perseus and Petrus often add illustrations or remarks of their own. They seem to owe relatively little in precise terms to the other theorists whom they name: principally 'Odo', Guido and Hermannus Contractus.

The non-musical sources are many. There are numerous references to Aristotelian treatises available in Latin by *c.* 1200, for example; those which are identified in the notes to this edition and translation include citations from the *Parva naturalia* (*De sensu et sensibilibus*), the *Ethica Nicomachea* (the books comprising the *Ethica vetus*), the *Topica* and the *Physica* (of which there is a very imperfect recollection at 883). These references point the way which learning was to go in the thirteenth century, but in the *Summa musice* they stand beside quotations from ancient poets that show the way which learning had come in the twelfth. Some of these were favourites with the grammarians and writers on poetry,[1] and

---

[1] Compare, for example, the texts edited in Faral, *Les arts poétiques, passim,* but particularly p. 186 (compare *Summa musice*, 2264–6).

they should give us pause if we are tempted to describe the *Summa musice* as a 'scholastic' work. Perseus and Petrus have absorbed some of the Aristotelian concepts which were systematically explored and elaborated by the schoolmen (the distinction between 'proper' and 'accident' is an example),[2] but they regard the logical techniques of Aristotle with the hostility which was sometimes felt by men of the early thirteenth century whose interests were mainly of a literary and schoolmasterly kind; in their judgement the syllogisms of the *Analytica priora* are only 'paralogical phantasies' (1025).

The union of verse and prose in the *Summa musice* is a schoolmasterly touch. 'We often speak twice on the same subject', says Quintilian in his *Institutio oratoria*, recommending to schoolmasters that they should set their pupils the task of paraphrasing verse into prose; 'brevity and copiousness each have their own peculiar grace, and the merits of metaphor are one thing and those of literalness another'.[3] The *Summa musice* exploits both qualities, for each chapter gives an account of its subject in prose and then follows it with a poem on the same topic, a *metrum de eodem*, sometimes expressed in densely metaphorical language. Viewed in these terms, the *Summa musice* begins to seem a greatly magnified version of what Janet Martin has described as the characteristic sentence of medieval Latin: '...the essential meaning is stated early, then elaborated; the movement is analytic and cumulative rather than synthetic and climactic'.[4]

The origins of the form which Perseus and Petrus have chosen for the *Summa musice* probably lie with the craze for versified manuals of elementary instruction which can be traced in the decades around 1200 and then well into the thirteenth century.[5] It

---

[2] See the Translation, n. 92. It is questionable whether the marginal terms 'questio', 'obiectio', 'solutio' descend from the authors' text or whether they were added by the scribe who (to judge by the other works that he copied in the manuscript) clearly had a taste for such things. These marginalia have been given the benefit of the doubt in this edition and retained, together with the frequent marginal marking *nota*.

[3] X:V, 7–8.

[4] 'Classicism and Style in Latin Literature', p. 545.

[5] For verse instruction it is still hard to improve upon older work such as Thurot, *Extraits de divers manuscrits latins pour servir a l'histoire des doctrines grammaticales*, and Paetow, *The Arts Course*, pp. 34–5.

was nothing new to explain plainchant theory in verse, of course, for isolated hexameters, clearly intended as mnemonics, are scattered throughout the musical treatises of the Middle Ages, and there are many examples of verse being used by theorists in a sustained and systematic way;[6] it was new, however, to present a sustained treatment of plainchant theory and polyphony in verse and prose making a coherent and systematic literary composition.

In this respect, the *Summa musice* can be interpreted as an attempt to create a place for music within a thriving tradition of writings on *Grammatica*, the subject to which *Musica* owed so much, within the context of a new fashion for basic instruction in verse. It was probably around the year 1200 that Eberhard of Béthune wrote a treatise on Latin grammar in hexameters, the *Grecismus*,[7] and no more than ten or fifteen years later that Geoffrey of Vinsauf completed his treatise on the composition of Latin verse, the *Poetria nova*, written throughout in hexameters.[8] The enormously influential *Doctrinale* of Alexander de Villa Dei, a versified textbook of Latin grammar that became a standard work during the thirteenth century, dates from the same time.[9]

Once such manuals became successful in the field of *grammatica* it was inevitable that someone would wish to create a musical handbook on similar lines. The musicians of the eleventh and twelfth centuries were taught to regard plainchant as a kind of applied grammar. A composer was to divide the musical phrases of

---

6 For the use of verse in theoretical writings before *c.* 1200, see Steglich, *Quaestiones in Musica*, pp. 93–9; Guido, *Regulae musicae rhythmicae* (Gerbert, *Scriptores*, II, pp. 25–34); Berno, *De varia psalmorum atque cantuum modulatione* (*ibid.*, pp. 60–61); Hermannus Contractus, *Opuscula musica* (*ibid.*, pp. 149–53); and Seay, *Carmen de musica cum glossis*.

7 Ed. Wrobel, *Eberhardi Bethuniensis Grecismus*. This versified treatise begins with a verbatim borrowing of the same passage from the *Disticha Catonis* that is used in the *Summa musice* (see the Translation, n. 1).

8 Text in Gallo, *Poetria nova*. On the poetry treatises see Kelly, 'The Scope of the Treatment of Composition'; *idem*, 'Theory of Composition in Medieval Narrative Poetry'; and Sedgewick, 'The Style and Vocabulary of the Latin Arts of Poetry'.

9 Ed. Reichling, *Das Doctrinale*. The manner of many passages in the *Doctrinale* is very close indeed to that of the *Summa musice*, and it is no surprise to learn that Alexander de Villa Dei may be the author of a plainchant treatise in Latin hexameters which has much in common with the style of our treatise. See Seay, *Carmen de musica cum glossis*.

a chant strictly according to the sense of the text (2171–4); as a
novice began his study of grammar with the alphabet, so he
embarked upon music with the letters of the gamut, itself called an
'alphabet' (*abecedarius*, 796); his musical phrases were called
clausulae, literally 'little clauses' (1194–8); the groups of neumes in
the books before him were compared to metrical feet; he was
warned against errors in the composition of chant with a wealth of
terminology borrowed from grammar and rhetoric such as
macrologia, or prolixity (2260–66). The study and performance of
plainchant was a discipline with its roots in the punctilious study of
the Latin language.

As it was taught in the eleventh and twelfth centuries,
Grammatica was more than the study of accidence and vocabulary
for it was also the study of the ancient authors: what constructions
they employed, what figures of speech they used and what wisdom
they had to impart. In strong contrast to most mensural writers of a
later generation such as Anonymous IV or Franco, the *Summa
musice* is animated by an impulse of literary humanism. In this
context, that humanism might be defined as a wish to evoke a
wisdom larger than the technical knowledge which is the ostensible
subject of one's teaching, a wisdom which resides in the great
literary works of antiquity where it must be sought in a
contemplative rather than an acquisitive spirit.

A brief analysis of the opening sentence of the *Summa musice*
followed by the corresponding passage in verse, will reveal some of
the qualities which the poetry of the treatise seeks to establish
(1; 44–5):

Prosa
Amicorum iusta et honesta petitio coactio reputatur.

Metrum
Cogere dicatur dum iusta precatur amicus;
Hic rogat, hortatur quem sermo terret iniquus.

Prose
The fitting and honest entreaty our of friends counts as a command.

Metre
When a friend asks for honest things he is said to compel; he entreats and
urges one who would be deterred by an unfriendly word.

To read the Latin verses aloud is to discover how carefully the poet
is patterning the sound. He is working to create what the twelfth-
century theorist of poetry Matthew of Vendôme calls a 'soothing of
the sense of hearing', a *blandimentum audientie*.[10] There are internal
rhymes which greatly increase our sense of chiming sound in the
passage:

...dicatur...precatur
...hortatur...

In lines 2 and 3 the internal rhymes are reinforced by parallel
syntax and construction:

Sic sceleris clamor...
Sed virtutis amor...

Techniques such as these, backed by abundant alliteration, help to
weave that 'festive garment of words' which Matthew of Vendôme
and other theorists regarded as one of the principal delights of
poetry. Words of related etymology are balanced against one
another ('coactio' is formed from the supine of 'cogere', used in
the first line of the Metrum); plurals become singulars or vice versa
('Amicorum...amicus') and some words remain still to emphasise
the changing relationships between the others ('iusta...iusta').

At its most difficult, the verse of the *Summa musice* defeats all
modern expectations of what makes good and lucid teaching by
compressing the subject matter until it becomes almost
unintelligible and expanding the means of expression into realms
of imagery that leave Quintilian's 'merits of literalness' far behind.
It is apparent, however, that the scribe who copied the unique
manuscript of the treatise gave the verse priority – contrary to our
instinctive expectation that the prose must be the lucid centre of
the work. The verse was always the first material that he copied on

---

[10] Faral, *Les arts poétiques*, p. 151.

each folio, using a large textura; only when he had completed this did he begin the prose, packing it around the verse in a cursive and heavily contracted script. The resulting pages look like a glossed copy of a poem in which the verse is the centre of study and the prose an ancillary aid.

In some places the poetry of the *Summa musice* achieves the aim which all good poetry can accomplish by restoring the metaphorical vigour to language grown tired (351–3):

> Fructus cantandi magnus perpenditur; usque
> Hoc attendentes Ignatius Ambrosiusque
> Decrevere deo quod in ecclesia celebretur
> Cantu qui mentem devotam concomitetur.

The first two lines rejuvenate the expressive power of the words which they employ. They might be translated

The great benefit of chanting is considered; turning their minds to this Igantius and Ambrose...

This is a possible translation, but it is based upon the transferred or figurative senses of the words 'fructus', 'perpenditur' and 'attendentes'. The literal meaning of 'fructus' is 'fruit', and the senses 'benefit' or 'result' are transferred ones. In the same way the literal meaning of 'perpendere' is 'to weigh carefully', while 'attendere' has the literal sense 'to reach towards, reach up to'. If we restore these primary senses to the translation then we find that there is a consistent metaphorical control:

The great fruit of chanting is carefully weighed; Ignatius and Ambrose, reaching towards this...

Many of the words which medieval Latin poets use – indeed many of the words in any language – are dead metaphors in that their literal sense no longer enlivens the figurative one. A poet can restore their life, however, by establishing a context in which the sense is borne by the figurative use of words whose latent literal meanings form a concatenation that gathers strength and comes to our attention simultaneously with the figurative sense. That is what happens in these lines.

Although the poetry of the *Summa musice* is frequently sententious, the tone of the verse is often more varied and supple than that of the prose. Indeed, the prose is generally rather monochromatic in tone, moving from one subject to another with formal transitions like 'Sciendum est autem' or some similar phrase. The verse, however, can encompass a grand manner (1884):

Non retro pungit fallacis acumine teli

It does not stab from behind with the point of a treacherous lance.

But it can bend as low as this (1566):

Exemplo careo; cum sit leve do quoque saltum

I lack an example; since it is simple I also leap.

The predominantly high tone of the verse owes much to the imperious subjunctives which turn a statement into an indirect command (cf. English 'let them enter'). The verse is also lent a higher tone than the prose by frequent reference to what might be termed the ethical dimension of theory as perceived by the authors. A prosa will say, for example, that something was done by the ancient inventors of music, but the metrum will not merely describe the achievement, it will celebrate the justice of it

The poetry is written in verse paragraphs of varying length, each comprising a set of hexameters bound into pairs by rhyme and (for the most part) by the distribution of the sense within the verse paragraph. In hexameters such as these the fifth foot is invariably dactylic, but the preceding feet may be either spondaic or dactylic. There is often a high incidence of dactyls to lighten the movement of a line ('Sed tamen hinc oculi nequeunt perpendere cantum'), and it is correspondingly rare to find five spondaic feet in a single hexameter. The third foot may begin with a syllable that is indifferently long or short, but which is generally long ('Musica dicatur ars que recte modulatur'; 'Fistula musa fuit olim pastoribus apta'). The hexameters reveal that Perseus and Petrus possessed a sound knowledge of quantity and a somewhat strict, conservative approach to their task.

4

The text and the edition

The *Summa musice* as we have it incorporates several layers of interpolation. At some stage an interpolator lengthened the Metrum of Chapter XX, splitting it apart in three places and inserting verse mnemonics, cast in hexameters, of the kind to be found in many medieval manuscripts (especially German ones) and mostly concerned with modal finals, the modal classification of various antiphons and related matters. Gerbert printed the interpolated lines as if they were part of the Metrum, but passages such as these destroy the rhyme scheme and seem very unlikely to have been part of the original text:

> Tertius est quinque quoniam Dominus Symeonem
> Quartus post Rubum pete Beata fidelia Syon
> Quintus Vox alma sextus notum Benedictus...

It is possible to demonstrate that these lines, and others like them, entered the text of the *Summa musice* some time after the second-layer chapter of *c.* 1225–37. At line 2123 the author of the second-layer chapter gives the total number of verses in the whole treatise as 860. The text edited here with the mnemonic hexameters deleted comprises 864 lines, and given the likelihood that the very last couplet is not to be included in the count (it is a kind of colophon, as noticed by the scribe who sets it well apart) then the total number of hexameters in this edition is 862, only two lines higher than the correct sum. Even with these deletions made the number of lines in the text is too high, so it is plain that interpolations have been made since the author of the second-layer chapter made his count. As the excision of the mnemonic lines from Metrum XX gives a result so close to the correct total, and since so many hexameters similar to those lines were in general circulation,[1] it is virtually certain that the mnemonics are not genuine.

The manuscript text is generally good but has the appearance of hasty work and the scribe's procedure has led to some lacunae. He first laid out the metrical portion of a chapter down the centre of a folio in a large textura, stopping at the bottom of the folio, whether he had reached the end of the Metrum or not. He then went back and wrote the Prosa into the right-hand margin of the folio and underneath the Metrum if it stopped short of the bottom of the leaf. Once the folio was full he turned over, breaking off the Prosa and taking up the Metrum again. Thus he was continuously turning from one block of text, often in mid sense, to begin another. As a result, portions of text were sometimes lost between folios where the change-over occurred (before 1565, for example). The scribe was also prone to drop lines in places where the poet writes several couplets with the same rhyme (after 676).

The text of the *Summa musice* presented here differs from Gerbert's edition in more than a thousand places. Many of these are changes in the readings which, I believe, have better authority as expansions of the scribe's contractions and which give better sense.

The aim of the edition is to provide an accurate text of the *Summa musice* as it was written by Perseus and Petrus, probably around 1200. The interpolations have been removed from the main text and placed in the apparatus; the second-layer chapter, added to the end of the work, is included. The orthography is based (but not slavishly) upon Classical Latin; this has the advantage of generally bringing a consistency to the scribe's orthography which is arbitrary in some respects (especially in the spelling of words of Greek origin and of words with geminated consonants). I have normalized *u* and *v*. The letter *j* is not used, nor the dipthong *ae*. Punctuation follows modern conventions and is designed to articulate the structure of sentences. Paragraph marks in the manuscript have not been reproduced and in many

---

[1] See Huglo, *Les tonaires, passim.*

places have been ignored in favour of clearer divisions of the
material. Capitalisation also follows modern conventions, being
principally reserved for proper names. All departures from the
manuscript text are indicated in the textual notes and variants
apparatus.

The translation is in prose throughout, the gain in fidelity to the
sense of the original being adequate compensation, in my view, for
the infidelity to its form. A verse translation of the Metra would
inevitably have wandered away from the sense of the original. An
attempt has been made to capture the tonal range of the Latin,
which is mostly serious and schoolmasterly. Translations which may
seem less than obvious (of which I hope there are very few) are
discussed in the notes to the Translation.

Each paragraph of the translation is tied to its Latin original by
line numbers. The translation is intended to be a self-sufficient
means of studying the treatise, and therefore notes have been
added to indicate the sources of citations and other borrowings,
together with a commentary of necessarily modest proportions.
The Latin text is supplied with a selection of parallel readings
which give a more detailed picture of the interrelations between
the *Summa musice* and other treatises.

Summa musice: The translation

[PROLOGUE]

[lines 1–42]

1-10 The fitting and honest entreaty of our friends counts as a command. When I have been urged by such entreaty towards what needs to be compiled, written and taught about the art of music, I have replied that for the most part people appropriately skilled in this art are to be found in any important ecclesiastical foundation, and if I were to presume to teach some trifling thing about music they would perhaps attribute it to my arrogance or to habitual rashness, and the question would be put to me, both in my presence and in my absence, which is sometimes put to the foolish and to the ambitious, namely whether they would call for a better bread than a wheaten loaf and a better drink than wine.

11-19 However, I have frequently noticed so many of my friends and pupils wandering badly in the path – that is to say in those things which are the principles of music, namely the knowledge of intervals which are produced either from equality of pitch or from raising and lowering – I thought that I would try to be a help and source of counsel for their obvious ignorance, principally so that they should be able to sing properly constituted chant in a well-informed way, and should receive as much honour when they sing amongst the uninformed as do the most expert.[1]

20-33 The following are the matters which I shall not discuss because they are beyond the power of boys and need a more thorough investigation: whether music be a liberal art or not; the *subiectum*[2] of music and the distinctive property of that *subiectum*; how the intervals are founded and established according to the properties of numbers; the consistency[3] of music. I will attempt to write just as certain Ancients and Moderns have done in treating fittingly of these things and of others planned for this work – chiefly Odo, Guido, Salomon and Hermannus[4] – leaving aside the

---

[1]   The general posture of the Prologue – one has been urged by friends to write and has finally agreed to do so; one writes to teach the young; one enters a field dominated by acknowledged masters with a modest awareness of one's own limitations – is highly conventionalised. Compare the Preface to Quintilian's *Institutio oratoria*.

   The passage 'However, I have frequently noticed...as do the most expert' is based, almost verbatim, upon lines from the Prologue to one of the most popular of all medieval schoolbooks, the *Disticha Catonis* (I:31), a collection of nearly 150 pithy phrases in Latin verse, compiled in the third century AD but attributed to Cato the Elder. The book was used in the teaching of Latin. The prominence of such a substantial borrowing from this book emphasises the schoolroom nature of *SM*, a text undoubtedly written for a master to expound to a class of boys.

   The treatise has other ambitions, however, as revealed by the almost verbatim dependence of the third paragraph of this Prologue upon Boethius' translation of Porphyry's *Isagoge*, a standard introduction to Aristotle's *Categories*. Perseus and Petrus use several terms and concepts with a deep Aristotelian colour (see n. 92 below), and make numerous references to the Philosopher's works – generally, it must be said, for pithy and proverbial remarks rather than for any closely argued term or point.

[2]   The *subiectum* is the essence, that which underlies all the accidents of a thing (see n. 92 below). The question of the *subiectum* of music is discussed in a page of notes on f.30v of the manuscript which contains *SM* (and it is clear that the compiler of these notes knew *SM*; the notes are printed in Gerbert, *Scriptores*, III, pp. 285-6). These notes define the *subiectum* of music as number correlated with sound. The *subiectum* which Perseus and Petrus do not choose to discuss therefore comprises the arithmetical basis of intervals.

[3]   *Consistencia* has the senses 'mass, matter, material', and presumably denotes the physics and acoustics of sound.

[4]   Odo: medieval theorists frequently refer to a certain Odo, but the name was borne by several musicians whose identities have been confused. The principal text in the Odo complex is the *Dialogus* (Gerbert, *Scriptores*, I, pp.

more lofty questions and discussing the simpler ones in a plain fashion. I will omit many things which they have said, and I will include from out of the conduit of my small wit some things which they have left untouched when I judge them to be advantageous.[5]

33-42 In return for this labour, however small it may be, I neither hope nor ask to be rewarded by the whisper of fame[6] or by another's purse, but rather by Him who allows no work to go unrewarded if it is undertaken with a virtuous intent, to whom nothing is past and nothing to come, who comprehends all human actions in His eternal present without an instant of forgetfulness. May He look kindly therefore upon my flimsy coracle and may He bring it to port, for as Augustine says, whatever power we may have to put evil from us, no one can do good without God,[7] and as Solomon says, all wisdom comes from the Lord God.[8]

A POEM CONCERNING THE SAME

[lines 43–71]

44-55 When a friend asks for honest things he is said to compel; he entreats and urges one who would be deterred by an unfriendly

251–64) long attributed to Odo of Cluny but now regarded as the work of an anonymous theorist working *c.* 1000 in the region of Milan (Huglo, 'L'auteur du *Dialogue sur la musique* attribué à Odon'). *SM* does not seem to derive any of its material directly from any 'Odonian' treatise.

Guido: this is one of several references to the most celebrated of all medieval music theorists, Guido of Arezzo (†1033). *SM* seems to derive little or nothing directly from any work by Guido and sometimes attributes teachings to him that cannot be found in any of his surviving works.

Salomon: presumably Elias Salomon, whose *Scientia artis musice* was completed in 1274 (Gerbert, *Scriptores* III, pp. 16–64). This treatise and *SM* cover much of the same ground, but this is to be expected since they are both plainchant treatises composed within a few generations of one another. As with 'Odo' and Guido, there seems to be no evidence that the authors of *SM* took anything directly from Elias, and if the theory proposed above concerning the date of *SM* is correct, Perseus and Petrus cannot have known the *Scientia artis musice.*

5   Echoing John (HGJ, p. 102).
6   Evoking the Whispers of Fame in Ovid, *Metamorphoses*, XII:61.
7   Citing, perhaps, the *Liber de predestinatione sanctorum* (PL 44, column 963).
8   Ecclesiasticus 1:1.

word. The summons of a wicked man leaves me with a cold heart, but the love of virtue repels everything which gives annoyance.[9] Perhaps it will make one audacious? God himself will help. I say small things to the small and so this work will not burden me. It would not be simple to describe the *subiectum* of music and its distinctive property, to describe how it relates to mathematics like a fourth part,[10] and especially to describe the sound of the vast bodies amid the secluded region of the heavens or explain why the discord of their motions gives concord; these concerns are too lofty and they would also leap, as it were, beyond the mental powers of boys.

56-71 Those [authors] who are not to our purpose, we will let them sleep; those fruits which are too high, we will leave on the tree. Let us consider intervals, however, and those things which follow and precede, and how they arise; but when practice follows the candle of theory that leads the way as an alternative to wandering in darkness, that candle will be here, and to discover why each detail must be described as it is let us proceed further with sounds as with notation (*vocibus ut notis*). Be with me therefore, O God; lead my sails to harbour and reveal to me the subject for me to expound well. Let not the pipe of fame be my reward for writing, nor do I seek any other worldly thing. May you be my reward, without whom there is nothing in any place which may be known to have the essence of goodness. To me the past counts for nothing, for nothing also the future; wherever I may be in the billows, O God, I choose you to be Palinurus.[11]

PREFACE TO THE CHAPTERS

[lines 72–84]

72-84 Since music requires many distinctions in comparison with the other arts, it suffices in many cases to put part for whole so that the

---

9 'Sed virtutis amor pellit quodcumque molestat' (Latin, line 47). The sense of this line is not entirely clear.

10 For music as the fourth division of mathematics, see the passage from the *Institutiones* of Cassiodorus translated in Strunk, *Source Readings*, I, p. 88, n. 6.

11 A skilful pilot of the ship of Aeneas in Virgil's *Aeneid* (III:202 etc).

reader may more readily discern the substance of what is being said. Since the subjects discussed below are laid out in chapters, it will be useful to set out the headings of those chapters here, observing the same order.[12] It is plain that music needs distinctions to avoid error, because any fault is the worse the more public it becomes; in comparison with the other arts, music is cultivated with great noise and a fault in music is therefore perceived more quickly and is carried further afield, causing greater infamy.

THE HEADINGS OR TITLES OF THE CHAPTERS

[lines 85–121]

1. What music is and by whom it was invented.
2. What music is useful for.
3. Who first employed music in the Church and why.
4. Concerning the division of music into 'natural', 'instrumental', 'celestial' and 'human'.
5. Concerning 'human' music.
6. Concerning the neumes of plainsong, what they are and for what they were devised.
7. Concerning the six solmisation syllables of the hexachord degrees and their sufficiency.
8. Concerning the palm, or musical hand, and its lines and spaces.
9. Why the hand is the preferred implement of music and not some other member.
10. Concerning intervals and their species.
11. Why there are no more intervals than nine and why no more connectives than nineteen.
12. Concerning the representations of intervals arranged by various people in various ways.
13. Concerning the stratagems with which a new and untrained singer learns chant.
14. Concerning the invention of the modes and their number according to both the Ancients and the Moderns.

---

[12] Compare John (HGJ, p. 102).

15. The *claves* and *viceclaves* which serve as the finals of the modes.
16. Concerning the initial *claves* of the modes, how [the modes] should ascend and descend, and by how much.
[17. How much the authentic and plagal modes may ascend and descend.]
18. How an authentic chant is distinguished from a plagal one through distinctive *claves*.
19. Concerning 'turn', tenor and *cauda* which are heeded in chant.
20. How and where the *Gloria* [*patri*] of the modes is begun, and concerning the mediations.
21. How, and in how many ways, one may go astray in chant.
22. How new chant should be composed and elaborated.
23. The faults which should be avoided in new chant.
24. Concerning polyphony and its various forms.
[25. The symbolic garment of music.]

1 WHAT MUSIC IS AND FOR WHAT IT WAS INVENTED

[lines 122–86]

122-33 For our purposes music may be defined as the art of measuring sounds distinctly, and the first thing to examine is the origin of its name and the identity of its inventors. Next, we must speak of its usefulness, and then of how music is to be divided and what things precede it and follow from it. So, in honour of the number three, this treatise has a threefold structure because of the three principal subjects to be investigated.[13] Three is a prime and odd number which cannot be divided into two equal parts; it is the first number with a mean that is 1, and for that reason it is hallowed by the scholars named above.

---

[13] *SM* could be said to have a 'threefold structure' in that the authors consider the name of music (Chapter I), the usefulness of the art (Chapter II) and then musical practice (Chapters III–XXIV), but this is neither a neat nor a convincing division of the material. The manuscript gives no indication that any formal division into parts was intended, and for these reasons no attempt has been made here to divide the treatise into three parts.

134-42 Having said that, it should be noted that different authorities hold different opinions about the word 'musica'. Some say that 'musica' is equivalent to 'moysica' from 'moys', which means water,[14] because when rain water (or any other kind) falls upon different kinds of substance – now upon roofs, now upon stones, now upon land, now upon water, now upon empty vessels, now upon the leaves of trees – it produces different sounds, and the Ancients are said to have devised music by bringing these sounds together.

143-63 According to some, music is named after the *musa*,[15] an instrument which they describe as the most excellent and perfect of all musical instruments. They say that music is named after it (after a thing more worthy, as it were) by antonomasia.[16] Others say that music [takes its name] from the poetic Muses because of the various ways of writing which they offered to poets, but music was invented before the practice of versemakers. The most judicious solution is that *musica* is derived from *musa*, a very rudimentary instrument discovered by shepherds around the beginning of the world and made from a marshy reed or cornstalk. These instruments, differing in length and breadth, and with various positions of fingerholes, first taught the shepherds to appreciate the diversity of musical sounds. Etymologically, indeed, *musica* may well be interpreted to mean 'strengthening the singer by practice'. Petrus Riga mentions the invention of the *musa* by shepherds 'so that pastoral labour might thereby rejoice',[17] and since this was the first musical instrument, it is appropriate that music should be named after it. Moses attributes the invention of

---

14 See Swerdlow, 'Musica dicatur a Moys'.

15 Compare John (HGJ, p. 105). In Old French the word 'muse' is generally used to denote a bagpipe (*Dictionnaire de l'ancienne langue Française*, ed. Godefroy, 'muse'; *Altfranzösisches Wörterbuch*, ed. Tobler and Lommatzsch, 'muse'). Here it seems to mean a simple pipe made from a reed or cornstalk.

16 Antonomasia is the substitution of an epithet for a proper name, and conversely, the use of a proper name to indicate a general idea (for example, when a writer is called 'a Shakespeare'). It is the latter which Perseus and Petrus imply.

17 A line from the celebrated verse-paraphrase of the Bible, the *Aurora*, by Petrus Riga. The first edition was issued *c.* 1170. See Beichner, *Aurora*, line 468.

this pipe to Jubal who is said to have been the father of those who play the *cithara*.[18]

164-73 Others attribute the first discovery of music to Methuselah.[19] Occupied with the work of digging waterwells, he heard the many different kinds of sounds made by the hammers and shaped them into the practice of music. Boethius ascribes the invention of the art to Pythagoras;[20] as he was walking past a forge he heard the manifold sounds of hammers and noticed that they differed in pitch; he selected numerous hammers of variable size and weight, and having ascertained the mathematical basis of their varied sounds he shaped them into the art of a musician. Some attribute the invention of music to Amphion the Theban[21] and some to Orpheus the Thracian.[22]

173-86 With regard to all of this, let us fittingly say, with Aristotle, that the beginnings of all arts, and implements at the time of their invention, were crude and meagre, each successive innovator adding something new.[23] In this manner the trickle of an ultimate source, enlarged by a confluence of waters, can be turned into a river carrying ships, and it could have been, as Moses says, that Jubal was the first, from whose name we derive both 'iubilus' and 'iubilare', and that the others mentioned, coming afterwards, added something new and so on up to the present time. Just as it says in the *Categories* that it is permitted to invent names,[24] so it may

18 Genesis 4:21.
19 There seems to be no other trace of this story.
20 *De institutione musica*, I:1. Compare John (HGJ, p. 106).
21 Amphion, son of Jupiter, said to have been the inventor of music by Pliny (*Natural History*, VII:204). Compare John (HGJ, p. 106).
22 Unaccountably, Gerbert prints 'Orpheo Cretensi' for 'Orpheo Trecensi', but the manuscript reading is clear and the Thracian home of Orpheus is not in doubt (see Horace, *Odes*, I:XXIV).
23 Perhaps a passage in *De sophisticis elenchis*, Chapter 34: 'For in the case of all discoveries the results of previous labours that have been handed down from others have been advanced little by little by those who have taken them on, whereas the original discoveries generally make an advance that is small at first...'.
24 'in Predicamentis licet nomina fingere' (Latin, lines 182-3). The *Predicamenta* are Aristotle's *Categories*, the reference here being to a passage in Chapter 7: 'we must state all correlative terms with exactness. If a name is already to hand, then the statement will prove to be easy. If no name already exists, then I think it is our duty to invent one.'

be said of the new manner of singing that something has been assented to by the Moderns which was not invented by the Ancients because, as Priscian attests, 'the younger a man is, the keener is his sight'.[25]

A POEM CONCERNING THE SAME

[lines 187-217]

187-99 The art which measures sound accurately and distinctly should be called *musica* and it bears this name by right. The pipe called *musa* was once the proper instrument of shepherds; it entranced the ear and the mind with its sound. The long [*musa*] and the short, the greater and the lesser, teach plainly; the first shepherds heard this gladly and frequently bound these harmonious [pipes] together,[26] however disparate they seem and clearly are. Others say that music takes its name from the Muses who used to guide the many emotions of poets; others claim that *musica* derives from *moys*, which means water, whose manifold sound teaches the new, first beginning of music.

200-207 Jubal, Methuselah, Pythagoras, Orpheus and Amphion taught music, and were the first. One was the very first; they were not all the first in time, but they can be grouped together because they enlarged the first beginning of the art. As there are many living today endowed with that gift, so a new line is produced from the point of origin.[27] Music takes its name because it strengthens

[25] *Institutio grammaticarum*, I:1. This aphorism, taken from one of the most fundamental grammar books of the Middle Ages, is often quoted by the theorists, including John (HCJ, p. 107). For the uses which medieval music theorists made of it, see Smits van Waesberghe, *Adelboldi episcopi...Epistola cum Tractatu*, pp. 64–5.

[26] Perseus and Petrus seem to be thinking of panpipes.

[27] 'Sic nova protrahitur ab origine linea puncti' (Latin, line 205). One of the many difficult lines to be found in the Metra. This metaphor is presumably derived from geometry, where lines are produced from points ('linea...protrahitur...puncti'); in the same way the inventiveness of musicians draws music forward from its point of origin. There is also presumably a word-play in the case of 'punctum', since this word has the sense 'musical note, neume, melodic phrase', while 'linea' is the standard term in medieval Latin for a staff line.

singers by practice[28] and through its enchanters it produces an auspicious omen.

208-17 The name of music, and its inventors, will be clear from what has been said; now the usefulness of music follows in fitting fashion. The end [of the chapter to come] advises and exhorts the slothful; it validates the whole art through what is achieved by one small part. The third part [of the treatise] follows, subdividing the art, giving practical instruction and explaining the things which an unwary musician generally mishandles. This is what the ternary structure takes up and it occupies the whole book, the fortunate author representing the Godhead by a propitious token. This prime number drives all evil before it, nor is it empty of significance in its mean, symbolising virtue.

2 WHAT MUSIC IS USEFUL FOR

[lines 218–60]

218-25 Those who explore the usefulness of music should note what Horace says concerning the good poet; only praising him, he says that 'the one who combines the useful with the delightful wins all the applause'.[29] These two things are found in music. It is delightful, because no other art gives pleasure so quickly; it is useful, because its practitioner, that is to say the *musicus*,[30] can

---

[28] The word 'musica' is here being etymologised as a compendium of initial and medial letters in the words 'strengthening singers by practice', in Latin 'muniens usu canentem'.

[29] *Ars poetica*, line 343.

[30] Medieval theorists derived their concept of the 'musicus' from Boethius, *De institutione musica*, I, Chapter 34, where the *musicus* is defined as a student of theory, and by implication as a gentleman connoisseur who has no contact with the menial trade of practical musicianship. Given the practical obligations of monks and secular clergy, however, who were required to sing the choral liturgy, this lofty disdain for music-making (which is essentially a disdain for *work*) could not be accepted in the clerical culture of the Middle Ages without some redefinition. *SM* expresses the favourite medieval modification of Boethian teaching whereby the *musicus* is understood to be one who knows the theory behind the plainchant which he sings, while the *cantor* merely sings the chant without understanding such theoretical concepts

compose new and correctly formed chant, can judge the same and can emend music that is not correctly formed.

226–41 The difference between a *musicus* and a *cantor* will now be plain to the attentive reader. Every *musicus* is a *cantor*, but the reverse is not the case. A *cantor* who is a *musicus*, that is to say a theorist and a performer, comes into this category, but a *cantor* who is not a *musicus* should not be called a performer, save by an abuse of the term, because performance is required to follow the science of theory which advances first. This is explained in the *Isagoge* of Johannitius.[31] A *cantor* without theoretical knowledge is like a drunkard trying to find his way or a blind man who wants to beat a dog. However, we have seen many singers of this kind and they exemplify what Boethius says about the unskilled in his book *On the Consolation of Philosophy*: such people tear the garment of Philosophy, and when they have stolen a tatter from her they swagger and say that she yields to them and that they possess her entire cloak.[32] Returning to our subject, however, let us briefly consider the usefulness of music.

242–60 Music has medicinal properties and performs miraculous things. Music cures diseases, especially those which arise from melancholia and sadness. Through music one can be prevented from falling into the loneliness and pain of despair. Music gives comfort to wayfarers and discourages villains and thieves, putting them to flight. In battle, the timid take heart when they hear music; those who have been routed and defeated rally when they hear it, and we read that Pythagoras used music to calm a man when he was maddened with lust,[33] for there is a species of music which banishes lust and there is another that invites it, just as there is a kind of music which lulls watchmen to sleep and another which

---

as mode. See further Page, '*Musicus* and *Cantor*'. It should be noted that while the authors insist upon the distinction here, their discussion of chant composition uses 'musicus' and 'cantor' as interchangeable terms. See Chapter XXII (Latin, lines 2105 and 2122).

[31] This should be the medical treatise entitled *Isagoge ad artem Galieni* by Johannitius, which became part of a standard corpus of medical texts in the early twelfth century, but there is nothing corresponding to this in the modern edition of the *Isagoge* by Maurach ('*Ysagoge ad artem Galieni*').

[32] *De consolatione philosophiae*, I, Prosa 3.

[33] Once again, the source is probably Boethius, *De institutione musica*, I:1.

can waken those who slumber. Music calms the irascible, gladdens the sorrowful, dissipates anxious thoughts and destroys them. What is greater still, music terrifies evil spirits and banishes them, just as David the string player, according to the Book of Kings, expelled the demon from King Saul when he was possessed by a devil.[34] It is no wonder if Man, a rational creature, is delighted by music, since flocks of four-footed beasts, certain birds and some fish are evidently charmed by the delightfulness of the art.

A POEM CONCERNING THE SAME

[lines 261–99]

261–79 If you wish to taste the fruit of this art, remember the true words of Flaccus: he who combines the useful with the beautiful will enjoy praise. Music adheres to this precept; it is rightly held to be praiseworthy. Music caresses the ears and soothes the mind; musical practice is useful and can thoroughly purge its devotee of harm. The *musicus* is a judge of music, a composer, and also one who can correct all errant melodies in the art of the proper paths. The *musicus* is a *cantor*, but if you reason this with yourself you must not reverse that statement to produce a counterfeit meaning.[35] The *cantor* who lacks art must not be praised; he is deceived, believing that the part he sees is the whole. A *cantor* is like a drunken man arriving at the crossroads of a town; the *musicus*, however, knows thoroughly what he sings in a thousand places. Declare that a *cantor* who lacks art is like a blind man; Fortune rules both of them as they proceed. Anyone who wishes to know what – and how much – music can achieve, may find what he seeks through synecdoche.[36]

280–99 Music heals the sick and comforts the healthy; it exhilarates the infant and the youth, be they human or canine. It especially soothes and alleviates nervousness and diseases of the brain,

---

[34] I Samuel, 16:23. Compare Page, *The Owl and the Nightingale*, pp. 159f.

[35] 'quod non convertere debes/Subiecto quevis pro signo si tibi prebes' (Latin, lines 270–71). Another extremely difficult passage.

[36] The rhetorical figure in which part is put for whole or vice versa.

banishing and palliating them. So it was that Pythagoras cured a wanton man; with melody he compelled the befouled individual to abandon his shameful doings. That is the kind of music which swells lechery; there is another which restrains lasciviousness and knows nothing of licentiousness. Music reassures the sad man, comforts the traveller and makes him climb the steep mountain of life. It discourages criminals and forces thieves to flee; it expels fears and often makes them perish altogether. In battle music heartens the fearful and recalls those who are fleeing; it urges the bold, seeking the palm of victory in war, to advance. Moreover, Bucephalus[37] dances to music amidst the enemy, and in the van he casts down foes as dead as posts. Through the intercession of music the unclean spirit flees, revealing that he is a discordant creature now just as he was before; so it was that David calmed the raging demon in Saul, showing with a melody the miraculous power of his *cithara.*

3 WHO FIRST EMPLOYED MUSIC IN CHURCH AND WHY

[lines 300–350]

300-313 Since so many, and indeed innumerably more, recommendations of music may be found, Ignatius,[38] who was the first, and then St Ambrose,[39] archbishop of Milan, decreed that God should be served in the Church with music for His greater reverence and honour. They set out to establish what was to be sung in church, how much was to be included, when it was to be sung and how it should be performed. They decreed that in the Divine Service before the Lord in Holy Church music should not be sung with levity, laughter or dancing, but should rather be performed in a lowly and devout fashion. Ambrose composed chant specially assigned and proper to each day of the year, and he

---

[37] One of the horses of Alexander the Great.
[38] Presumably St Ignatius of Antioch (†c. 110). This section owes much to John (HGJ, pp. 136–7).
[39] St Ambrose of Milan (†397).

decreed that all the churches under his jurisdiction should festively perform it.

313-25 After that St Gregory,[40] bishop of the Papal See, composed chant to be promulgated throughout the Roman Church and sent it first to the cathedral churches. Peter the Deacon saw a dove sitting on Gregory's shoulder when he was writing with the needs of the Church in mind.[41] However, Gregory did not make his chant prolix in the way that St Ambrose is reported to have done. Some say that this was on account of weariness induced by maladies, for Gregory was often subject to a quartan fever and he was also troubled with fainting fits and gout. Others say (and perhaps they come nearer the truth) that whatever Gregory wrote, both music and text, derived its content, extent and quality from the Holy Spirit.

326-40 The singing of the ancient believers, both in the New Testament and the Old, provided Gregory with his authority for the use of singing in worship. The Book of Daniel tells of the three young men singing praises to God in the furnace.[42] The Book of Exodus relates that the Hebrews crossed the sea and witnessed the Egyptians as they were overwhelmed and drowned;[43] then Miriam, the sister of Moses, sang praises to God with her brother, relating the mighty works of their protector in their singing. Again, King David sang and played his *cithara* before the Ark and before the Lord, calling upon others with diverse musical instruments, saying: 'Sing a new song to the Lord' and so on, and further: 'Sing and rejoice and make music', and again: '[Sing] to the Lord on the *tympanum* and the *chorus*, on the *psalterium* and the *cithara*, on the resounding *cymbala*, on strings and on the *organum*, on ductile *tube* and with the voice of the *tuba* made of horn'.[44]

---

40 Gregory I (†604). For a readable but penetrating account of Gregory and the beginnings of chant, see McKinnon, 'The Emergence of Gregorian Chant'.

41 Text in PL 75, columns 57–8. Peter the Deacon was a constant companion of Gregory. It is generally accepted that the passage in Peter's *Vita sancti Gregorii magni* relating to the dove on Gregory's shoulder is a later interpolation (BHL, 3640–41).

42 Daniel 3:51–90.

43 Exodus 15:1–21.

44 II Samuel, 6:5; Psalms 33:3, 96:1, 98:1, 149:1 and 150:16.

340-50 In the New Testament, after one angel had announced the birth of Christ to the shepherds, a group of angels sang together with him, in case the authority of one should seem insufficient, 'Glory be to God in the highest'.[45] There is also the song of Zacharias, that is to say *Benedictus*,[46] the song of Mary, *Magnificat*,[47] and the song of Simeon, *Nunc dimittis*,[48] which are called 'songs' with good reason. The manner of singing reveals the devotion of the singer and arouses a feeling of piety in the listener if he is well disposed, and so music is deservedly and rightly used in the Church in a lowly and devout fashion.

A POEM CONCERNING THE SAME

[lines 351–94]

351-65 The great fruit of chanting is carefully weighed; Ignatius and Ambrose, reaching towards this, decree that God should be worshipped with music that befits a devout spirit. Ambrose contributed the liturgy proper to each day with prolix chant. Then came Pope Gregory, the Roman, who delighted in worship where no man may stand like a mute, for it is fitting that the Saviour of the world, three persons and one, should receive the triple gift of our observance: the heart must yearn, the mouth sound, and the whole mechanism of the body strive which so devoutly prays to the Lord in this way.[49] Anyone who thoroughly strives in his praying with mind, voice and works is deservedly called a *citharista* in the Temple of the Lord.[50]

366-79 The Pope arranged the new and completed chant in order; the Holy Spirit taught him how to accomplish what was done there, for Peter [the Deacon] saw that a beautiful dove sat touching the

---

[45] Luke 1:14.

[46] Luke 1:68–79.

[47] Luke 1:46–55.

[48] Luke 2:29–32.

[49] For this view of chant performance as a prayerful occupation of the whole mind and body, see the discussion of monastic reading, prayer and meditation in Leclercq, *Love of Learning, passim*.

[50] By analogy with David, *citharista*.

ears of the Pope whenever he gave admonition. Some attribute the
brevity of his chant to his maladies; others cite the mercy of God as
the cause, for however brief it may be there are some who evidently
do not know it [by heart], and yet they show themselves to be
expert singers.[51] It is better that no great confusion has arisen
concerning this; I consider that this confusion has been forgotten
by the grace of God. Fainting and a quartan gout commanded
Gregory to be silent sometimes and forbade him to sing. What he
sang in the front must therefore be sought at the rear; with what
could he fill the vacuum that could not be allowed to remain?[52]

380-94 He took as an authority the three who sang in the furnace,
and Moses, when his pursuers perished under the waters. King
David taught that one should serve before God with every kind of
music, and holding a *cithara* he played it, frequently summoning us
to sing; he iterated the word 'sing' (*verbum cantandi*) in his praises,
foreshowing what [the music of the liturgy] would thereafter be
called [i.e. 'chant', *cantus*]. Also, when Christ was born during the
hours of night, the angelic citizens, instructed in this melody, sang
Gloria to the shepherds and to us, through them, by oral and
written tradition (*dictum scriptumque*). If ecclesiastical chant is
devout and virtuous it gives pleasure and brings great advantage
immediately. The listener whose mind is exalted in prayer loves it
while he strives, as it were, to join the angelic songs. If he is not
virtuous it displeases him and he feels troubled; either he sorrows,
guilty, or he laments because he is sad.

---

51 Here, as in numerous other places, Perseus and Petrus emphasise the
importance of knowing chant by heart. Compare Chapter 13 (Latin, lines
1209-10), and the second-layer chapter, number 25 (2420-24), where the
unknown author of that chapter compares those who can sing without a book
to those who must rely on written copies and who are therefore vulnerable to
changes in the availability of chant books.

52 'Quo decet impleri vacuum quod nescit haberi?' (Latin, line 379). A very
difficult line, largely because 'nescit' does not seem to give good sense.

4 CONCERNING THE DIVISION OF MUSIC INTO 'NATURAL', 'INSTRUMENTAL', 'CELESTIAL' AND 'HUMAN'

[lines 395–424]

395–407 Music is divided into two categories: 'natural' and 'instrumental'.[53] One kind of natural music is 'human' and another 'celestial'. Celestial music arises from the diversity and concord of sounds produced by the movements of heavenly bodies, for just as scholars have said, such bodies could not move so rapidly, and so continuously, without emitting sound. Since the firmament and the planets have spiritual[54] and different motions, producing both spiritual and different sounds, they generate a kind of harmony within themselves which is called celestial music.

408–24 There are many kinds of 'artificial' instruments and they are divided into three classes: some are called 'stringed instruments', some 'instruments with apertures' and some 'instruments made from vessels'. Stringed instruments are those which are played with strings of metal, silk or gut; examples are *cithare, vielle* and *phiale, psalteria, chori,* the *monocordium*, the *symphonia* or *organistrum* and instruments like these.[55] Instruments

---

53 Compare John (HGJ, pp. 105–6).

54 The adjective 'spiritual' is not easy to interpret at this point, although the reading of the manuscript certainly seems to be 'spirituales' both here and in the next line (Latin, lines 404–5). Since it is fundamental to Christian doctrine that anything 'spiritual' corresponds to the spirit in its superiority over sensible nature, the point being made is presumably that the music of the planets is not audible like the grosser, sublunary music of voices and instruments.

55 This valuable passage is the earliest reference to silk strings in the West, and a very early reference (but not the first) to metallic strings. On the chronology of string materials in the Middle Ages as revealed by literary texts, see Page, *Voices and Instruments,* Appendix 4.

The identities of some of these instruments can be established with reasonable certainty. The Latin word 'cithara' is generally associated in medieval word-lists and translations with some form of the (ultimately) Germanic word 'harp(e)', usually denoting a pillar-harp in northern and central Europe before the fifteenth century. The distinction implied by 'vielle' (the plural of 'viella') and 'phiale' is unclear; in accordance with prevailing medieval usage, 'vielle' presumably denotes bowed instruments as a group, or possibly one

with apertures are those whose different notes arise from the diversity of holes; such are *muse, syringe, flaiota, tibie, cornua, fistule, tube* and others like these.[56] Instruments made from vessels are those which lack both holes and strings and are formed in the manner of hollow pots; *cymbala, pelves, campane, olle* and such, which emit various sounds according to the diversity of their form and material, are of this kind.[57] But of all musical instruments the

specific type. The word 'phiale', the plural of 'phiala', appears to be the standard Latin word for a phial or vessel, presumably pressed into service as a name for a musical instrument under the influence of 'viella' and in response to a need for a distinction between instruments called 'vielle' and others. Several bowed instruments could be involved, or it may be that the distinction implied is between bowed instruments and instruments of similar morphology played by plucking. 'Psalteria'(the plural of 'psalterium') are certainly psalteries, probably trapezoidal at this date rather than shaped in the familiar 'pig-snout' form. The meaning of 'chorus' cannot be established beyond that it is a stringed instrument. The 'monocordium' is surely the pedagogue's monochord. The terms 'symphonia' and 'organistrum' may be synonymous here, both denoting forms of hurdy-gurdy. There appears to be no firm foundation for the view, frequently encountered in modern histories of instruments, that the word 'organistrum' was reserved for hurdy-gurdies played by two men and 'symphonia' for those manipulated by a single player. The identity of the 'sistrum', mentioned in the Metrum to this chapter (Latin, line 438), is mysterious, although there was a tradition, clearly discernible in fourteenth- and fifteenth-century France, of identifying the word 'sistrum' with the lute (Page, 'Early Fifteenth-Century Instruments', p. 349, n. 17). For the detailed evidence on which these identifications and judgements are based, see Page, *Voices and Instruments*, Appendix 1, and *idem*, 'The Medieval Organistrum and Symphonia', Part II.

56 The grounds for identifying these instruments are less secure than in the case of the stringed instruments discussed in the previous note. On the 'musa' (vernacular 'muse'), see n. 15 above; Perseus and Petrus seem to be thinking of simple reed-pipes. Prevailing medieval usage would suggest that 'tube' are trumpets of some kind while 'cornua' are horns. The remaining terms ('syringe', 'flaiota', 'tibie' and 'fistule') presumably denote various kinds of reed-pipes and flutes, but it is impossible to be precise.

57 Of these percussion instruments, 'cymbala' are presumably the rows of small bells so often shown in medieval psalters, although one should remember La Rue's warning that such sets of small tuned bells, struck with hammers, may never have existed ('The Problem of the Cymbala'; for a very different view see Smits van Waesberghe, *Cymbala*). 'Campane' are probably tower-bells. The word 'pelves' means 'basins', so these may be cymbals, often rather deeply domed in the Middle Ages. 'Olle' means 'pots' or 'jars', so these may be drums of some sort.

human voice is the most worthy because it produces both pitch and words, while the others serve only for sound, not for a note and words.

A POEM CONCERNING THE SAME

[lines 425–53]

425–41 Music comprises instrumental [music] and natural; in this way it offers two kinds. It also befits natural [music] to bear two [kinds]: it contains celestial [music] and human within itself. Heavenly bodies produce celestial music by their movement in a vast continuum; they never pause at any time. Human music should not delay us much; instrumental music is evidently to be considered first. Three things give three species to it: string and vessel and aperture. The string goes first and its name is more worthy than the rest. I have seen [strings of] gut, silk and metal which I regard as the best and I do not believe that I am mistaken. The *psalterium, chorus* and *sistrum* should be classed with the *cithara* for these evidently sound with a similar striking motion. The bow gives sound to the *phiala* and wheels to the *monocorda*; these instruments are indeed hollow vessels but they resonate with a string.

442–53 There are also many instruments with apertures and by no means do the greater and lesser examples differ only in form. The *tibia, flaiotum, syringa, fistula* and *musa* are played only by the common people who have long been busied with them. *Organa* or *tube* and *cornua* with vigorous sound smite our ears with a powerful gust of wind. We should also recognise music produced by small vessels, distinguished by their weight and set into vibration by a strong blow. There are *cymbala, campane, pelves* and *olle*. However, you can see that the human [instrument] takes pride of place for it provides words that carry meaning to lie beneath the note.

5 CONCERNING 'HUMAN' MUSIC

[lines 454–88]

454–70 Having spoken of instrumental music, let us return to human, our principal subject, so that something may be said of it. Although music is a discrete arrangement of sounds, the word 'discrete' should be understood in the strict sense. If it is broadly interpreted, so that 'discrete' means the same as 'distinct' (that is 'distinctly made'), then music would also be the fit property of irrational creatures like the birds which distinguish clearly between different sounds in their song. If, however, [the word 'discrete'] is understood in the strict sense, then 'discrete' is equivalent to 'made with discretion', and music defined in that way is only fitting to Mankind, for Man is the only creature that sings and performs other actions with rational judgement. We say that the nightingale 'sings', so too the parrot, the lark, the blackbird, the crane, the swallow, the cock and birds like these, but they only sing when they are prompted or urged by Nature. Man, however, sings with discretion, joining words to his song with well-formed sense.

471–88 The word 'cantus' means 'a sounding action' and 'canor' 'travail with breath'. The inventors of song and the first preceptors accordingly considered the pipe of the trachea, the instrument of the human voice, to be capable of emitting a threefold music according to a triple disposition. Sometimes it is very relaxed and emits a low sound; sometimes it is very tense and produces a very high sound; sometimes it is disposed between these two and gives a high sound. They called this triple music *diatonicus* as if from the property of the modes (*tonorum*). They discarded music lower than the *graves* as being worth little or nothing because of its slackness, and they called it *organicus* because the organ of the human voice is deficient in it. In the same way, they devoted no further attention to music higher than the *acute* because of the insupportable labour of producing it and because no pleasure is to be found in it. They called this kind of music *enharmonicus* because, situated beyond the harmoniousness of diatonic music, it exhausts and vexes both the singer and the listener, giving no pleasure of restful delight.

A POEM CONCERNING THE SAME

[lines 489–507]

489–507 Having said the above, it is fitting that we return to human [music]; it is more to our purpose and we should examine it more closely. [Human music] will teach us to measure sounds with a judicious mind, and it adds words; no such thing is fitting to birds for they are taught to sing by Nature; they have no power of reason, whatever the sounds they sing. Thus the nightingale sings, thus the lark, the cock, the swallow and many others that I do not name but which may nonetheless be said to sing from the depths of their heart. Human [music] is more worthy than these because it accomplishes more; it teaches song with words and Reason is involved in that. He who sings badly does not care to follow Reason.... [He who sings well] puts the organic register aside and discards the enharmonic; one is too dark and the other tears at the throat. Between these two there is *gravis, acutus* and *peracutus*, and it is this kind of music that fittingly follows its own modes (*tonos*). It is therefore deservedly called 'diatonic'; correctly performed it can be pleasing to all.

6 CONCERNING THE NEUMES OF PLAINSONG, WHAT THEY ARE AND FOR WHAT THEY WERE DEVISED

[lines 508–39]

508–22 The musicians among the Ancients did not strive only to gain as much enjoyment as possible from music; they also diligently considered how they might teach others to sing. They therefore devised certain figures which, assigned to any syllable of the words, could denote the individual notes as their own specific signs, whence they are also called 'marks' (*note*) or 'little marks' (*notule*). Because music proceeds in many ways – sometimes by unison, sometimes ascending or descending – the marks are formed in various ways and given different names. One is called a *punctus*, one a *virga*, one a *clivis* major or minor, one a *plica* major or minor, another a *pes* or *podatus* major or minor, one a *quilisma* greater or lesser, and one a *pressus* major or minor.[58]

523–40 The *punctus* is formed in the manner of a point and is sometimes joined to a *virga*, to a *plica* or to a *podatus*, sometimes one only and sometimes many equally, mostly when the pitch is descending. The *virga* is a onefold (*simplex*) mark that is elongated like a rod. The *clivis* is so called from *cleo*, that is 'I bend', and it is composed of a mark and half a mark, indicating that the sound (*vox*) must be inflected. The *plica* derives its name from 'folding' (*plicando*) and contains two marks, one above and the other below. The *podatus* contains two marks, one below and the other above ascending. *Quilisma* means 'a bending', and it contains three or more marks either ascending and then descending, or the reverse. The *pressus* takes its name from 'pressing' (*premendo*); the lesser contains two marks, the greater three, and it should always be performed evenly and rapidly. But, to this point, a chant can only be imperfectly recognised by these signs, nor can anyone learn a chant from it in solitude; it is necessary that the music be frequently heard from another and learned through long practice, and on this account the practice of this chant took its name.[59]

---

[58] The names of the neumes in *SM* show several divergences from modern textbook terminology. The *quilisma*, in particular, appears to be a porrectus ('three or more marks either ascending and then descending, or the reverse'). The nature of the neume which Perseus and Petrus call *plica* is obscure, save that it comprises two notes. The mysterious remarks about the *clivis* ('composed of a mark and half a mark, indicating that the sound must be inflected…the mark at its end denotes a dark sound') are puzzling indeed. Since the authors describe the *clivis* as a neume that 'always wishes to descend', it is plain that, in principle, it is the same neume as the *clivis* of the modern textbook. There are no studies of the neumes described in *SM*. Wagner (*Neumenkunde*, p. 43, n. 2 and p. 68, n. 4) quotes two passages and discusses them very briefly, as does Fleischer (*Die germanischen Neumen*, p. 50 and p. 57, n. 3). Floros (*Universale Neumenkunde*, II, p. 172) quotes a section of *SM*, corresponding to lines 510–18 of the Latin below, in an imposing place, but offers no discussion of the *SM* evidence.

[59] Another reference to the derivation of the word 'musica' from 'muniens usu canentem' ('strengthening the singer by practice'). See n. 28.

A POEM CONCERNING THE SAME

[lines 540–60]

540-60 In former days singers delighted in music so much that they wished to teach the rules of the art to their descendants. They therefore devised new figures to record the various movements of notes. They called them 'marks' because from that moment the syllabus of vocal music was secured. Their names are *clives, plice, virga, quilismata, puncta* and *podati*; the *pressus* [notes] should be classed with these. The *pes*, growing, wishes to stretch upwards with two marks; the high one, liquifying, abandons what it represents.[60] The *clivis* always wishes to descend with two marks, and the mark at its end denotes a dark sound (*obscurumque sonum*). It avoids a pause or lingers in the mouth of one who is pausing, as if it enjoyed the status of a complete mark.[61] If you ignore the *virga*, all the other signs denote a plurality [of sounds] for minor and major forms are frequently encountered. However, up to this point, the eyes cannot encompass a chant unless the ear be enlisted and also the voices of those who sing it first. Because it builds up through use of this kind, the chant which the discipline of *musica* does not acknowledge is called 'practice'.

7 CONCERNING THE SIX SOLMISATION SYLLABLES OF THE HEXACHORD DEGREES AND THEIR SUFFICIENCY

[lines 561–640]

561-72 As I have said, and as daily examples show, there are some singers who should not be called *musici* because they do not follow the rational principles of music and they cannot learn a chant unless it is sung to them repeatedly by another, perhaps a teacher or a colleague. The inventors of music therefore applied their

---

60 'Deficit illa tamen quam signat acuta liquescens' (Latin, line 550). A difficult line whose meaning is far from clear.
61 'Precedit pausam vel stat pausantis in ore' (Latin, line 553). Even more obscure than the previous.

minds, with the utmost diligence and with much searching, to make it possible for anyone keen to remedy his ignorance of music to proceed in an informed way, according to the rules of the art, and thereby learn a chant (that is to say a piece of notated music) without a teacher, and further learn to ponder it, to judge it, to commend it when properly ordered and to correct it when imperfect.

573–81 The first preceptors therefore devised six syllables, *ut, re, mi, fa, sol* and *la* which are the names of the six hexachord degrees if they are considered without any reordering or mutation. If necessity requires that they be reordered, then they name and signify all notes, both above and below, to infinity. The French, the English, the Germans, the Hungarians, the Slavs, the Danes and others on this side of the Alps use these names for the hexachord degrees;[62] the Italians, however, are reported to use other degrees and names; inquire of them if you wish to know what they may be.

582–94 These six names of the hexachord degrees are enough, not only because the number 6 is noble but also because superfluity in art is thereby avoided. Arithmeticians have stated and proved that the nobility of the number 6 rests upon it being the first perfect number. Furthermore, Moses says in the Book of Genesis that because God created Heaven and Earth, that is to say the four Elements, during the course of the first day, for the next five days He adorned them.[63] On the seventh day He rested from all the labour that He had undertaken, and Moses says 'therefore Heaven and Earth were completed'.[64] Since it pleased God to complete the work of creating the world in many days rather than one, this certainly had to happen in six days because the number 6 is, and may be declared to be, perfect, so that this might prove His work to be perfect. On account of this [Moses] fittingly adds: 'and He rested'.[65]

595–601 Necessity also, or convenience, requires that there should not be a larger number of hexachord degrees because superfluity is considered to be a fault in any art, as may be proved thus. When,

---

[62] On the significance of this list of nations see above, Chapter 1.
[63] Genesis 1:1–31.
[64] Genesis 2:1.
[65] Genesis 2:2.

beginning with *ut,* the melody moves (of which more must be said later) up to *la,* if there were any further ascent then a semitone would be placed next (of which more later). But a semitone was placed earlier; thus the same thing would be put twice in a useless fashion and would be deemed a fault in art.

602-10 Perhaps someone will ask why the semitone is located in the middle of the six hexachord degrees; why should it not stand at the beginning or at the end? To this it should be replied, with Aristotle, that Art imitates Nature;[66] it is the same in the natural world where soft organs are placed in a medial position and are enclosed: the brain within the cranium, the intestines and the respiratory organs within the ribcage, the marrow within the bone. The semitone has a soft sound in comparison with the tone and therefore it is located in their midst rather than at an extremity.

611-31 It may also be asked why these syllables, rather than others, are the names of the six aforesaid degrees of the hexachord, that is to say: why are these letters put into the syllables? Some would reply that this arrangement is fortuitous and without any rational basis, but I do not believe that. Perseus says that some people, seeking consolation for their incompetence, declare that the positions of the parts of speech are fortuitous and that it is not possible to transgress in the matter of their order. That is a foolish opinion, however, as can be proved. Solmisation syllables[67] are the signs of notes (*voces*), and since vowels (*vocales*) derive much from the voice (*vox*) from which they take their name and are called vowels, it is fitting that all the vowels be placed in these solmisation syllables. There are six syllables, so it is necessary that the first of the vowels should be repeated to the last of the syllables. These vowels are not disposed in these syllables as they are in *orthographia*; there they are arranged according to the position of the vocal organ, but here they are disposed according to whether they produce a greater or a lesser sound and so that there may be a progress from a less open sound to a more open one, just as has

---

66 *Physica,* II:2 'But if, on the other hand, art imitates nature...'. Compare Guido's remark in his *Micrologus* (HGJ, p. 59).

67 It is curious that, in this section, Perseus and Petrus give no indication that they know the origin of the solmisation syllables *ut re mi fa sol la* in the lines of the opening verse of the hymn *Ut queant laxis.*

been said, because first there is *cantus gravis*, then *acutus* and then *peracutus*. So it is clear to anyone who looks into the matter that the vowel *a* is repeated in the sixth syllable, in preference to any other, because it is more sonorous.

632–40 Concerning the consonants [used in the solmisation syllables], it should be noted that mute consonants are also placed there, but only those which have the most sound when they are pronounced, that is to say *t* and *f*. [The syllables] also contain four semivowels [*r, m, s, l*] and so all the species of letters are included, showing that they are generally accepted in chant for all distinctions of notes. In this way the number and sufficiency of the hexachord degrees is apparent. Neighbouring vowels are not placed adjacent to one another, but are rather mingled [with consonants], to stop neighbouring sounds, sung in a more or less similar way, introducing cacemphaton[68] or a wearisome quality through hiatus.[69]

A POEM CONCERNING THE SAME

[lines 641–80]

641–61 The preceptors of the art called *musica* approved the kind of music which may be taught with rational principles. They disdained mere practice as something which is both often and excessively wearisome, and whose watchword is 'because it is so', never proving anything with 'therefore'. A rational structure removes such error immediately, producing a fixed and specific course of music. A quadruple rule[70] was devised with fixed spaces related to fixed marks by a fixed principle. *Ut, re, mi, fa, sol* and *la*: a sixfold naming of degrees. These suffice and all music may be made with them. There is nothing extraordinary in that, for the number six is deemed to be perfect. We are told that the

---

[68] A term of rhetoric for an ill-sounding expression.

[69] The break between two vowels coming together, without an intervening consonant, in successive words or syllables.

[70] Presumably this 'quadruple rule' (*Quadrupla...regula*) is the staff, although that invention has yet to be reached in the authors' survey of notational history.

mechanism of the universe is founded upon it. You may prove with this argument that six [hexachord degrees] are sufficient if you wish to continue a degree beyond *la*, because, in ascending further, you will repeat what has already been put or – which is an excess – you will employ what is redundant in art, the semitone;[71] since it went before, this also follows: it is better that what has gone before [i.e. the pattern whereby a semitone lies between two tones on either side, TTSTT] be repeated. [The preceptors] established six hexachord degrees and a medial semitone; if we judge correctly, they were guided by Reason.

662–71 It is fitting that soft materials be enclosed within hard ones; Nature does this to guard against harmful things. The soft-sounding [semitone] *mi fa* is evidently such [a soft material], and it is rightly assigned a medial position within the hexachord degrees. If anyone should ask why these letters are placed in the syllables and are put in this order, [it may be replied that] the grammarian offers *a* first and *u* last; lady Music sails forward signalling the same but with a reversed oar. [The grammarian] notes the disposition of the vocal organ, but [lady Music notes] the types of sounds; [*musica*] *gravis* is primary and is put as the first of them.

672–80 Whatever opens the mouth most resonates most and is placed next. The vowel [in each solmisation syllable] is joined to a mute or to a liquid consonant. *U* is first, and then comes another which evidently resonates more, and the fourth vowel [*o*] is placed in the fifth seat [*sol*]; it is apt, however, that [*a*] be repeated in the sixth position [*la*]...They are mixed together [i.e. the vowels in the solmisation syllables are mixed with consonants] lest hiatus, arising from likeness, give offence; euphony requires that the vowels be not placed adjacent to one another. These solmisation syllables require three species of letters, for in their wanderings they touch the extremes[72] of triple melody.

---

71 This section is perhaps the most glaring example in the whole treatise of the difficulty which the authors of *SM* encountered in trying to explain the technicalities of chant theory in metaphorical language and in quantitative verse.

72 The word 'extremes' corresponds to 'gades' in the Latin (line 680). Gerbert capitalised this, 'Gades', as if it were the name of the Spanish port of Cadiz. The word 'gades' is indeed derived from the Latin name of Cadiz, but is here

8 CONCERNING THE PALM AND ITS LINES AND SPACES

[lines 681–811]

681-90 We have explained the six hexachord degrees which suffice for the expression of any melody, and which are placed in lines and spaces. But we have neither mentioned nor explained the names of the lines and of the interposed spaces, nor have we said how many names there are. I say 'interposed', because it is impossible to notate anything below the lowest of the lines or above the highest. In order to clarify this we should first consider the expert attention which the ancient preceptors gave to the question of how they might educate their descendants.

690-706 They reasoned that every craftsman achieves his aim more efficiently with the help of a well-designed implement, and so they contrived to have the rudiments of music attributed to the inner part of the hand, and to the left rather than to the right, if Nature has not erred in forming it (that is to say, if the hand is not malformed with too many fingers or too few). When there are nineteen junctures of the fingers (the tips, ends or summits, which I take to be the same) they may be called connectives.[73] The

being used in a common medieval sense of 'limit' or 'boundary', a sense nascent in Classical Latin and inspired by the position of Cadiz, the western extreme of the known world. The use of the term here provides no clue to the provenance of *SM.*

73 In what follows the authors employ no term corresponding to modern English 'staff', nor indeed is there any concept of the staff as such, but only of lines and spaces (*in lineis et spaciis*, 683), each of which has its own name (*nomina linearum et spaciorum*, 684). Indeed, the puzzlement which we may feel in contemplating the terminology used in *SM* (and in many other plainchant treatises) principally arises from the intrusive references to naming, all bearing the implication that it is somehow important to keep the name and the thing named distinct in our minds but without ever indicating what that importance is. We are simultaneously assured that we are dealing with an elaborate system of signs which must be kept in the front of the mind, and yet in the authors' own usage the system is completely assimilated and is sometimes distorted. It seems that precision is being sought, and yet the terminology used in *SM* is not rigid nor, despite the emphasis on naming, do we always find names where we would expect them (the absence of any term for the staff being an example).

preceptors assigned nineteen positions of hexachord degrees to these, giving each one its own name composed from the letter, which is the name of the *clavis*, and from the name or names of the hexachord degree or degrees which that *clavis* involves. They declared the first connective to be a line, the second a space, and so on until the end; in the layout of any page, however, line and space show more differentiation than the hand.

707–74 They accordingly located a point of reference, that is to say a point to which a hexachord degree may be assigned, on the tip or on the end of the thumb and called it gamut Γ *ut*, which is said to be composed from Γ, which is a Greek letter called *G* by the Latins and which is the letter of this connective, and from its hexachord degree which is *ut*, the handmaiden to this letter. This letter has no more hexachord degrees.

Each line and space has a name compounded from two elements. Firstly, there is a letter of the gamut such as A, B or C (*littera*, 701, but also *clavis*, 710, a usage that survives, for example, in modern English 'clef'). Technically, the *littera* is the name of the *clavis*. In what follows 'littera' has generally been translated 'letter' and 'clavis' 'note', the latter being consistent with modern English usage for one can still speak of 'the note A'.

The second element in the name of a line or space comprises the hexachord degrees (called *note vel notule*, 702) which lift the letter of the gamut away from what is (theoretically) a state of meaningless neutrality and locate it in the scheme of *musica recta*. Thus *E la mi* comprises a *littera/clavis*, E, followed by the two *note/notule*, *la* and *mi*, which fix it as either *la* in a hexachord beginning on gamma or *mi* in a hexachord beginning on C. In what follows the terms 'nota' and 'notula' have been translated 'hexachord degree(s)', for there appears to be no significance (or at least no consistent significance) in the use of the diminutive 'notula'.

A compound name such as *E la mi* is called an *articulus*. Since the hand was used as a mnemonic to help singers remember all these compound names and since each name was assigned to a joint or tip of a finger, the word 'articulus' as used in medieval music theory always retains a strong colouring of its literal sense, a 'joint of the finger'. The transferred sense is 'a point of reference where a letter is joined to its hexachord degrees mnemonically related to a joint of the finger'. I have chosen the translation 'connective' because it suits both the literal and the transferred, technical senses of *articulus*.

The terminology is flexible. In a compound name such as *E la mi*, the *clavis* is technically only what is denoted by the letter E, and yet the term 'clavis' can denote a whole compound name as a shorthand (794–5). A *nota* is a neume, but it is also used to denote a compound name such as *E la mi* (699), and also used for the hexachord degrees which form only part of such a compound name (702 *et passim*).

Further, on the central joint of the thumb, they put *A re*; *A* is the letter and *re* the hexachord degree. This letter has no more degrees.

Next, *B mi* was put on the root of the thumb. *B* is the letter and *mi* the hexachord degree. This seat, or this connective, has no more degrees.

Next, they placed *C fa ut* on the root of the index finger. *C* is the letter, while *fa* and *ut* are the names of two hexachord degrees which belong to it: *fa* in relation to lower letters and *ut* in relation to higher ones.

Next, *D sol re* is placed on the root of the middle finger, and *D* is the sign (*figura*) or letter, while *sol* and *re* are the hexachord degrees which are due to it; *sol* in relation to the lower ones and *re* to the higher.

Next, on the root of the third finger, they put *E la mi*, and *E* is the letter, while *la* and *mi* are the hexachord degrees which are due to it, *la* in relation to lower letters and *mi* to higher ones.

Next, *F fa ut* is located on the root of the little or smallest finger – which is the same thing – and *F* is the letter while *fa* and *ut* are the hexachord degrees which are due to it, *fa* in relation to lower letters and *ut* in relation to higher ones.

Next, *G sol re ut* is situated on the first joint of the little finger. *G* is the letter, while *sol, re* and *ut* are the names of the hexachord degrees which accompany it, *sol* in relation to lower letters, *re* to those above and near and *ut* to those above and much higher.

Next, *a la mi re* is placed on the second joint of the little finger; *a* is the letter, while *la, mi* and *re* are the names of the hexachord degrees which accompany it, *la* in relation to the lower, *mi* to those above and near and *re* to those above and much higher.

Next, *bfa♮mi* was sited on the tip or on the end of the little finger; *b* and ♮ are the names of the letters, but taken in diverse ways, for round *b* is named *fa* and square ♮ is named *mi*.

Next, *c sol fa ut* is placed on the tip of the third finger; *c* is the letter, while *sol, fa* and *ut* are the hexachord degrees which accompany it, *sol* relating to those far lower, *fa* to those which are lower but near and *ut* to those higher.

Next, *d la sol re* is placed on the tip of the middle finger; *d* is the letter, while *la, sol* and *re* are the names of the hexachord degrees, *la* relating to those lower, *sol* to what is lower but near and *re* those higher.

Next, *e la mi* is placed on the tip of the index finger; *e* is the letter, while *la* and *mi* are the names of the hexachord degrees which are due to it, *la* relating to the lower letters and *mi* to the higher ones.

Next, *f fa ut* is installed on the second joint of the index finger; *f* is the letter, while *fa* and *ut* are the names of the hexachord degrees; *fa* relating to the lower letters and *ut* to higher ones.

Next, *g sol re ut* is impressed on the first joint of the index finger; *g* is the letter and *sol*, *re* and *ut* are the names of the hexachord degrees which accompany it; *sol* relates to the lower, *re* to the higher but near and *ut* to those far higher.

Next, ♮ *la mi re* is placed on the first joint of the middle finger; ♮ is the letter while *la*, *mi* and *re* are the names of the hexachord degrees, *la* relating to lower letters and *mi* and *re* to higher ones, but in a different fashion if they are continuous. If round *b* is above then the said ♮ *la mi re* is solmised as *mi*; if there is an ascent through square ♮ then it should be solmised as *re*.

Next, ♭ *fa* ♮ *mi* is placed on the first joint of the third finger; ♭♮ is one letter, but there is a distinction. If it is round ♭ then it will be solmised as *fa*; if it is square ♮ then it is just solmised as *mi*.

Next, ç *sol fa* is installed on the second joint of this same third finger; ç is the letter, while *sol* and *fa* are the names of the hexachord degrees, both of which relate to lower letters, *sol* to what is near while *fa* reaches down to those far below.

Finally, ♦ *la sol* is rooted on the second joint of the middle finger; ♦ is the letter, while *la* and *sol* are the names of the hexachord degrees and they relate to what is below in different ways: *la* to letters far removed, while *sol* wishes to be linked to those placed nearby.

775-83 Among other things it should be known that a seat or connective is said to be 'on a line', as are *G*, *B*, *D* and so on; a connective may equally be 'in a space', as are *A re*, *C fa ut* and others like them. The letter of any connective is said to be 'on a line' for the reason that it is the principle of a line which keeps the name of that connective to itself up to the point where [the line] ends or changes. Similarly, any letter is said to be 'in a space' which is the sign of a connective and the principle of a space which takes its name from that connective up to the end of the space or up to its perceived change.

₇₈₃₋₉₃ A space is defined as a surface designating an even-numbered connective from Γ *ut* up to ♮ *la sol.* From this it can be seen that above ♮ *la sol,* and below Γ *ut,* there is no space that can be used as a point of reference, as has been said, because a space in music is nothing other than a surface actually or theoretically enclosed between two adjacent lines. I say 'theoretically', because it sometimes happens that an upper or lower line is actually added to the four lines [of the staff] and another which could be put, but is not written, is understood as lying beneath. The space interposed in this way should be called 'notable', that is 'assignable to notes'.

₇₉₄₋₈₀₁ It should also be known that the Ancients sang at first from within *A re* and then *B mi,* and so, in ascending, they devised a second sequence of letters taken from the alphabet. Afterwards, indeed, they noticed some chant descending to *A re,* such as the antiphon *O sapientia* and others of its kind, but there cannot be a space on the staff capable of bearing notation unless it is enclosed within defined limits, and for this reason they devised Γ which removes the error beneath this *A re.*

₈₀₁₋₁₁ Anyone who does not know, or does not prearrange, the purpose of his journey or of any labour goes astray. It should also be considered that the letters in the connectives are neatly defined within three boundaries. The first boundary contains Γ *A B C D E F G,* and these are called the *graves* because they are employed with a sound that is low and muted relative to others. The second boundary contains *a b c d e f g,* and these are called the *acute* because they customarily produce a high sound relative to those just given. The third boundary contains ᵃᵇᶜᵈ, and they are called *peracute* because they are higher than the *acute.* For the moment this is enough about the letters.

A POEM CONCERNING THE SAME

[lines 812–54]

₈₁₂₋₃₆ No one knows an art if the principles of that art are not acknowledged. Knowing these things, one does not know everything but only a part; [the singer] desiring to know the hand which music seeks will be able to see into the subtle hearts of the preceptors. They distinguished ten – add a further nine – connectives of the fingers filled with hexachord degrees and with melody. They put the Greek Γ *ut* on the top with the thumb; let Γ be your letter and *ut* your hexachord degree; thus it will be correct. The first [preceptors] ordained *A re* on the first joint of the thumb; *A* is the letter and *re* the hexachord degree. They taught their pupils this. The root [of the thumb] gives *B mi*; it lays *B* open and gives *mi* as the hexachord degree. *C fa ut* follows on from this but it will also stand at the foot of the index finger. Let *C* be your letter; *fa* looks towards lower letters and the hexachord degree *ut* towards what follows, hardly at all to the lower. So it is with the rest; let the letter, the *clavis*, be first; one of the hexachord degrees tends upwards, and another searches downwards. Here, however, make an exception of ε *sol fa* and high ♮ *la sol*, for they cannot leap above themselves. Even as they mount they only look behind; when the path fails it is no flight to turn one's back. It is clear that this is not so with *bfa♮mi*, for there the duplex *b* is regarded as a double letter. The soft, round *b* hastens to be the first; if ♮ is made square it requires *mi* and it is thus also hard.

837-54 The line [that is to say the staff] will show whether it be round or square; music must have a space for both the soft *b* and the hard. When a connective is even-numbered then it will hold a space; if it is odd-numbered then a line will have its name. There are nine spaces, but the tenth line exceeds [this number], and you should not look for any resources beyond that. A space should be enclosed, either theoretically or actually; otherwise the garment of the notes will be found to be full of holes at every touch. Although you have been wise, consider the objective of your travels in advance; to what end do you walk thus? Confusion in these things is injurious. The line or the space runs; it is as if the whole page, not distant from the clef, teaches like a clef.[74] It is sought in the palm why a line is not varied; however, the page may often allow

---

[74] 'Linea vel spacium currit quasi pagina tota/Ut clavis docuit que non est clave remota' (Latin, lines 848–9). A contorted passage; the translation is tentatively offered.

this when it is written out.[75] There is a complete explanation for this; it is because only the palm remains unchanged, nor can four lines easily convey [all] music. It cannot be doubted that many can accomplish more than a few; thus it is in the great affairs of men that a crowd is petitioned.

9 WHY THE HAND IS THE PREFERRED IMPLEMENT OF MUSIC AND NOT SOME OTHER MEMBER

[lines 855–90]

855–76 Reflecting upon the arrangement and usefulness of the hand, the palm of music, it is no wonder if someone should ask why the first teachers chose to found the principles of music upon the hand, an organ and part of the human body, rather than upon some external implement. This question can be answered firstly by interpretation and secondly by reason. It is not true that the principles of music can only be known by means of the hand; there is also the monochord. However, not everyone owns a monochord, nor is one always readily available; furthermore, these principles may be more easily and promptly encompassed and employed by means of the hand. The preceptors therefore considered that among the five senses, as Aristotle says, there are only two which can receive instruction, that is to say sight and hearing,[76] both of which can comprehend teaching which must be put into practice by the hand. A man seeing and hearing, then diligently reaching out with his hand, can grasp much profit. By means of vision he discerns the signs, differences and intervals of the connectives, and through hearing he discerns and contrasts the diversity of sounds. Whence Horace says in the *Ars poetica* that 'we discern the correct sound with finger and ear'.[77]

---

[75] 'Pagina sepe tamen, cum scribitur, hoc patiatur' (Latin, line 850). Another example of compression. Reading passages like this it is important to remember that they are meant to be difficult and to possess a riddling quality. During teaching the *magister* would expound the verses.

[76] *Parva naturalia* (*De sensu*), Chapter 1.

[77] *Ars poetica*, line 274.

877-90 It should also be noted that music brings some benefit to a deaf man who can see – but not much – if he possessed hearing before his deafness and if he was then not ignorant of music. Similarly, this art is of some benefit to a blind man who can hear because his hand can learn by exploring with touch, however ignorant it may have been before. If, indeed, he be deaf, and has never possessed hearing, then music is of no benefit to him, nor is the hand. Aristotle says that 'a blind man does not argue about colours',[78] and we may add in the same way nor does a deaf man [argue] about sounds. A sounding thing is the special province of hearing, just as a coloured thing is of sight. As for external musical instruments, they are of no use to a deaf man, however skilled he may formerly have been in the art of playing them. Nonetheless, a blind man who can hear can play some instruments, but others hardly at all, which is easy to understand and examples are not lacking.

A POEM CONCERNING THE SAME

[lines 891–901]

891-901 The hand is declared to be more useful than other [instruments]; it is much more serviceable and is always nearby. The principal senses are useful with the help of this art: hearing through touch and sight through the medium of appearances. This art is worth nothing to a deaf man, although a blind man can engage with it, both learning and teaching, since he is seen to sing. Make a sound to a deaf man, or lay a colour before a blind one, if it suits you to waste time in vain. Many blind men play musical instruments, but the deaf man must sing sustained by no melody.

---

[78] A confused memory of a passage in *Physica*, II:1, which says exactly the reverse: 'A blind man from birth might reason about colours'.

10 CONCERNING THE KINDS OF INTERVALS

[lines 902–83]

902-9 Having spoken of the connectives, which are also called the seats of the hexachord degrees, let us also consider the hexachord degrees which were assigned to the connectives.[79] One, two or three hexachord degrees must be assigned to each connective, but no more, even though [a note] is only a single vibration or striking of sound. We must further consider how we should refer to a melody composed from two hexachord degrees, and in how many ways may it be varied.

910-20 A combination of degrees is referred to by the general term 'interval', and there are nine kinds: unison, semitone, tone, minor third, major third, fourth, fifth, minor sixth and major sixth. The octave is added last of all. Unison is the beginning and the foundation, so-to-speak, of the intervals, but it is not one of the nine because it is not sung by moving up and down the degrees of the hexachord. It is called 'unison' because the majority of hexachord degrees sound identically when they are continously placed in the same line or space, as for example *re re, fa fa, sol sol* and so on. It is called 'unison' from 'unity of sound'.

921-30 The reverse is true of the semitone, but because the semitone is less than the tone and may be compared to a state of privation, the tone being the habitual state, and because privation cannot be perceived save in relation to what is habitual, we must first consider the tone. The word 'tone' is ambiguous in many respects. A tone in grammar is an accent, which the Ancients divided into acute, circumflex and grave, while the Moderns distinguish acute, moderate and grave. 'Tone' is still used ambiguously in music, denoting the 'tone of two [notes]' and the 'tone of many notes', [that is to say it is divided into] both the minor tone and the major tone.

931-42 The minor tone is a perfect and prime consonance of two dissimilar notes whose relationship of sound is called an interval and thus 'an intervening space' or 'a standing apart'. The tone is called a 'consonance', as it were 'sounding together', because if

---

[79] Compare John (HGJ, pp. 110–12).

the melodic movement of a tone is broken by a long gap it destroys the essence and nature of the tone and it should not be given that name. In this definition, therefore, 'consonance' indicates the genre [of the musical sound], while 'dissimilar notes' excludes the unison. The distinction 'perfect' excludes the semitone and the detail 'prime' excludes the minor third and the other following kinds of intervals.

943–52 It should accordingly be noted that the semitone does not take its name from 'semis', which means 'half', but rather from 'semus, –a, –um', which means 'imperfect', because it is an imperfect tone. It is more than half a tone. Thus it was said of the Trojans [that they were] 'Phrygian eunuchs', and again '[Shall] we [endure] a Phrygian eunuch',[80] and so on. They were called 'imperfect men' [semiviri] because they dressed in the manner of women. Having said these things about the minor tone it remains to speak of the major tone.

953–6 A major tone [i.e. a plainchant mode] is the harmonious relationship of the many notes of one melody; its character is chiefly concentrated towards the end [of a chant]. However, no more of that now for let us not interrupt the subject announced; many things will be said about the matter in due course.

957–70 The minor third (semiditonus) takes its name from 'semis', which means 'imperfect', and 'ditonus', as in re fa and vice versa. The major third (ditonus), means 'double tone', as in mi ut and vice versa. The fourth (diatessaron) takes its name from 'dia', which means 'from', and 'tessaron', which means 'four' or 'square', because it proceeds by four to a note four steps away, as in la mi, fa ut, mi la, sol re and vice versa. The fifth (diapente) takes its name from 'dia', which means 'from', and 'pentha', which means 'five', thus 'made from five notes', as in re la and in other such. The minor sixth (semitonium cum diapente) is so called because it joins a semitone to a fifth, as when a melody moves from the fa which is in c sol fa ut to the mi which is in E la mi among the graves. The major sixth (tonus cum diapente) is a consonance comprising a tone and a fifth, as if the la in a la mi re were joined to the ut which is in C fa ut among the graves, and so on in other instances.

971–83 The ninth and final interval is the octave (diapason), taking its name from 'dia', which means 'from', and 'pan', which means

---

80 Virgil, Aeneid, XII:99; Statius, Achilleidos, line 78.

'all', and 'son', which means 'sound', whence 'containing all consonances', because it encompasses all the connectives of all the other intervals. Others say that it takes its name from 'dia', which means 'from', and 'pasin', meaning 'similar' or 'equal', because it proceeds from like to like. No matter how diversified the connectives may be, the initial letter of any connective, that is to say its *clavis*, has another letter similar to it either eight degrees above or eight degrees below with which it makes an octave; for example, Γ *ut* has *G sol re ut, A re* has *a la mi re, B mi* has *bfa♮mi*, and so on; a musical sound moving from any letter to its peer, whether it ascends or descends, produces an octave.

A POEM CONCERNING THE SAME

[lines 984–1008]

984–96 Each of the connectives has one, two or three hexachord degrees; none contains more. Let there be a hexachord degree and let one be there as often as the pitch is changed; for this reason a pitch that is sung continuously does not require a change of hexachord degree.[81] The degrees can be twinned together; if they are joined in this way then nine intervals, no more, are recognised. Unison is first, and the semitone waits upon it; the tone follows, but its meaning is variable. A 'tone' is an accent [or it is] a defined melodic movement of hexachord degrees [and it may therefore be] either major [i.e. a plainchant mode] or minor [i.e. the interval of a tone]. O minor [tone], be only [an arrangement] of two [notes] which are perfect, continuous and dissimilar. The semitone is smaller and cannot be cut away evenly from these.

997–1008 When a tone is major it will encompass many hexachord degrees, stretching forward to the final from which it will take its name. Let this tone lie and return to the intervals; what has been said before prompts us to consider their names. The major third (*ditonus*) may be understood by the reader to be a double tone; however, the 'ditone' which is joined to the word 'semi' [i.e. the

---

[81] A somewhat expansive and explanatory translation of a compressed original: 'Fit nota, fit totiens quotiens fuerit sonus ictus;/Hoc fine continuus etiam non est nota dictus' (Latin, lines 987–8).

semiditonus, or minor third], precedes this. The fourth [interval, for unison is not counted] associates with the fourth note and then diatessaron comes forward; you should associate the fifth [interval] with the fifth and thus diapente will be produced. The minor sixth follows immediately afterwards. Briefly, there follow the major sixth and the octave. The octave falls into the ninth category, either because it contains all these others or because it contains letters bound in likeness to one another.

11 THE REASON WHY THERE ARE NO MORE INTERVALS THAN NINE AND NO MORE CONNECTIVES THAN NINETEEN

[lines 1009–74]

1009-25 Since two notes are combined in nine ways, so that nine intervals may be formed from them, it would not be foolish if anyone were to ask why the trained musician (*musicus*) is content with only nine intervals, since hexachord degrees can be combined in many ways, both above and within the octave. We may answer that it is the same in every art. Whatever hinders the attempt to illuminate the final purpose of an art should be rejected. Just as in grammar, whose purpose is harmonious utterance, barbarism and solecism are declared to be errors and (what is more striking) cacemphaton is also avoided, so also dialectic, which strives to make doubts out of a matter, discards useless conjunctions of propositions, when hunting down a logically inevitable conclusion, such as the collocation of two affirmations in the second figure and other paralogical phantasies of this sort.[82]

1025-36 Something of this principle operates in all the arts and it is so in music; its principal aim is to give delight, and it therefore rejects and condemns anything that seems to interfere with that

---

[82] The 'useless conjunctions of propositions' are Aristotle's second figure of syllogism in which the middle term is the predicate of both premises. In the *Analytica priora,* I:5, Aristotle states that if both propositions are negative, or if they are both positive, then there is no syllogism. Perseus and Petrus are referring to this when they write of 'the collocation of two affirmations in the second figure'.

aim. Pairings of hexachord degrees which do not constitute any of the nine intervals described above are rightly avoided by a trained musician; they are not the genuine material of melody but produce a hateful dissonance and are judged hostile to the aim of music. Such an interval is *fa* in soft *b* with *E la mi*, both above and below, should it be joined to it in the manner of an interval. Another such is *a la mi re* with *b mi* and vice versa, and a similar verdict must be passed upon similar intervals, and the same must be said of the interval that surmounts the octave [i.e. the ninth].

1037-54 Again, although the ancient preceptors established nineteen connectives or seats of hexachord degrees, it may be asked whether there can be more and whether more should be devised. To which it may be replied that nineteen suffice but there certainly could be more. Since music is classified into the *graves*, *acute* and *peracute*, and since eight letters serve for the *graves*, seven for the *acute* and four for the *peracute*, it can scarcely arise for anyone to have a voice of such strength that he may run through all of the letters in singing and ascend to further ones – even if they were invented – without crossing the break in his voice. If a singer fails to begin a chant in the required low manner, but mounts into the higher letters by beginning it in an incompetent fashion, he does not complain that anything is lacking; he should take the lowest, nearest letter complying with the same letter in place of the upper letter which he seeks but has not found, and he will find in that the octave of the pitch desired. This can be seen with musical instruments that only have seven or eight distinctions of hexachord degrees but which can play any melody.[83]

[83]   Medieval monastic or collegiate choirs, generally working without an organ at this date, and possibly not wishing to interrupt the musical momentum of the liturgy (not to mention its propriety) with the sound of a small bell or some other means of setting pitch, must often have begun chants too high in their voices and have been compelled to abandon the effort; for an early fourteenth-century description of this fault, see Page, *The Owl and the Nightingale*, p. 244, n. 13. Perseus and Petrus seem to be recommending (or at least describing) a technique of octave transposition of the kind used by instrumentalists. This instrumental practice is well attested. See the *Commentarius anonymus in Micrologum Guidonis Aretini*, p. 122 (which mentions the *cymbala* and *organa*), and Jerome of Moravia's account of the playing technique of the five-stringed *viella*, or fiddle (text, translation and commentary in Page, 'Jerome of Moravia', pp. 90–91, Latin text line 446, where the reference is to octave transposition *upward*).

1055-74 Some explain the nineteen hexachord degrees in terms of the nineteen articulations of the hand; they maintain that no more seats of hexachord degrees can be invented because the hand has no more joints. However, it is clearly foolish to believe such things, for there are different kinds of joints both beyond the hand and within it. Let us also remember that Guido added three connectives with hexachord degrees to the nineteen in his *Musica*; for he called our *c sol fa* '*c sol fa ut*', while he called our *d la sol* '*d la sol re*'. Above these he added *e la mi*, *f fa and g sol*.[84] This is the reason that he gives for doing so. Since we can have an octave in the *graves* from Γ up to *G*, and again in the *acute* from *G*, which is the limit of the *graves*, to *g*, which is where the *acute* end, Guido said that it is necessary to have enough connectives among the *peracute* that the octave can also be fulfilled in them, or because music is deficient in this respect. To which it may be replied, as we have said before, that since we can manage without those connectives they are apparently superfluous. Art desires to supply deficiencies but it is also concerned to discard superfluities.[85]

A POEM CONCERNING THE SAME

[lines 1075–99]

1075-87 The joining of two notes, if it is done, will produce nine intervals that sound well. However, their number could be extended further and it may be asked why the use of these does not please. Things which hinder a final purpose cause disturbance; art therefore shuts them outside and the things which we have been discussing should be considered in this light. Soft *b fa*, as it sounds, is contemptuous of having *E la mi*, so too *C fa ut* and, not looking above, *a la mi re*. Each one of these will resound in the manner of wolves; they are excluded from here and we shall not mention their names. If, perhaps, you sing the interval which

---

84 These last three additions to the gamut are not advocated in any authentic Guidonian writing.

85 Compare Aristotle, *Nicomachean Ethics*, II:6 'Thus a master of any art avoids excess and defect...'.

transcends the octave [i.e. the ninth] you will think that you have
let loose the braying of an elephant rather than song.

1088–99 There are nine plus ten connectives of hexachord degrees;
it might be asked whether their number could be enlarged. Guido
answers 'yes'; he taught us to supplement them with three more,
the others having been left behind. The nearest is *e la mi,* then *f fa*
and *g sol* follows; he added these so that an octave might be
achieved with them, for with this arrangement you can find it
among the *graves, acute* and *peracute* with these three [*e, f* and *g*]
following at the end. Since, however, there seems no good reason
for these notes there is no need for us to teach them in this art; a
singer is rarely required to mount so high that he cannot mutate
his chant into the remaining letters.

12 CONCERNING THE REPRESENTATIONS OF INTERVALS ARRANGED BY VARIOUS PEOPLE IN VARIOUS WAYS

[lines 1100–169]

1100–109 From what has been said it will be clear that the intervals
employed in chant proceed according to arsis and thesis, so it is
convenient to measure them within defined boundaries; otherwise
there would be no apparent difference between the space of a
greater and the space of a lesser [interval].[86] Representations
(*signa*) are therefore required which allow the various kinds of
intervals to be recognised, and something must accordingly be said
about them. In musical instruments the representations of
hexachord degrees are established in different ways according to
the various properties of the instruments.

1109–25 Wind instruments have no greater continuous
[representation] than tone or semitone according to how they are
disposed, progressively arranged. *Organa, tibie, cornua, muse, syringe,
flaiota* and others are of this kind. Certain stringed instruments are
also progressively tuned, like *cithare* and *psalteria,* the *organistrum,
monocordium* and others like these, and they have their own
representations of their hexachord degrees. Percussion

[86] Compare John (HGJ, pp. 146–51).

instruments recognised according to their arrangement and disposition are also of this kind, like *cymbala*. There are more stringed instruments, which are barely distinguishable by the ear from others, and they are tuned in the consonances of octave, fourth and fifth; by stopping the strings in various positions with the fingers the players of these produce tones and semitones, and so it is with the rest [of the intervals].[87] A singer, however, has the connectives on his hand and distinctions of pitch for his representations, and with these he can either write a melody on a page or can learn it and sing it from notation if he wishes. Clearly, he is lacking in signs which indicate the duration of sounds.

1125–40 The Ancients used various representations in various ways, and as a demonstration of what follows it should be noted that the first preceptors were accustomed to form the letters of all the connectives in various ways. They represented *G* by the Greek Γ and next they placed the single letters *A B C D E F G* and assigned them to the *graves*. Then they established the *claves acutas* with the letters *a b c d e f g*. Finally, they formed the *claves peracutas* with the four doubled letters ♮ ♭ ♮ ♭, and it is obvious that the letter of each connective retains its own individual form. After this, some of the Ancients who wished to notate chant without lines for their own use, not for others, simply wrote the letter as a notational symbol. It is easy to see, from what has been said, how a melody was notated with letters above the words, but it is apparent that this manner of singing is too unwieldy for it requires a double labour.

1141–8 Concerning the difficulty or diversity of the letters devised by the Ancients, we say that it is not necessary to represent all the letters differently. When anything is notated beyond Γ in single letters, and when both the *graves* and *acute* are written, it suffices to observe one distinction, namely that the letter which is on a line among the *graves* is to be found in a space among the *peracute* and vice versa. Among the *peracute* it is useful to employ capital letters

---

[87] With the exception of Jerome of Moravia's chapter on the *rubeba* and *viella* in his *Tractatus de musica*, this is the only solid piece of medieval Western evidence pertaining to the tuning of fingerboard instruments before the later fifteenth century. The testimony of Perseus and Petrus supports the evidence of Jerome in that they do not mention the use of thirds or sixths, major or minor, but only fourths, fifths and octaves. For an interpretation of this evidence see Page, *Voices and Instruments*, pp. 126–33.

to distinguish them from the *graves* in case the resemblance between the two may cause error.

1148-56 After the time of the said singers, Hermannus Contractus notated music in a different way without lines. For an equal sound or unison (which is the same) he put *e*; for a semitone *s*, for a tone *t*; for a minor third [*semiditonus*] he used *t* and *s*, that is to say *s* above *t* in this fashion *t^s*. For the major third [*ditonus*] he employed double *t^t*; for the fourth [*diatessaron*] *d*, and for the fifth *n*; for the minor sixth [*semitonium cum diapente*] he put *n^s*, and for the major sixth [*tonus cum diapente*] he used *n^t*. For the octave he employed capital *A*. These representations of intervals, when they lack points, signify an ascent.

1156-69 Up to this time, however, music was still shrouded in much obscurity, so Salomon, Odo and Guido invented other devices so that they might designate the connectives with lines drawn across the surface of the page with interposed spaces, and so that they might express the differences between intervals using the neumes of plainchant interposed between these lines and spaces. They therefore put clefs at the beginning of the lines designating these same connectives either to the end of the line or to the point where they changed. They also employed one further distinguishing sign, for they notated using colours: yellow for *c*, green for *a* and red for *F*. But much error arises from this system of changing colours, produced by the mutation of the lines and by the variability of music, both higher and lower.

A POEM CONCERNING THE SAME

[lines 1170–84]

1170-84 There is thesis, there is arsis and there is unison; the representations which entirely identify all species should be noticed first. Some of the Ancients placed the letters as markings, believing that novices might wish to sing using those. Others, in due course, notated intervals with ciphers; by means of these Hermannus wished to benefit future ages. Both teachings were at first obscure to small boys; eventually, others produced records with more effective musical notation. With Guido's help, lines and spaces, with clefs in an initial position, identify musical signs for us. [Guido] further wished that the lower notes might be separated from the higher ones by the use of different colours, but this manner of notation does not have many devotees because the renewal of the music, or of the line, gives rise to error.

13 CONCERNING THE STRATAGEMS WITH WHICH A NEW AND UNTRAINED SINGER LEARNS CHANT

[lines 1185–219]

1185-93 Anyone who has understood musical notation, and who wishes a quick remedy for his ignorance of chant, should consider the clefs first of all, then whether the first note is located on a line or in a space, and then how many notes should be assigned to one vowel.[88] I say 'to one vowel', and not 'to one consonant', for as in grammar, where the accent is principally placed upon the vowel rather than upon the consonant, so it is with the neume or neumes of music.

1194-8 Next, the singer should perform the phrase or group of neumes distinctly by itself, and when he pauses to take a breath he should not begin a syllable after a pause unless it is the first of a word; such splitting of syllables in singing produces barbarism and an unsuitable performance (*ostensionem*).

1199-204 Next, a junior singer of this kind should proceed very carefully so that he does not delay the placing of the semitone or place it negligently. He should be particularly cautious in dealing with soft *b* and hard ♮ to avoid going awry; these must be assigned [by scribes] to their proper neumes, for if they are not properly indicated, because of negligence, then they often lead a singer who does not know the music by heart into error.

1205-7 The novice singer should chiefly attend to this rule: that he hold one note as long as is necessary to consider fully where, and how, the next note should begin.

1208-19 The inexperienced singer should frequently study by singing with someone else, and must diligently consider the

[88] Compare John (HGJ, p. 151).

mutations and intervals. He should learn the chant by heart so that he may sing in a more accomplished fashion when he is alone. He should also study a chant beyond the matter of its intervals or whatever mode it may display, and if he does not have a supple voice but a harsh one, and if he has perhaps forfeited a teacher's offer of help and favour, then he should take extra care and also play musical instruments, especially those like the *monocordium* [and the] *symphonia* which is called *organistrum*.[89] He should also study to play the organ. On instruments of this kind the note cannot readily go astray, nor be twisted from its proper pitch, because the notes can easily be studied with the aid of fixed and labelled keys and then promptly performed by the singer without an associate or teacher.

A POEM CONCERNING THE SAME

[lines 1220–47]

1220-35 If the singer who gladly wishes to sing is inexperienced, then he should frequently sing with a friend or teacher so that he can learn how to perform a chant clearly. He should review the clefs, distinguishing them and fixing them in his mind to the point where the music which they define mutates or lasts; by these means he will be able to sing graciously. Next, he should examine the first neume to determine whether it is located on a line or in a space, and to see whether it is joined to anything. He should also study how to congregate the notes on a vowel and how to determine which [notes] may be rightly taken away from that vowel. A phrase carries many notes, called a *clausula*, and those notes should be performed alike; none should be left aside. He should sing a new [phrase] distinctly, but a syllable must not be begun after a pause unless it begins a new word.

1236-47 As for the semitone, in order not to be inept the inexperienced singer should keep strictly to the rule of the art

---

[89] For the use of the *organistrum* and *symphonia* in the teaching of chant to boys, see Page, 'The Medieval *Organistrum* and *Symphonia*', Part I, plate V (which shows the instrument being used by a boy *and* a songmaster), and bibliography there cited.

when he is inexperienced, whose best stratagem for the novice is clearly that he should hold the note until he is sure of the one seen next. He should learn the intervals by always keeping watch on *Ter terni*,[90] holding its essence not just in the hands but in the heart. Thinking he knows everything, he scarcely knows a part. 'Study hard, however much art you may have learned.' It is possible that the novice has a harsh voice and has therefore lost the favour of a teacher who has no wish to labour in vain. He should not abandon his studies, however; he ought to cultivate musical instruments and concordantly join vocal sounds to the touching of keys.

14 CONCERNING THE INVENTION OF THE MODES AND THEIR NUMBER

[lines 1248–350]

1248–62 It was said above that the word 'tone' is ambiguous, denoting both a major tone [i.e. a plainchant mode] and a minor tone [i.e. the interval of a tone]. The minor has already been discussed, so we now speak of the major, giving our attention to what it is and how it is divided. In part, we have touched upon the question of what it is because a major tone is a regulated motion of chant of many notes which is chiefly directed towards its end. 'Motion' denotes the type [of melody], while 'regulated' is added to distinguish it from music which exceeds the diatonic species either above or below; 'many notes' distinguishes [the major tone] from the minor which consists only of the musical relation of two [notes]. 'Chiefly directed towards its end' is added to refute the opinion of those who believe that a chant should be judged in relation to its beginning.

1263–75 Thus provided with a definition of a mode, it remains to be seen how it is divided. The Ancients of music divided the mode into four parts, namely into the Protus, Deuterus, Tritus and Tetrardus, that is to say the first, second, third and fourth, but one may ask what reasoning led them to make this fourfold division. To

---

[90] The first two words of a didactic song for learning intervals and their names, associated with Hermannus Contractus.

which it may be replied that these inventive preceptors studiously and carefully considered that music is founded upon a supreme and benign harmony of sounds. It is rationally organized therefore according to the number and proportion of things which are known to possess concord of a benign, supreme and primary order, that is to say the Elements whose union and mutually concordant discord form the Macrocosm, that is to say the Greater World.

1276–87 Fire is hot in the highest degree, Air moist, Earth dry and Water cold. Drawing the rationale of their number from this, the first preceptors divided the modes into four. The same fourfold division, also founded upon the Elements but differently arranged, is found in the Microcosm, that is to say in the Lesser World which is Man. He is constituted from four Humours, namely Choler, Blood, Phlegm and Melancholy, and these partake of the four Elemental properties just mentioned, but they are not arranged according to the disposition which is [explained] above and below. The Elemental temperament and disposition are also found in the four quarters of the year, month and day.[91]

1288–303 The [Ancients] also stipulated that chant of the Protus should have its final on *D*, of the Deuterus on *E*, of the Tritus on *F* and of the Tetrardus on *G*. But it may be enquired why chant is most appropriately brought to a close on these notes rather than others, be they higher or lower, and why on adjacent notes rather than separated ones. It may be replied that music was principally invented for the sake of delight, and it therefore entrusts its final purpose to the *graves*, rather than to the *acute* or to the *peracute*, which is designed to achieve this objective in a reasoned and delightful manner. But [chants] evidently show a contrary tendency when they rise a fifth to their final note. However, this is an inessential feature to ornament the end of a chant which is principally orientated towards the *graves*. It is a proof of this that while many can hold a melody securely when it lies among the *graves*, few can sing it a fifth higher; if it were the reverse it would be irregular.

91 The four quarters of the year, month and day will be the division of the year into four sections of three months, the division of the month into the four quarters of the moon, and the division of the day into four sections of six hours.

1303-14 Since chants of all the modes are accordingly brought to a close in a regulated fashion amongst the *graves*, they admit the higher notes of the *graves* [as their finals, i.e. *D E F G*] rather than the lower ones since, as will be explained afterwards, a chant very often descends below its final, and this would not be appropriate if it employed some final among the lower *graves*. The modes end on four notes rather than upon one, and those not separated but contiguous, because the modes are arranged in relation to the Elements which are not identical but have four positions: Earth the lowest, Water next, Air third and Fire fourth. Thus the Elements are not placed separately but adjacently, whence also the modes.

1315-23 The inventors of the four modes were followed by others, more perspicacious than the Ancients, who noticed that chant of the four modes sometimes ascends and descends a good deal. To avoid confusion they divided each mode into two: the Protus into the authentic Protus and the plagal Protus, the Deuterus into the authentic Deuterus and the plagal Deuterus, the Tritus into the authentic Tritus and the plagal Tritus, and the Tetrardus into the authentic Tetrardus and the plagal Tetrardus.

1323-34 'Plagalis' derives from 'plaga', which means a 'placing' or 'a lowering', because [a plagal mode] relates very much to the lower notes. 'Authentus' means 'extended on high', because [an authentic mode] ascends into the higher letters more, or perhaps *authentus* is as much as to say *authenticus* because it is more noble than a plagal and is like a master to it. Note that any authentic mode is odd-numbered, and if [a mode] is even-numbered then it is plagal. The authentic Protus and the plagal Protus have the same final, *D*, and they are the first and second. The authentic Deuterus and the plagal Deuterus, that is to say the third and fourth, have *E*; the authentic Tritus and the plagal Tritus, that is to say the fifth and sixth, have *F*; the authentic Tetrardus and the plagal Tetrardus, that is to say the seventh and the eighth, have *G*.

1335-50 Perhaps someone will ask about the rational basis of this eightfold division and enquire whether there is anything in Nature upon which this number and its property might be founded. It may be said in reply that this eightfold arrangement is deduced from the same reasoning as the fourfold arrangement [of the modes] mentioned above, but viewed differently. Although there are four Elements, and only four prime Elemental qualities, each Element has a principal quality and a secondary quality which is less innate and is less specific than the first. For example, Fire is principally hot, secondarily dry; Earth is principally dry and then cold, but Water is innately cold and then moist as a non-essential property. Air is described as principally moist and secondarily hot. In this way the eightfold number of modes is deduced, and just as an Element possesses one quality principally and the other secondarily, so two modes come together in one final, principally in the authentic mode, secondarily in the plagal.

A POEM CONCERNING THE SAME

[lines 1351–93]

1351-61 The Ancients declared there to be four species of modes; it may be asked how that number was deduced. The Elements of the Greater World are content with this number; add the humours of the lesser and the parts of the year, of the month and of broad daylight; with these you may compare modes which are of the same kind. They also have contiguous parts and are fixed in their order; consider the four species of mode thereby encountered. They will hold the highest letters of the *graves* for their boundary and they cannot properly be finished anywhere else.

1362-75 Those who came later noticed that the first [preceptors] had erred in the number of [modes] who, now lower and now in a high voice, intoned any of the modes, authentic or plagal; their successors declared one in each pair of modes to be less distinguished than the other. This one is called an authentic mode, as if to mean 'stretched high', while that one will be called plagal, 'pressed down' because slow to rise. A plagal is even-numbered, a dependent, and it walks and moves in a lowly fashion; an authentic is odd-numbered, a master, and it flies in front with wings. Thus the number increases, and thus an eightfold division goes forth; one [modal category] covers two as if beneath a veil. An even-numbered and an odd-numbered mode seek the same note so that they can eventually conclude a chant in the same fashion; a lord and a servant, although they are not united at table or in their burden, both sleep at night in the same way.

1376-93 Having said why there are twice two [modes] it must now be explained why there are eight, doubling the number. A tree puts forth its first, massive boughs, and sometimes a great one divides into a pair of lesser ones. Although Fire is primarily hot, it is secondarily dry, so divide Fire into two parts in this way, and Earth is firstly dry and explained as subsequently cold. So it is with the rest; let Water and Air be doubled. An eightfold arrangement, like the sun, rises up from this to be the first principle of two; the remaining one is a servant. The finals are given to the authentics first, so-to-speak; then, they are given to the even-numbered [modes] from the lowest up. Aristotle says that there cannot be more Elements, nor can there naturally be fewer. A circle drawn, when it is a perfect form, is no more and no less than what it customarily is. Whence it is plain that music is a splendid perfection which is founded on these things and has such fixed signs.

15 THE NOTES AND SUBSTITUTES WHICH SERVE AS THE FINALS OF THE MODES

[lines 1394–449]

1394-403 It has been said that the Protus ends on *D*, the Deuterus on *E*, the Tritus on *F* and the Tetrardus on *G*, and these finals are the exclusive property of the modes just described according to the rules of music.[92] I say 'exclusive' because a chant is sometimes ended in a fashion not its own. Occasionally, a chant which should end exclusively, and according to the rules of music, among the *graves,* has to be finished higher among the *acute,* and this is done because of a necessity that is principally created by the semitone.

1403-14 If a chant of this kind is placed amongst the *graves* it either lacks a semitone where it should have one or has a semitone where

---

[92] Here, as in many places in the discussion of modes, the authors employ an Aristotelian distinction between 'proper' and 'accident', the former denoting the essential, defining properties of a thing, and the latter denoting the non-essential properties. In the Latin of this passage, as in many other places in *SM*, the sense of 'proper' is conveyed adverbially by 'proprie'.

it should lack one. Accordingly, when a chant of this sort can find its desired ascents and descents amongst the *acute*, it is transferred from the *graves* to the *acute* so that it is not impeded by the semitone. But this arises as a grace, not as of right judgement; furthermore, this freedom is only granted to the Protus, Deuterus and Tritus, because *D*, which is [the final] exclusive to the Protus, has the very similar substitute *a*; also *E*, which is exclusive to the Deuterus, has hard *b* as a substitute in *bfa♮mi*; so too *F*, which is exclusive to the Tritus among the *graves*, has a substitute in *c* among the *acute*.

1414–21 The Tetrardus never avoids its final *G*, for on account of the proximity of a semitone, above and below, necessity never leans on it for its final to be located elsewhere, therefore it does not need a substitute and it can perform its proper task in the proper place. If a chant of the Tetrardus is sometimes seen to wander from its proper course, it should be attributed to the ignorance of the composer (*primi eius cantoris*) or perhaps of the scribe, and submitted to the correction of an experienced singer.

1422–38 To give some examples of the necessity just described, [we may say that] chant of the Protus goes astray among the *graves* in the second mode antiphon *Magnum hereditatis mysterium*, for necessity compels it to end on *a*. Note that if a chant ends higher, then the transposition (*translatio*) must begin higher according to the demands of the final. Since this often happens, as has been said, because of a semitone being wanting, some players of musical instruments place a semitone between *G* and *F* and some between *G* and *a*; they call this the 'false' *clavis*, and in chant this convenience chiefly pertains to the instrument which is called the organ.[93] It has no place in vocal, human music. Guido (most

---

[93] This use of what is clearly *musica falsa* terminology may cause surprise in a text composed *c.* 1200, for it is widely held that the *De mensurabili musica* (*c.* 1240) of Johannes de Garlandia contains the earliest instance of *falsa* in this sense (see, for example, *Grove 6*, 'Musica Ficta'). However, the term 'musica falsa' appears in the *Carmen de musica cum glossis*, which has been attributed, on the basis of sound arguments, to Alexander de Villa Dei (*fl c.* 1200). See Seay, *Carmen de musica cum glossis*, p. 19. Another theorist, the Seay Anonymous, discussing practices of the later twelfth century, refers to any singer who transgresses against 'the natural disposition of music' so that he may sing 'what cannot be notated in music' as a *falsus* (Seay Anon, p. 25). These two

expert in the art of music) included several things in his *Musica* which we do not need when he added three new letters to the *peracute* in order to create an octave with them, and he could easily have added the semitones [between *F, G* and *a*] if they were necessary.

1438–49 Accordingly, when necessity dictates that a chant of this kind cannot be finished amongst the *graves*, we may seek help from the *acute*. When a chant of the Protus cannot touch *D* in the responsory *Sancta et immaculata es virgo*, it requests the substitute final *a*, ascending from the *graves* into the *acute*. Again, a chant of the Deuterus does not observe its proper course in the communion *Quod dico vobis in tenebris*. Similarly, chant of the Tritus, sometimes leaving its proper course, takes *C* rather than *F,* as in the responsory *Tua sunt hec Christe*. If anyone begins and sings all of these on the substitute *claves* or affinities, he will come to the end without error. The Tetrardus, however, will not change its proper seat.

A POEM CONCERNING THE SAME

[lines 1450–65]

1450–65 Chant is finished among the *graves* by the law of the modes; they have three substitute finals among the *acute*. The Protus has *D*, but the Deuterus can take *E* for itself; *F* belongs to the Tritus but *G*

texts, taken together with *SM*, extend the terminology of *musica falsa* back to the second half of the twelfth century and possibly beyond.

This passage is the earliest evidence we possess of chromatic keys on the Western organ. Presumably they became particularly necessary when organists accompanied (or alternated with) a choir. This is the point explicitly made by the anonymous author of the *Cuiusdam carthusiensis monachi Tractatus de musica plana* (Coussemaker, Scriptorum, II, p. 441), a compendium surviving in a manuscript copied in the first years of the sixteenth century but having many points of contact with *SM*. For a late thirteenth-century reference to what may be the organ (*cum organis*) in the alternatim performance of sequences, see Page, *The Owl and the Nightingale*, p. 217, n. 84. By the time of Jacques de Liège (*c.* 1330) the tones on an organ keyboard were divided 'almost everywhere' (*quasi ubique*) into semitones (ed. Bragard, VI, p. 136). See further Hibberd, '*Musica ficta* and Instrumental Music'.

serves the Tetrardus. Aligned with the first three are *a*, ♮ and *c*, dissimilar in aspect, they are well in chant. The Tetrardus has only *G* and let it hold that alone; the singer who denies this should be sorry for his own error. If a chant of the Protus ends badly on *D*, its exclusive [final], you may ascend so that it can end on *a*. The Deuterus, losing *E*, seeks to have hard ♮; the Tritus, fleeing from *F*, wishes through *c* to please as it comes to a close. The seventh and eighth retain their own seat, for a neighbour does not draw them into another abode. It is better that the finals of chant be legitimately varied…[*some text missing at this point*].

16 CONCERNING THE INITIAL NOTES OF THE MODES, HOW [THE MODES] SHOULD ASCEND AND DESCEND AND HOW MUCH

[lines 1466–542]

1466-76 It has been explained that a chant of any mode is chiefly considered and judged in the region of its close. This means that however much a chant may display the characteristics of a particular mode at its beginning, and may yet move closer to that same mode in the middle, it is chiefly adapted to [its mode] at the end. Since we have already discussed the finals of modes – what they are and how many they are – we should now discuss the initial notes of their chant and by how many degrees they may cross the final above and below.

1477-82 However, it may be enquired why the finals of the modes were discussed first, in preference to their initials or those which relate to the middle. The appropriate answer is that this was done because of the greater worthiness of the final, for a chant is not so well judged in terms of its beginning or middle as in terms of its end.

1483-97 The authentic Protus has four proper initials: *C*, *D*, *F* and *a*. Every chant of the first mode properly begins either on *C*, as in the antiphon *Post excessum beatissimi*, or on D, as in the antiphon *Ecce nomen domini*, or on *F*, like *Venit lumen*, or on *a*, as in *Exi cito*. A chant of this mode never begins on *E* or *G*. Chant of the first mode descends as far as *A*, four notes below the final, as in the beginning of the responsory *Letetur omne seculum*. It ascends to the letter *g*, that is to say ten notes above its final, in the same responsory at the words *eternus amor*. Some are of the opinion that this chant is irregular because of its excessive ascent, but we may counter them by saying that this ascent is delightful and so does not overstep the goal of music, chiefly invented for the sake of pleasure.

1498–504 The plagal Protus has four initials or principals: *A, C, D* and *F*. It has *A* as in *Ecce advenit*; *C* as in *Fuit ad tempus*; *D* as in *O sapientia*; *F* as in *Consolamini*. Chant of this mode descends to Γ, which is not found in the others, as in *Collegerunt* and in the beginning of the sequence *Eya dic nobis*; it ascends to *d*, seven notes above the final, as in the responsory *Omnis pulchritudo*.

1505–9 The authentic Deuterus has three proper initials: *E, F* and *G*. It has *E* as in *Hec est que nescivit*; *F* as in *O gloriosum*; *G* as in *Te semper idem*. It descends only to *C*, as in the responsory [*O*] *magnum mysterium*, and ascends to *g* among the *acute*, as in the responsory *Virtute magna* at the word *testimonium*.

1510–14 The plagal Deuterus has five initials: *C, D, E, F* and *G*. It has *C* as in *Frange esurienti*; *D* as in *Tuam domine*; *E* as in *Vigilate animo*; *F* as in *Tota pulchra*; *G* as in *Post partum virgo*. It descends as far as *B mi*, as in the responsory *Tanto tempore*. It ascends as far as *c* among the *acute*, as in *Exequie Martini*.

1515–19 The authentic Tritus has three proper initials: *F* as in *Paganorum multitudo*; *a* as in *Solvite templum hoc*, and *c* as in *Sanctus, sanctus, sanctus*. It ascends to *g*, as in the responsory *Qui cum audissent*. It never (or rarely) descends below its final, something not found in the others.

1520–24 The plagal Tritus sometimes ascends to *d*, and among the *peracute*, but then it is brought to a close on *c*, the substitute final, as in the sequence *Verbum dei deo natum*. When it closes among the *graves*, however, it has two initials, *D* and *F*. It has *D* as in *Hodie scietis*, and *F* as in *O admirabile*.

1525–30 These modes have their own initials just described when they end in their proper fashion; nonetheless, when necessity compels, they are obliged to change their proper finals and to accept others. This variation is not found in the seventh and eighth modes.

1531–5 The authentic Tetrardus has four initials: *G* as in *Angelus ad pastores*; ♮ as in *Misit dominus*; *c* as in *Populus Syon* and *d* as in *Omnes sitientes.* It does not descend any further than *F fa ut,* as in the aforesaid antiphon *Angelus ad pastores.* It ascends, however, as far as *g,* as in the antiphon *Omnes sitientes* at the word *querite.*

1536–42 The plagal Tritus has six initials: *C* as in *Sapientia clamitat; D* as in *Spiritus domini; F* as in *Alleluia nativitas; a* as in *Quodcumque ligaveris; g* as in *Repleti sunt omnes; c* as in *Erat enim.* It ascends to *a* amongst the *peracute* as in the gradual *Miserere,* at the words *omnia ossa.* It descends to *C* where the antiphon *Sapientia clamitat* begins, and it always ends on the same, that is to say upon *G.*

A POEM CONCERNING THE SAME

[lines 1543–84]

1543–55 The end [of a chant] leads the way in higher state, and there should only be a mention of the beginning (not the first in esteem) and of the middle. The first mode begins on *C, D, F fa ut* or *a;* they authenticate *Ductus* [*est Iesus*], *Ecce* [*nomen domini*] and *Venit* [*lumen*]. Let *Exi* [*cito*] be appended like a tail. It seeks *g* in ascending but seeks *A re* in descent; should you sing *Letetur* [*omne seculum*] you can register both of these. The second departs from *A re* and the same [mode] submits to *C, D* and *F fa ut.* Long ago, some wished to add gamma to those now mentioned. However, this introit *Ecce* [*nomen domini*], *O* [*sapientia*] and *Genuit* [*puerpera*] will authenticate *Eya dic nobis,* which will sound through Γ, as Protus [chants]. Many a *Natus* and *Natalis* will sound through Γ, and many will begin what I have said on [*A*] *re.*

1556–71 A prudent man will follow the usage of the Church in the smallest matters, accommodating others lest he be always weighed down with strife. In *Collegerunt* [*pontifices*] you yield to gamma *ut;* perhaps, by singing *Omnis* [*pulchritudo*] you have sung to *d* among the *acute.* The third mode enters, *E* and *F* wish to be associated with *G,* always to attend upon *O* [*gloriosum*], *Pauli* and *Te* [*semper idem*]. It descends to *C,* and mounting touches *g,* to which eminence it leads you as you sing and follow. The fourth mode retains five [initial notes]: *C, D,* then *E* and it submits to *F* and *G...* it descends to *B* but easily mounts on high to *e.* I lack an example; since it is simple I also leap. The fifth mode has three: *F, a* and the *c* which is recognised by a line. It never steps lower; it is found at *g* among the *acute*. The sixth mode, taking *F* as its primary final, will take *D* or *F* as a beginning; descending, it seeks low *C.* Hence the introit *Hodie* [*scietis*], *Testes* and *Benedictus.*

1572–84 Notes are changed above when [the final of the sixth mode] is taken from *c;* let it be so in these cases if it is necessary, but you will not move the Tetrardus from its proper seat for you will see it ending always and everywhere on *G.* The seventh mode enters on *G;* next you may join ♮, *c* and also *d.* This is witnessed by Caput [*draconis*], Misit [*dominus*], Populus [*Syon*] and Omnes [*sitientes*]. The seventh mode touches its neighbour, *F,* and mounts to *g; Angelus* [*ad pastores*] and *Omnes* [? *sitientes*] will make a secure chant for you to sing. The eighth mode is richer in beginning than the rest; if it seeks a lodging it beholds six as it travels. It enters on *C* or *D,* both *F* and *G,* and asks for both *a* and *c.* It descends to *C* but stretches up to surpassingly lofty *a. Sapientia* [*clamitat*] gives the former and *Miserere* supplies the latter.

17 HOW MUCH THE AUTHENTIC AND PLAGAL MODES MAY ASCEND AND DESCEND

[lines 1585–614]

1585–605 The regular range and constitution of the modes have been discussed in specific terms, but this can be retained more concisely through general rules. I define 'regular range' or 'constitution' in chant as fixed ascent or descent, that is by how much any of the modes may be stretched or relaxed, that is to say by how much they may properly or improperly ascend or descend, that is to say according to rule or to concession. It should therefore be noted that an authentic chant may sometimes ascend through an octave, eight notes above its final, and as a licence [it may ascend] to the ninth and eventually to the tenth degree, but rarely. What anyone possesses by rights he may frequently use; the wise man, however, employs what is conceded to him with both restraint and caution. A plagal chant, however, may sometimes ascend through a fifth and up to the sixth degree, and as a licence it may mount to the seventh and eventually to the octave, but rarely. Plagal chants, moreover, descend to four notes below their final – that is to say through a fourth – and also down to the fifth note, but this rarely. Authentic chants, indeed, descend to the fourth [below the final] which is [the region] of the plagals.

1605-14 The third mode is an exception, for it does not cross below the note just under the final, and so is the fifth [mode], which is never required to descend below its final. However, although it has been said that the authentic modes may ascend through an octave and sometimes further, and the plagals through a fifth and sometimes further, one should not conclude that this must always be so but rather that it may be done in this way, just as we say that a bishop may ordain both the greater and the lesser Holy Orders on four occasions; this does not mean that he must do so on all four occasions, but only that he may.

A POEM CONCERNING THE SAME

[lines 1615–29]

1615-29 You may believe that you know the regular range and law of the modes when you know where their regular course should proceed and how much it may extend. The authentic modes have the right to climb an octave; one [note] may be added, or perhaps two. It befits the wise man to use sparingly what is conceded to him, but you will be able to employ what is yours in safety and well beyond that. It is right for a plagal mode to ascend through a fifth; it is allowed one extra note or two, also three without difficulty. A plagal mode will have twice two notes below the final; one further is added but it will rarely see five. Give four [notes below the final] to the authentics; the third mode is an exception, joining itself to one. The fifth mode is friendly to none. Nobody will think that it is always done to ascend and descend in this way; he will rather note that it can be done.

18 HOW AN AUTHENTIC CHANT IS DISTINGUISHED FROM A PLAGAL THROUGH DISTINCTIVE NOTES

[lines 1630–711]

1630–46 Although there are four proper finals of the modes, that is to say *D*, *E*, *F* and *G*, I say 'proper' because, when necessity compels, the Protus, Deuterus and Tritus have substitute finals corresponding to themselves through a fifth, as if having its harmoniousness, which are *a* ♮ *c* among the *acute*, through which there is some excuse for the defect in *D*, *E* and *F* among the *graves*. Someone will ask how the first [mode] can be distinguished from the second, since each of them accepts *D* as its final. The same question may be asked of the third and fourth, whose final is *E* among the *graves*, so also of the seventh and eighth, both of which adopt *G* as their final. But if it is both a good and a difficult matter to distinguish in this matter then art is lacking. Aristotle says that it is not very difficult to draw a distinction between very dissimilar things, but rather between those which are mostly alike.[94]

1647–55 With reference to this it should be noted that just as there are four finals, so also there are four distinctive notes of the modes. Much has been said above concerning the finals. The distinctive notes of the modes are contained in the little finger, and they are *F*, *G*, *a* and hard ♮. There are four, indeed, no more and no less, because although there are eight modes, each distinctive note serves to differentiate two modes. *F* distinguishes the first from the second, *G* the third from the fourth, *a* the fifth from the sixth, and hard ♮ the seventh from the eighth.

1656–63 Perhaps someone will ask why these, and not others, are established as the distinctive notes, to which it may be replied that a plagal chant wanders more through the lower notes and an authentic [chant wanders more through] the higher, and on this account the distinctive notes are deservedly arranged so that two of them are the last of the *graves* and the other two the first of the *acute*. Accordingly, by understanding this rule (with a certain exception that will now be mentioned) you will distinguish an authentic chant from its plagal.

94 Untraced.

1663-73 If a chant of the Protus has more notes above *F*, then to that extent it is authentic and of the first mode; if more below, then to that extent it is plagal and of the second. Again, if a chant of the Deuterus has more notes above *G*, then to that extent it is authentic and of the third mode; if more below, then to that extent it is plagal and of the fourth. Again, if a chant of the Tritus has more notes above *a*, then to that extent it is authentic and of the fifth mode; if more below, then to that extent it is plagal and of the sixth. Again, if a chant of the Tetrardus has more notes above hard ♮, then to that extent it is authentic and of the seventh mode; if more below, then to that extent it is plagal and of the eighth.

1673-82 The qualification 'to that extent' is added because, according to its own quantity, the majority of notes above the distinguishing pitch draws a chant towards the nature of an authentic mode; if the majority lies under the distinguishing note then, according to its own extent, it draws a chant towards the nature of a plagal mode. I say 'according to its own extent', because it will happen as I have described if the 'turn' (*tropus*) concords with the regular range of the chant; if indeed the 'turn' and the regular range of the chant do not agree, then we must yield to the 'turn', putting the regular range aside.

1682-92 But since nothing has yet been said as to what a 'turn' may be, a subject which will be fully discussed in due course, it should be noted for the present purpose that an authentic chant descends in a well-bred and gradual way to its close.[95] The final purpose names the action, and for that reason antiphons like the following are judged to be of the first mode and not of the second: *Volo pater, Reges Tharsis* and *Circumdantes*, even though they have more notes below *F* than above. A plagal chant inclines to its end more by falling or tumbling, as through a minor third or through some other, greater interval; therefore, the authentic law having been repealed, it takes to itself only the property of a plagal, as happens in the communion *Tu puer propheta.*

1693-703 Odo and Guido say a noteworthy thing concerning the difference and distinction of the modes, namely that if a chant touches the fifth above its final five times or more then it should be assigned to the authentic category, and not to the plagal, however

[95]   Compare John (HGJ, p. 139).

much it may run according to the plagal law.[96] This is shown in the antiphon *Ecce tu pulchra es* and in the responsory *Deus omnium exauditor,* and it is so in very many others. This does not apply as a general rule; we have mentioned it to establish that a plagal chant should rarely touch the fifth [above the final], and in this way the privileges of ascent are given to the authentics as if to the masters of the plagals.

1704-11 It should also be noted that a chant which is called doubtful by some – not easily recognised as either authentic or plagal – should always be called authentic; a name ought to be taken from the nobler by right, which is apparent in the antiphon *Circumdantes* and in similar instances, and in the introit *Deus in adiutorium* which should be regarded as seventh mode rather than eighth. The greater and primary honour is to be accorded to the lord, not to the servant.

A POEM CONCERNING THE SAME

[lines 1712–47]

1712-29 Just as four notes are introduced as finals, so four are readily found to be distinctive and they are *F* and *G* among the *graves,* but we call *a* and ♮ *acute.* This number is sufficient because each of these notes distinguishes two modes. The first mode wishes there to be more above *F* and the second duly wishes there to be more below. The third [mode] stands apart from the fourth through the mediation of *G;* the fifth [mode] also differs from the sixth, the letter *a* having given its aid. It is taught that the seventh [mode] differs from the eighth through ♮. The odd-numbered [mode] stands above but the even-numbered is kept down. If you count correctly, the given, fixed rule suffices if the final phrase (*finalis neuma*) is found to be in agreement [with the regular range of the chant]. If, perhaps, it is begun near the end, then the prior law of the authentic is nullified and it is thence called plagal. The reverse also happens; the point extends more languidly and then the plagal law wrought by what has gone before is nullified.

---

[96] Compare John (HGJ, p. 122).

1730-43 Thus the first mode gives a name to *Nisi* [*ego abiero*] and to *Dominus* [*quidem Iesus*]; this final phrase is seen to give the mode at the end. Odo and Guido, however, say that if a chant is bent down as it moves under the plagal law, if it is nonetheless drawn upwards to a fifth [above the final] four times, or more than that, then it is called authentic by rights. Let the rule not disappoint; [the matter] may be verified thus if the final phrase is recognised as a concordant end to an authentic mode. If a chant is a doubtful case – if you cannot tell what it may be from the notes – then it grows in stature to be authentic, for it befits a commentator to give the benefit of the doubt in undecided cases, shunning the worse. That is what I wish to do; let any chant be of the primary kind, however much it may be subject to the plagal law. This and the final phrase make a chant a friend to its close.

1744-7 If the end [of the chant] does not deviate from the constitution [of the chant up to that point], then you can quickly and easily determine the mode which a chant obeys. But if [the constitution of the chant and the end] do not accord, then let credence be given openly to the end; the constitution of the chant yields to the end what it is poorly able to direct.

19 CONCERNING 'TURN', TENOR AND *CAUDA* WHICH ARE HEEDED IN CHANT

[lines 1748–860]

1748-55 Having considered how the modes all properly end among the *graves*, and incidentally among the *acute* (save the seventh and eighth, which do not vary their position), three other properties of chant, as it is customarily sung in the Church, must be considered, whose names are these: 'turn' (*tropus*), tenor and *cauda* (which some name from the word 'finis').

1756-65 'Turn' is an equivocal term signifying many things. The grammarian and the rhetorician call a 'turn' a figure, manner or certain figurative manner of speaking. A 'turn' in music, however, is a declaration of melodic identity which is sung in a particular mode. It is chiefly deployed towards the end; indeed, whatever the beginning or middle of a chant may have been, the intention of a skilled singer nonetheless always turns the chant towards the proper ending of any particular mode that is particularly intended. This kind of turning or declaration is called a 'turn' as if to denote a redirection towards the mode intended by the singer.

1765-81 This 'turn' sometimes begins at the start of a chant and never conflicts with the constitution or the regular compass, as in all the antiphons of the Trinity, and there only fools are in doubt about the modes concerned. Sometimes the 'turn' arises in the middle of a chant, sometimes before the end not far from the close as can be seen in the responsory *Preparate corda vestra domino* whose beginning is of the authentic Protus, that is to say of the first [mode], but which closes on *E* and therefore moves from the Protus to the Deuterus, the third mode. So too in the responsory *Gaude Maria*, because at the beginning and in the middle it is of the authentic Deuterus, the third mode, but it is assigned to the third plagal mode at the end, however, that is to say the sixth.[97] Aristotle says 'the final purpose is the best in a thing', and again 'whose beauty is the final purpose',[98] so it deservedly happens that a chant is most efficiently recognised by its end. Anyone who does not wish to regret his judgements should beware of judging quickly. Whence Solomon: 'My son, be quick to listen but slow to judge'.[99]

1782-96 Custom, rather than Reason, causes certain chants to be bent to the character of one mode by some while others pull them in a different direction and finish them on a different note; then, as has been said, we should accept – or at least endure – the customs of churches in order to avoid the arguments of those on different sides. This has to be done in such chant because different singers use different 'turns' in coupling together different modes; for example, the antiphon *Et respicientes* is finished by some so that it is of the third mode and by others so that it is of the eighth. In a similar way, the end of an antiphon like *Bene fac* is sometimes concluded by some singers so that it belongs to the fourth mode, and sometimes so that it belongs to the eighth. Similarly, the antiphon *Germinavit* is sometimes finished so that it is of the first,

---

97 Compare John (HGJ, pp. 103–4).

98 *Nicomachean Ethics*, I:1 '…in all arts the ends are to be preferred, for it is for the sake of ends that the arts are pursued'.

99 Not from Proverbs, as the citation implies, but from the Epistle of James, 1:19.

sometimes so that it is of the fourth and sometimes so that it is of the eighth. We shall not put down examples of these in our text for they are easy things for any singer to find.

1797-803 From what has been said it will be plain to the attentive reader that there are two ways in which doubt can arise about a chant as far as the diversity of the modes is concerned. Sometimes the final note of the chant for each case of doubt is the same [when performed by all singers], and then doubt arises as to whether a chant is authentic or plagal. In these [cases] the position of the majority of notes [relative to the distinguishing note] is generally a guide.

1803-40 Sometimes, however, a doubt arises about a chant which has one final *clavis* when performed by some and is conducted to the proper mode for such a final. Among others the same chant, using a different final (and perhaps a different initial) is judged in terms of the mode which is the servant to that final. For example, there is doubt as to whether the antiphon *Gloriosi principes* is of the sixth mode or of the eighth according to whether it is begun and finished on *F* or on *G*, but it is most properly of the sixth. It is the same with the antiphon *Nemo te condemnavit mulier*. If it is begun and finished on *F* then it is of the sixth mode; if, however, it is begun and ended on *G* then it is of the eighth, and it is most properly of the eighth. In a similar way the responsory *Genti peccatrici* is a doubtful chant, for some sing the verse like this:[100]

Esto placabilis [music missing]

Others sing it thus:

Esto placabilis [music missing]

and in these things one should assent to the usage of the Church and to the book examined. The word 'tenor' also has many meanings.[101] The gist of a speech or its principal meaning is called

---

[100] The example is derived from John, who gives the music (HGJ, p. 134, with transcription). In letter notation, the examples are:

c cd c c aca c cd c c

de fed cdc c c ...

[101] Compare John (HGJ, pp. 117–18).

a tenor. A tenor in music, however, is a certain aptness of melodic construction holding a chant within the bounds of its mode. The tenor keeps guard upon a chant by means of the two words 'seculorum amen' and chiefly through these and not through others, because they are the end of the versicle which is most frequently performed. There is a distinction between a 'turn' and a tenor because a 'turn' sometimes appears at the opening of a chant, sometimes in the middle, sometimes near the end; it is also clear that the final phrase (*neuma finalis*) discussed above is the same as a 'turn', and every mode has its proper 'turn' near the end. I said 'near the end', and not 'at the end', because a plagal mode and its authentic counterpart share one final note; they cannot therefore be distinguished by that. And although there are as many tenors as there are modes, nonetheless the beginning of one tenor is sometimes good for many continuously, sometimes not, as in the beginning of the second tenor, as I state:

[se- cu- lo- rum A-men]

The beginning of the first, fourth and sixth tenors is *a* among the *acute*; of the third, fifth and eighth *c* among the *acute*, while *d* among the *acute* begins the seventh.

1841-9 Someone will ask why the second and seventh modes have special initial notes (*litteras*) for their tenors, marking them out from the other modes. It may be replied that this is done to show that these two modes extend themselves very differently from the others, for the second descends further than the others and the seventh, entirely within itself, ascends more than they do. I say 'entirely within itself' because the sixth mode sometimes (but not often) is found to touch *d* among the *acute* as has been said above, but is often found to be lower than the seventh.

1850-60 A *cauda* [literally 'tail'] or 'end' (*finis*) in a chant is a certain melodic movement which is customarily made, when a chant is finished, to distinguish its mode and to commend its tenor which follows; because a tail is the end (*finis*) of an animal, and the *cauda* is named *finis* after that, therefore a *finis* of this kind is customarily added to the *final* antiphon. For this reason the antiphon in Compline, when there is only one antiphon for the psalms, must not have a tail, and if what is more conspicuous is not [tailed], then neither is what is less conspicuous, and therefore on account of this, and since the antiphon after the psalms in Compline must not be tailed, nor the one after the *Nunc dimittis*, similarly, and for the same reason, the antiphons of the Hours should not be tailed.[102]

A POEM CONCERNING THE SAME

[lines 1861–89]

1861–73 Having said what a mode is and where it may go, the well-informed singer must know three other things. He knows what a 'turn' and what a tenor is, and last of all a tail; let him remove the ambiguity [of the word 'tenor'] and see what [sense of the word] 'music' requires. In chant, a 'turn' is a certain twisting of the voice through which I may trust a chant to touch the chosen end. Now [the 'turn'] springs up at the beginning, now it arises towards the end; through the medium of a 'turn' a chant customarily seeks a harbour for itself. The 'turn' in final position may be recognised here as the final phrase (*neuma finalis*), which earns a rightful place for itself as the close of the mode. Whatever goes before to bear the first burdens, when the 'turn' arises then it is proper for the 'turn' to give the name [to the mode].

1874–89 There is a tenor of words [i.e. the gist of a speech] and we are taught that there is a tenor of notes; through the latter a chant is held within the loose texture of a mode. *Secula* gives a name to it, if you join Amen [to *secula*] in the genitive, but I am depriving this [explanation] of music. This sound is more often in a singer's mouth than the others; it should also, therefore, flourish in the honour of its name. Before the end is the 'turn' and the tenor waits upon the end; it confirms the mode, as if doing homage to a liege lord, and the mode receives its proper 'turn' and tenor as tribute; a tail, a final melody, should follow with due observance. It

---

[102] The Latin text of this last paragraph is contorted and elliptical.

does not stab from behind with the point of a treacherous lance...[*text missing*]. Whatever happens before or behind, it will be found a faithful friend; it is not to be called an enemy. A tail sometimes signifies harm, destroys and deceives; it is arrayed like a peacock, a capon and a bird of prey. Let it be so in chant because the tail cannot harm. It endorses chant and adorns it, so it should by rights be approved.

20 HOW AND WHERE THE *GLORIA* [*PATRI*] IS BEGUN, AND CONCERNING THE MEDIATIONS AND THE *DIFFERENTIE* OF THE MODES

[lines 1890–951]

1890-99 Since the tenor of any mode – which is also the *seculorum amen* – is the end of the versicle *Gloria patri*, it will be clear from what has been said how that versicle is brought to a close. We should also therefore consider how it should be begun, especially in relation to what is due to the psalm. The Church is required to employ psalmody above everything else, and this [chapter] is to investigate how the psalm should be inflected according to the tenor of each mode.

1900-16 The *Gloria* [*patri*] of the first, fifth and sixth [modes] begins on F, of the second on C, of the fourth on E, of the third and eighth on G and of the seventh on hard ♮. Although we have assigned one *seculorum* to each single mode as a tenor, nonetheless the tenor of each mode either has one *differentia* or many, with the exception of the second whose tenor is sufficient for it without any *differentie*. That one tenor may have more *differentie* than another is because the beginnings of the antiphons of one [mode] are more diversified than those of another and they therefore need many *differentie*; thus an easier transition may be made to the beginning of the antiphon, the psalm having been set according to such and such a tenor or *differentia*. The number of *differentie* assigned to the tenors varies according to the customs of various churches, being sometimes fewer, sometimes more, and therefore you should 'do as the Romans do when in Rome; when you are elsewhere you should sing as they do there'.[103]

1917-25 Just as there are eight modes and eight tenors of the modes, so also there are eight mediations (*hemitonia*) which take their name from 'hemis', which means 'half', and 'tonus'. Just as modal melody is considered in relation to the beginning and end, so it is also considered in relation to its middle. However, Custom rather than Reason dictates that two beginnings and two mediations are assigned to the eighth [mode], for a special mediation is assigned to the *differentia* of the antiphon *Nos qui vivimus* and such like, differing from the mediation of its tenor and its other *differentie*.[104]

1926-31 The mediations of the second, seventh and eighth modes are inflected in various ways according to the usage of churches in different regions, which is not surprising since ways of speaking and dressing also vary. In all satisfactory things, anyone who is content to leave such things alone will also be pleased to change them, for 'with the passage of time a wise man modifies his ways without wrongdoing'.[105]

1932-51 The mediations used in the *Benedictus* and *Magnificat* differ from the mediations used for psalms in the first, fourth, sixth and eighth modes; in the remaining cases they agree with the mediations of the psalms. Examples would be given here if it were not disagreeable to mix chant with prose, 'but may you, by your will, conceive more things than my words say'.[106] If you wish to have direct experience of these things, turn to a Tonary and there 'study hard no matter how much art you may possess'[107] until the arrangement [of the Tonary] becomes a way of life. Anyone who is studying these matters closely should also consider that just as the inflections of the psalms vary according to the diversity of the modes, so also do the verses of the responsories. In a similar way both the psalm and the *Gloria* [*patri*] of introits vary according to the various modes. But because such things are more or less demonstrated to the eye in more or less any church with the aid of

---

[103] For a variant of this saying see Walther, 28521.
[104] A reference to the *tonus peregrinus*.
[105] *Disticha Catonis*, I:7.
[106] Ovid, *Remedia amoris*, line 360.
[107] *Disticha Catonis*, IV:21.

a Tonary, it is appropriate to leave whatever might be ascertained about these matters in a more diffuse way because, as Horace says, 'you shall not linger on the everyday and common round'.[108]

A POEM CONCERNING THE SAME

[lines 1952–78]

1952–66 Since it has been explained what a tenor is, which is said to be the end, then by rights *Gloria*, the beginning, should not vanish away. Because the tenor of each mode is varied once or many times – although the second is an exception – we are taught that the *Gloria* [*patri*] is to be finished with varied melody so that it may be assimilated more easily to the beginning of the antiphon. The singer should not only pay close attention to the beginning and close [of a psalm tone]; he must also give careful heed to the middle where [the psalm tone] offers a pause. The first, fourth and sixth mediations stand apart from the rest, and the eighth is added in the *Magnificat* and *Benedictus*. responsories appoint verses and they appoint the *Gloria*, but they do not all seek the same final notes; this is done after the verse because the chant repeats the part whose beginning is served by the end of the verse.

1967–78 All introits have verses and a *Gloria* [*patri*] to which they are securely joined in their final. The third is an exception, the fourth and fifth being joined, prepared to change their final notes on account of the beginning. Without using musical notation I do not know how to readily teach in poetry what turn of chant the *Gloria* [*patri*] should have. This is something which it is fitting for the Church to teach both sufficiently and plainly; anyone who wishes to know should seek and freely sing. If you wish to know fully – to quickly distinguish how, and by how much, any one of the tenors may be varied – the Tonary teaches these things in a fuller fashion and with musical notation; I advise that you always have it to hand.

---

[108] *Ars poetica*, line 132.

21 HOW, AND IN HOW MANY WAYS, ONE MAY GO ASTRAY IN CHANT

[lines 1979–2065]

1979-98 Since it is often the case that the integrity of chant is not respected by all, one should consider the number of ways – and the kinds of ways – in which error can arise.[109] Error is sometimes caused by powerlessness, sometimes by negligence, sometimes by obstinacy and sometimes by ill-breeding (*incuria*). Chant is badly performed through powerlessness by old men, by boys and by the infirm, and this is a venial thing because natural inability excuses such people, whence Perseus teaches that 'a fault arising from Nature is not to be mocked'. Chant is performed badly through negligence by drunkards, by the indolent, and by those who scorn to perform their chant in a more diligent manner and who are also excused by those who judge everything from an ill-considered point of view; they are scarcely to be pardoned, or they deserve no pardon whatsoever. Concerning the first of these, Aristotle says 'let the drunkard be punished with a double penalty';[110] it is aptly said of the others that 'being ignorant he will be ignored'.[111] Against the last it is said 'let him come to nothing, I pray, who thinks that deeds are to be judged by their result'.[112]

1999-2004 Some chants are begun in the same way but finished differently,[113] like the two antiphons *Benedicta sit creatrix* and *Gloriosi principes*, so also *Cantabant sancti* and *Sub trono dei*. So it is also with *Iste puer* and *In odore*. However, all of these differ according to the 'turns' of the modes as may be plainly seen at the end of each [chant].

2005-15 Chant is badly performed through obstinacy by those who cast aside the proper constitution (*lex*) of a chant and follow the

[109] Compare John, chapters 15 and 22 (HGJ, pp. 129–33, and 152–9).
[110] *Nicomachean Ethics*, III:15 'Indeed, we punish a man for his very ignorance, if he is thought responsible for the ignorance, as when penalties are doubled in the case of drunkenness.'
[111] Untraced.
[112] Ovid, *Heroides*, II:85–6.
[113] Compare John (HGJ, p. 132), and for the source of some of the examples cited in the next two paragraphs, pp. 129–31.

movement of their own fancy (*motum animi*), perverting things that have been correctly composed, and thus they teach falsities to others and draw them into a practice which cannot be corrected; then it is not the use but the abuse of these singers that is regarded as authoritative. It is said against such people that 'he who sins in teaching how to sin, sins twice: both in himself, who is accused, and through those whom he causes to be accused'. Aristotle speaks of these individuals when he says that 'some were born to be disruptive', and then people of this kind are the first to leap up, defending their pernicious opinion with raised voice.[114]

2016-30 Those who have been overcome by boredom sing badly through ill-breeding, so too those exhausted by their labours.[115] They pull down whatever must be raised; sparing not the chant but rather themselves, or impelled by a kind of impudence they ineptly raise what should be lowered and complete their chant absurdly and in a way which does not accord with what has been sung before. An example of the first is the gradual *Qui sedes domine*, at the words *super cherubim*; when it should be sung higher they sing lower and go astray. Another example is the communion *Principes persecuti* at the word *concupivit*; what they sing on soft *b* they should sing higher on *c*. Another is the gradual *Probasti domine*, at the words *igne me*, for when they should begin on *c* they begin on *F*. In the same way they elevate what they should depress, as in the antiphon *Cum appropinquaret dominus Ierusalem*, at the words *si cognovisses et tu*. Similarly in *Terribilis* [*est locus iste*], at the words *et porta celi*, they ineptly raise what should be sung among the *graves*.

2031-45 Again, they do wrong through ill-breeding who begin a chant with an insipid or rough voice and twist it from its legitimate

---

[114] For the saying see Walther, 21061c. The reference to Aristotle (assuming it is accurate) has not been traced.

[115] The words 'ill-breeding' translate 'incuria', whose Classical Latin meaning is 'lack of care, negligence'. With the development of the sense 'royal or aristocratic court, whether ecclesiastical or lay' for 'curia', a development which is a medieval innovation, adjectives, nouns and adverbs built upon 'curia' (such as 'curialis', 'incurialis', 'curialiter', 'incuria') come to possess a broad range of related meanings, founded upon the idea of cultivated and urbane behaviour. On the adverb 'curialiter', used to describe a certain kind of melodic motion in *SM*, see above, Chapter 2. For this paragraph, continue to compare John (HGJ, pp. 129–31).

course, which usually happens in the antiphons *Cum inducerent puerum* and *Cum audisset Iob.*[116] Since they are of the first mode, if the melody is distorted too much they become like *Qui de terra est* and *Quando natus es,* which belong to the third mode. Again, scribes often sin damnably through ill-breeding, and make as many others err as possible, when they ignore the initial and final notes of the chant, beginning it so carelessly that they cannot lead it to its proper close, or they corrupt it during its course, or twist it away from its proper final and sometimes bend it into another mode. As an example of this malefaction let any chant be brought to mind which, of necessity, is borne across from the *graves* to the *acute,* if anyone should begin it otherwise it must go wrong, first when it is written and afterwards when it is sung.

2046-58 Again, they offend through ill-breeding who believe and declare that the melody does not lie. Such singers, moreover, attribute one mode to all chants; they do not so much sing as whinny like horses or bellow like oxen. Horace speaks of such people in his *Ars poetica* when he says that 'he who is always at fault upon the same string is ridiculed'.[117] Such people are unaware that, among other things, the melody of a chant performs the same function as a figure of speech in verse. The intention of one who performs a chant and of one who declaims verse are of the same kind: it is that the voice [*vox*] should accord with the matter of its text. For if the matter of a chant text is joyful, then the music must be light and joyous like the chant of the Virgin Mary, of St John the Baptist, of Epiphany, of the Resurrection and of others such as these.

2058-65 However, if the text treats of some matter which is arduous in either its deep meaning or its surface meaning (*vel secundum virtutem vel secundum apparentiam*), then the music should be grave (*gravis*) and should cross from soft *b* to hard ♮ and vice versa. This is plainly seen in *Fabrice* and in *Collegerunt,* and in the prolixity of the verses of the responsories of St Stephen and in such like. When the matter [of the text] is a mean between these two extremes then the chant should also strike the mean, something which fools believe to be without any rational basis.

---

[116] Compare John (HGJ, p. 132).
[117] *Ars poetica,* line 356.

A POEM CONCERNING THE SAME

[lines 2066–96]

2066–82 The infirm, boys, and those trembling with age go badly astray in chant and are feeble in it. Let no one blame this because it is evidently natural; nobody is expected to ridicule a weakness that arises from Nature. Thus, when chant is sung negligently, it must be a harsh and inept thing, received by the ear as if it had more aloes than honey. The drunkard, he who does not employ art and he who thinks that he knows everything having glimpsed only a part – these persons sing and defile the beauty of chant with error; in singing thus the singer will forfeit a singer's office. Some singers are obstinate. Lacking rational judgement, they pervert the chant and defend their error with a forceful word; nor do they capitulate when advised. They claim that they sing well, and many believe them. In this way fault practice is spread wide. It achieves written form and Reason cannot find a way to lay the writing aside.

2083–96 Through such people *Deus* [*in adiutorium*] and *Misit* [*dominus*] take a point of departure from *G*, and then they give themselves an inappropriate refuge lower down. What is badly sung is due to ill-breeding when weariness comes first or care from crushing labour. Most often these singers lower what should be raised, but in an impudent manner they raise what should be lowered. There are also those who change a 'turn' with foul presumption; they are happy to alight upon a final in any way. Some are reported to have said that the melody cannot err, and they say the same today, but they lie. For truly, just as it is fitting that a likeness of God should be seen to be a resemblance, so a melody is assimilated to some extent to the matter [of a text]. A joyous [melody] is music for a joyous matter, not something arduous; you will represent matter that strikes a mean with a medium melody (*colorem*).

22 HOW NEW CHANT SHOULD BE COMPOSED AND ELABORATED

[lines 2097–184]

2097-104 Having understood the nature of chant, someone will think it not enough to sing chants composed by others and in former times. Impelled, perhaps, by the quickness of his own ability, or drawn by the requests of others, he will undertake to compose the text for a chant with appropriate music, or at least to join a fit chant to a text accepted from another.

2105-21 The composer (*cantor*) of this [chant] must therefore consider how he may adapt his own chant to a pre-arranged mode, for just as men do not all delight in the same dish but some in sweet things, some in bitter, and some in those which lie between, so it delights some to hear the fastidious and courtly wanderings of the first mode, others [to hear] the falling and dark profundities of the second.[118] Some are more fortified by the austere and haughty dancing of the third; the sound of the fourth attracts some as if in a caressing and flattering way. Others are soothed by the delightfulness of the saucy fifth; others are moved by the voice of the sixth as if by a sweet lover's plea or by the song of the nightingale. To others, the extrovert leaps of the seventh seem delightful; others willingly attend to the seriousness of the eighth, beyond all other modes, as if to the instruction of a schoolmaster or of a father. Terence, considering the various dispositions of various individuals, accordingly says 'there are as many opinions as there are heads; to each his own humour'.[119]

2122-32 When a composer (*musicus*) is to compose a chant at anyone's request, if he seeks to satisfy the petitioner's wish he will first make a diligent attempt to ascertain what kind of music chiefly delights him; he ought then conform his chant to the mode proposed. If he does not know as much about the petitioner's character as he knows about the matter [of the text], he should consider what Horace says in the *Ars poetica*, because one cannot use one manner of versifying for every subject. Horace [*sic*] says

---

[118] Compare John (HGJ, pp. 137–9 and p. 133).
[119] *Phormio*, line 454.

that 'valiant wars rejoice to be sung in Maeonian metre', and again 'he errs who plays Thais for Andromache'.[120]

2133-44 The composer of chant should exercise a similar caution to ensure that any subject matter receives the chant appropriate to it. If the matter is sad, the appropriate music will be low-lying and ponderous as in the responsory *Libera me domine*, and in the antiphon which proclaims the lament of David, *Doleo super te*, so also in the lament of Dido, *O decus, O Libie regnum*. For this reason the tracts of the Mass are of the second and eighth modes. tracts must be sung either in the Mass for All Souls or on a day of fasting, and on these occasions the appropriate chant will properly be either mournful or at least grave, and therefore these modes pertain to tracts before all other kinds of chant.

2144-56 If the subject is joyous, however, the music should conform to it among the *acute*.[121] This is done at Easter time when *Alleluia 'Surrexit pastor bonus', Cum rex glorie* and others like them are sung. If indeed the matter is joyous and jocose, the music matches it with a leap, as in *Veterem hominem* for Epiphany, *Propter insuperabilem* for St John, and *Gaude mater* for the Blessed Virgin. If, however, the material strikes a mean, let the chant properly conform to it. Chant has been composed by some to traverse the individual modes so that its first section must be assigned to the first [mode], the second to the second, and so on with the others. This is done so that composers may reveal the skill of their magisterial office, or because they consider that sameness is the mother of dislike since variety whets the appetite.

2156-60 A second cause of this diversity may be cited giving consideration to texts in which there is some good fortune and some bad, as may be seen in the chant for St Catherine, of St Gregory, of the Transfiguration of the Lord, and such as these.

2161-8 It should also be noted that some composers of chant place a special mark in their chant; some give pride of place to a particular melody in the repetitions of the responsories which was

---

[120] The correct reference is to Ovid, *Remedia amoris*, lines 373 and 384. The 'Maeonian meter' is the hexameter, the meter of Homer, the Maeonian poet. Thais was a famous courtesan of Athens who accompanied Alexander in his Asiatic conquests. Andromache, wife of Hector, was a heroine whose tragic life is recounted in Homer's *Iliad*.

[121] For this section compare John (HGJ, p. 138).

not present in the responsory that preceded it, as for example in the responsory *Descendit de celis*. The chant for St Lambert is like this throughout.[122] Others only wish to erect the structure of their chant upon a foundation of rhythm and metre, examples of which will be easily found by anyone who looks for them.

2169–84 Others declare the tenor of the mode of the antiphon in the versicle which accompanies the antiphon. This may be seen in the chant of St Lawrence, of St Paul and of the Holy Trinity. It is also opportune for the composer of chant – if he wishes to compose and lay out a delightful melody – that he establish pauses in the chant where the text itself requires a moment of pause.[123] This teaching is well observed in the antiphon *Cum esset desponsata*, and also in *Cum inducerent puerum Iesum*; a similar observation may be made about similar chants. Moreover, if the sense of the text evidently hinders the melody and vice versa, then both the singer and the listener will tire of it. A composer should also note that the intervals of fourth and fifth are delectable ones, as may be seen in *Alleluia 'Vox exultationis'*, and these intervals may often be employed; the octave may also be used to delightful effect if its limits are rigorously observed, but on account of its difficulty it should be employed rarely.

A POEM CONCERNING THE SAME

[lines 2185–223]

2185–91 One man knows how to sing and he sings freely; it is enough for him that he can sing in a fitting way. Another, however, is not satisfied to proceed along a fixed mountain track; he wishes to linger in a shady valley. I count the singer as nothing who desires to sing what nobody has heard before unless he sings with skill.

---

[122] That is to say the Office for St Lambert composed by Etienne de Liège. Perseus and Petrus are referring to prosulas, texts created to fit melismas in chant. The responsory *Descendit de celis* is one of the responsories most frequently supplied with prosulas. For the chant for St Lambert, see Auda, 'L'école musicale liégeoise'.

[123] Compare John (HGJ, p. 139).

2192-201 A composer who undertakes to compose a chant must consider what mould will give the proper form to the chant proposed. The character (*virtus*) of the text teaches this first; the music which follows should advance as the text makes its way along. A sad matter gives a sad and low-lying [melody], a joyous matter a joyous melody; what strikes the mean commands a neutral melody. When a tract must express lamentation, or ar least a serious subject, then it will by rights be assigned to the second mode; the eighth mode also touches upon this. The sixth mode wishes to have *Vox exultantis* and *Rex* [*seculorum quem laudat*]; truly, it desires to impart the greatest joy through music.

2202-9 Nonetheless, every mouth does not praise every flavour; this man judges a melody to be such as he flees from, while that man shows that he finds it better. There is something in a particular mode which one delights in; another, loving something else, asks another chant to give that gift. The composer, therefore, making whatever is requested, does not always complement the matter of the text in singing. Perhaps he will excuse himself from the entreaties of the petitioner, but I have more praise for the behaviour of one who fears to offend [against the rules of art] in any way.

2210-23 There is sometimes a novice composer, and when he composes chants he gathers all the modes together for himself and depicts (*pingit*) all things in all ways so that the first mode may retain its first seat, and the rest [of the modes] the remaining [seats], until the chant duly arrives at the lowest. Perhaps they put on a show because they are skilled in this art, or alternatively they compose in that way because diversity is pleasing; I prove it in terms of food. Bitter things are thus joined to sweet, sad things to happy; the rose stands with the thorns, the silver-fir with the brambles of hazels. Some think their chant to be worthy of praise and are glad to display their own mark in it; sometimes writers of poems also fix a special, gracious mark in books. Perseus and Petrus are taught to observe this, for they adorn their verses with their tokens (*signa*).

23 THE FAULTS WHICH SHOULD BE AVOIDED IN NEW CHANT

[lines 2224–73]

2224-33 It will now be clear how new chant should be composed, and how it must incline towards the matter of its text, unless for some external reason it must be shaped otherwise. As Aristotle says in the *Topics*, 'it springs from the same impulse to love one's friends and to despise one's enemies',[124] so also to incline towards the properties which belong to chant by right and to avoid the faults which interrupt a chant by perverting it. And yet it is difficult to be wary of anything unless it be known, so the composer should attentively and diligently avoid the things which are faults in chant.

2234-43 Accordingly, the new master of chant should be careful not to attach a conflicting 'turn' in the course of a mode, for if he does then a chant whose beginning and middle are of one mode will be judged to be of another when it comes to a close. This teaching is well observed in the chant of the Trinity, but badly in the communion *Principes persecuti sunt me* which sometimes has the constitution and regular range of the third mode, sometimes of the sixth, and at the end has a 'turn' of the first and is thus of the first mode. This fault in music can be compared to the kind of solecism in grammar which arises from incoherence in the accentuation of words.

2244-9 There is another fault which should be avoided in new chant, and that is the use of some irregular interval that differs from the nine noted above, such as a movement from *E* to soft *b* and vice versa. This kind of fault may be compared to a false proposition of the kind which is rigorously avoided by the dialectician. Such irregular music is rightly called *musica falsa* and it should be scrupulously avoided.

2250-9 Again, in the creation of new chant the same interval should not be pointlessly repeated,[125] as in the tract *Qui habitat*, at the words *refugium meum deus meus*, and similarly in the introit

---

[124] *Topics*, II:7 'the doing of good to friends is not contrary to the doing of evil to enemies, for both courses are desirable and belong to the same disposition'.

[125] Compare John (HGJ, pp. 138–9).

Miserere mihi domine. It should be known, however, that one
repetition of an interval or a phrase may be heard with pleasure; it
may therefore be repeated once, but not often, as in *Alleluia
'Surrexit pastor bonus'* at the words *pro ovibus,* and in the chant for
St Nicholas [*Qui cum audissent* at the word] *clementiam.* Consider
this vice to be like *nugatio,*[126] something a rhetorician greatly
detests.

2260-73 Again, a new composer should diligently avoid both
truncated brevity and tiresome prolixity, and these two faults are
evidently comparable to ellipsis and *macrologia.*[127] Horace distances
these from the good poet when he says 'I strive to be more brief; I
become obscure. He who chases after smoothness loses all his
vigour.'[128] If some (or indeed all) of the aforementioned faults are
to be seen daily in ecclesiastical books then let all such error be
imputed to the first composers of those things as may be somewhat
excused by their authority. The Moderns should realise that they
are not allowed everything which was allowed to the Ancients, and
this is clear from the books of the Ancients as much in the
construction of their proses as in the figures of their verses.

A POEM CONCERNING THE SAME

[lines 2274–94]

2274-94 Having described what is fitting when a chant is begun, this
[section] has now considered, in broad terms, what corrupts a
chant, for the wise traveller wishes at least to know the pitfalls so
that he who delights in a safe track may cross it. No 'turn' should
be allowed to force the course of the chant from its seat in a hostile
fashion; it is more harmonious if the 'turn' be in accord with it
everywhere. A leap of the sort condemned by rule is another fault.
This is a 'false' manner; let him declare it so who knows. The same
note should never be repeated more than twice, although you may

---

[126] A term of rhetoric denoting vacuous repetition.
[127] Ellipsis is the omission of one or more words in a sentence which would be
     needed to complete the grammatical construction or fully express the sense.
     Macrologia is the use of redundant words or phrases.
[128] *Ars poetica,* lines 26–7.

make an exception of unison because it is iterated here more frequently. Excessive brevity and prolixity both retire without praise; the one kind of chant stirs nothing, the other does harm through its tedium. Virtue in the midst of vices evidently pleases; it also teaches us to observe moderation in chant by right. Someone asks why these things are prohibited now since it is evident that the Ancients kept to them often enough. He should hear this: many things which the Ancients long ago wrote down in their notebooks are not permitted to the Moderns. To be sure, they often used many kinds of verbal expression which are faults in some respects because they are [?comparable to] faults of chanting.

24 CONCERNING POLYPHONY

[lines 2295–359]

2295-300 So far we have spoken of monophonic chant, called monophonic (*simplex*) because it is either sung by one or by many in one manner. Now, proposing to put an end to this work, lest we may seem to be wholly ignorant of polyphony let us say a little concerning what it is and how it is divided.

2301-6 The term 'poliphonia' is derived from 'polis', which means 'plurality', and 'phonos' which means 'sound', for it is nothing other than a manner of singing by a plurality [of singers] observing diverse melody. It is divided into three species: diaphonia, triphonia and tetraphonia, that is into double, triple and quadruple chant.

2307-15 Diaphonia is a manner of singing in two ways, and it is divided into 'basilica' and 'organica'. Basilica [diaphonia] is a manner of singing in two ways so that one singer continuously holds one note which is like a foundation melody for the other singer; his companion begins a chant either at the fifth or at the octave, sometimes ascending, sometimes descending, so that when he pauses he accords in some way with him who maintains the foundation.

2314-19 Organica [diaphonia] is a music of two or more singers in two ways so that one must ascend and the other descend, and vice versa; however, when they pause they chiefly converge either on the same [note] or on a fifth or on an octave. It is called 'organica' from 'organum' which denotes the [vocal] instrument used in singing, because in music of this kind [the voice] has to work hard.

2320-27 Triphonia is a music or manner of singing by three or more, and in three ways so that one note is continuously held by one or many as a foundation, and the same chant is begun by another one or more at the fifth. They sing the same melody in this way until the end. The same chant is continuously begun by a third one or more at the octave, and the course of this same chant may be legitimately brought to a close in [unison with] the first voice, and this manner of triphonia is similarly called basilica triphonia.

2328-38 Organica triphonia is a music or manner of singing employing three or more and in three different ways. One or more must lay the foundation among the *graves* with held notes (*notis pausatis*); let another one or more begin a more convoluted (*distortius*) and 'organic' melody at the fifth or perhaps at the fourth, and another one or more should begin a different 'organic' melody at the octave. The third part, converging with the second 'organic' part, uses in relation to it – as in relation to the first part – any concordant pause either at the fifth or at the octave. It can also be that a part like the 'organic' part and the dissimilar third part is sung in the three parts together, and this manner of singing is aptly named organica triphonia.

2339-45 The teaching is similar with respect to tetraphonia, in which four different parts are varied. The [first] part begins lower down among the *graves*, the second begins the same chant at the fifth, the third, with respect to the first, begins at the octave, and the fourth, with respect to the second, begins at the octave. Thus the four parts, coursing through the chant together, should pause together and finish the chant together, each one in the manner described above.

2346-59 'Organica', as has been said, takes its name from the vocal organ because different voices resonate in different ways, just as each man has his own distinctive appearance. 'Organica' is nothing other than a disparate concord of chant running forward in various fashions. In this kind of chant, when one part ascends a good deal then the other descends a good deal and vice versa. They pause together, as has been said, either on the same note or at the fifth or at the octave. If it so happens that they pause elsewhere – which is rarely seen – the note should not be held for long but should hastily spring away from the pause. It often happens in 'organica', however, that the lower part has few notes and the upper many; in those cases the few are to be protracted and the many sung rapidly. Thus, at length, the parts come together at the end, either on the same note or on the fifth or fourth.

A POEM CONCERNING THE SAME

[lines 2360–86]

2360-86 There is monophonic chant which is familiar from what has been said, and it is not to be associated with two-part, three-part or four-part music. If there is one manner in what is sung, then it is termed 'monophonic' (*simplex*) after the [single] melody which is not varied by a plurality of singers. There is also double [chant], but it is not so called because there must be two singers in it; indeed, it is a twofold manner cultivated by those who delight in their skill. One holds a note, the other circles in an apt fashion and this delights the ear which is enticed by a great sweetness. Or, each part sings concordant and discordant with its fellow; you can call this kind of polyphony, with this kind of melody, 'organic'. In this way a triple music with a threefold movement arises, not because there must be three singing; it swells with a greater number. Either the first part maintains a note and the two following parts sing together in a way that differs from the first but is concordant with it, or the first sings in an 'organic' fashion and thus, in tripling the parts, [the techniques employed for the various parts] do not differ save in their notes and in their relative pitch (*cantumque gravando*). The fourth manner of chant is for the sake of a fourfold melody, nor may any of the aforementioned techniques be disposed in this arrangement (although in three-part music the singer must be on his guard when he sings in an 'organic' fashion for that is the greatest labour). [In tetraphonia] the first part sings among the *graves*, the second at the fifth, while the third and the fourth are not slow to add the octave [of the other two parts]. The third [part] replies to the first, but the fourth to the second; nobody should sing such things who does not have a willing spirit. They should both pause together and are seen to end together; and we are ready to end this book here.

25 THE SYMBOLIC GARMENT OF MUSIC

[lines 2387–565]

2387-93 As the Philosopher has said, like rejoices in its like and spurns its contrary. Accordingly, since we have explained how music was invented and by whom, what it is, what its essential matter is, and what its final purpose is, it does not seem out of place that we should now consider if there is anything which it resembles.

2394-6 Music, to speak tropologically,[129] is seen to be similar to the Church and this is plain in the things which are both rooted in the same species of number.

2397-407 Music is one science, even though it has many parts; in the same way, although the Church has many members, it is one, rooted in the unity of the Catholic faith. Solomon says in the *Song of Songs* 'My dove, my beautiful, is one'.[130] In this way he speaks figuratively of the Holy Spirit and of the utter simplicity and unity of the Church. There is a binary structure to be found in music inasmuch as it is divided into *mundana* and *humana*; in the same way, one can demonstrate a binary structure in the Church because it has two Testaments which it reads and studies by matching them together, and in this way it labours and joins their walls with signs of the cornerstone, which is Christ.[131]

---

[129] That is to say in terms of allegory. More specifically, however, 'tropological' has a technical meaning in terms of the fourfold interpretation of Scripture. Tropological interpretation is that which refers the scriptural narrative to the deeds and circumstances of Christ, especially by connecting Old Testament events with New Testament ones.

[130] Song of Songs 6:9.

[131] Matthew 21:42 '...the stone which the builders rejected, the same is become the head of the corner...'.

2408-27 Again, there is a further binary structure in music because it is divided into *naturalis* and *instrumentalis*; so in the Church there is another binary structure to be found because it employs the Contemplative Life and the Active Life. *Naturalis* may be likened to the Contemplative Life, and *instrumentalis* to the Active. Music which a person has learned by heart, so that he is able to perform it without books, is comparable to the Contemplative Life; in the same way, music which the singer can only perform with the aid of external tools, such as books, is comparable to the Active Life. Concerning this, however, it is said that '[Mary] has chosen that good part for herself which will not be taken away from her';[132] so neither is the cultivation of music taken away from him who performs it by heart. And just as the life of Martha, which represents the Active Life, is more perilous than the life of Mary, because [Martha] was evidently exposed to greater danger, so too they who cannot sing a chant without books are speedily brought to grief in that they seem to become dumb and know nothing of chant when the books are elsewhere or are not ready. But because 'it does not fall to every man to travel to Corinth',[133] I advise that anyone who cannot be Mary in his chanting should at least be fully prepared to get Martha's spirit for himself.

2428-34 There is a further binary structure in music according to whether a chant is authentic or plagal; similarly, and comparable to this, there is a twofold love in the Church, that is to say of God, which is comparable to an authentic mode, and of one's neighbour, which is comparable to a plagal mode, for the love of God and an authentic mode evidently look up to those things which are above; love of one's neighbour and a plagal chant are directed towards lower things.

---

[132] Luke 10:42, the last verse in the episode where Martha and her sister Mary receive Christ in their house, Mary listening to Christ's words while Martha is busied with preparations. When Martha complains to Christ that Mary has left her to serve all alone, Christ replies with the words quoted. In medieval commentary Martha was associated with the Active Life and Mary with the Contemplative Life, as here. Compare, for example, the responsory *Relinquens Maria* (**WA** 336, etc) and the interpretation of Luke 10:42 given by the *Glossa ordinaria* (PL 114, column 287).

[133] *Ars poetica*, 25-7, alluding to the fame of Corinth as a place of sophistication and luxury.

2435-40 Again, there is a ternary structure to be found in music, for chant is divided into *gravis*, *acutus* and *superacutus*; similarly, a ternary can be found in the Church – in contrition of the heart, which can be compared to the *graves*, confession of the mouth, which can be compared to the *acute*, and the fulfilment of penance, which can be compared to the *peracute*, because these three things are arranged in ascending steps.

2440-46 Again, there is another ternary division in music according to whether instrumental music comprises stringed instruments, instruments with apertures and instruments made from vessels. So in the Church there is another ternary, that is to say Faith, Hope and Love, and in these harmonious things the Church celebrates and festively rejoices in the manner of a *citharista*.

2447-53 Again, there is a third ternary division to be found in music, for the beginning, end and middle [of a chant] are considered in that art; there is a comparable ternary in the Church because it is believed and demonstrated that the Father is as the first, the Son is as the second, and the Holy Ghost is as the third, each of whom is not nor will be nor was without the other. And just as the three sections of chant constitute a unity, so also these three constitute the one substance of the one sole God.

2454-60 Further, there is a fourfold division in music because the modes are divided into Protus, Deuterus, Tritus and Tetrardus. So also in the Church there are four Virtues, that is to say Prudence, Temperance, Fortitude and Justice, in signification of which Moses, adorning the exterior of the Tabernacle, made coverings and curtains of four colours which are purple, fine flax, blue and scarlet.[134]

2461-5 Again, it is customary in music for the most part that four lines are drawn above the text without which the notes cannot be informative to the singer; so in the Church there is the quaternary of the four first Evangelists, through which the works of the faithful are guided to blessedness.

2466-7 Again in music there are seven final *claves*; so also in the Church there are seven Hours established.

2468-74 Further, in music there are the seven initial letters of all the connectives, that is to say *A B C D E F G*; so in the Church there

[134] Exodus 26:31.

are seven sacraments, named in this way either from their effect, because they sanctify the Church, or because they are the tokens of a sacred matter; one thing is perceived by bodily sense and another holy thing is understood behind it. These [seven sacraments] are the Eucharist, Baptism, Confirmation, Unction, Ordination, Matrimony and Penance.

2475-9 Again there is another septenary in music to the extent that chant among the *acute* is founded on seven connectives. Similary, the Seven Gifts of the Holy Spirit constitute a septenary in the Church: the spirit of fearing the Lord, of piety, of knowledge, of fortitude, of counsel, of understanding and of wisdom.

2480-6 Further, an eightfold division can be seen in the modes which is founded upon the quaternary of the modes. So in the Church there are eight Beatitudes which are rooted in the four Virtues mentioned a moment ago; it is plain to anyone who reflects carefully upon these matters that each one of the Beatitudes granted by the Lord can be reduced to one of the four Virtues.

2487-98 Further, nine intervals of musical sound are distinguished in music and it has been adequately said above what they are and how they are distinguished from one another; similarly, the Church recognises nine distinct orders of angels; they are Angels, Archangels, Thrones, Dominations, Principalities, Powers, Virtues of the Heavens, Cherubim and Seraphim. Again, in music there are nine spaces; and according to what is most frequently and generally found in the Church there are nine lessons, nine responses and nine Psalms; I said '[according to] what is most frequently found', on account of the liturgical usages of the monks who have altered the ancient custom for the most part.

2499-520 Further, ten lines can be seen in music; similarly, in the Church there is the Decalogue – that is to say the joining of the ten precepts of the Law – which are written here, and may be read, to remedy the ignorance of those of lesser learning; many things are evidently unneccessary – even superfluous – as far as learned readers are concerned, but are useful to the less learned.[135] 'Thou shalt have no other Gods before me', that is to say have me only as God. 'Take not the name of thy God in vain', that is to say do not

---

[135] Commentaries upon the Ten Commandments abounded in the Middle Ages. The source of this one is unknown.

swear in a false or unnecessary way. 'Remember to keep the day of the Sabbath holy', that is to say hold it as sacred and do no base labour on that day. 'Honour thy Father and Mother', that is to say in reverencing them and supplying them with what they need. 'Thou shalt not kill', which should be glossed 'on your own volition'; this can be done by the hand, the counsel, or the agreement of the highest judge. 'Thou shalt not commit adultery', that is to say you should have no carnal knowledge of any woman – be it in the flesh or in thought – unless she be the proper one. 'Thou shalt not steal.' This should be glossed '[thou shalt not] either in wish or deed secretly and unlawfully take away the property of another'. 'Thou shalt not bear false witness against thy neighbour', and such false witness is not acceptable from a brother at any time. 'Thou shalt not covet thy neighbour's wife' – and if it is not legitimate to covet it is not legitimate to possess – nor his servant, nor his serving woman, nor his ox, nor his ass, nor anything whatever that is his, moveable or immoveable; plainly you may transgress in this.

2521–31 Further, in music there are nineteen connectives; that is to say eight among the *graves,* seven in the *acute* and four in the *peracute.* Similarly in the Church there are some degrees, which are lower, some higher, and some in a middle position between them; in these degrees God is constantly worshipped by the guardians of the true faith. The first degree comprises devout laymen who exist in a state of mutual love with one another. The second degree comprises journeying pilgrims. The third is the Order of the Brothers with the Sword; the fourth is the Order of the Templars, the fifth is the Order of the Hospitallers, the sixth is the Order of the Holy Trinity, the seventh is the House of the Teutonic Knights, the eighth is the order of Lepers and these are comparable to the eight letters among the *graves.*[136]

---

[136] On the Order of the Brothers with the Sword, see above, Chapter 1. The Order of the Knights Templars was founded in 1119, called into existence by the needs of the Latin Kingdom of Jerusalem. The Order of the Knights Hospitallers was founded in imitation of the Templars, initially as a fraternity to serve a hospice for poor and sick pilgrims in Jerusalem. The Trinitarians, founded in 1198, were regular canons of a sort whose principal objective was the release of captives from heathen hands. The Order of Teutonic Knights, created in the Holy Land in the wake of the Third Crusade, penetrated the

2532-7 Again, there are seven Orders in the Church comparable to the letters among the *acute*. The first is the Order of secular clerics, the second of St Augustine, the third of St Benedict, the fourth of St Bernard, the fifth of the preachers, the sixth of St William, the seventh of St Francis, and these Orders are with good reason compared to the *acute* for they are higher than the *graves*.[137]

2537-46 Again, there are degrees in the Church which are comparable to the four letters of the *peracute*. The first is the degree of the Barbarians, the second of Anchorites, the third of Hermits, and the fourth of Christians captured by pagans or heretics.[138] These are comparable to the *peracute* because they surpass the others in tribulation and in the severity of their pains. In music, *claves* are signs of their own connectives; so in the Church each of the said orders has a specific habit so that it may be distinguished from the others.

2547-59 Again, music reaches after delight; so, every day, the Church [reaches after] the delight which is only found in the blessed state; it sighs when it says 'Thy kingdom come'. Concerning this joy St Paul adds 'I desire to be dissolved and to be with Christ'.[139] In music, there is a distinguishing note in a medial position which divides plagal chant from authentic; in the Church Christ the mediator divides the goats from the sheep, the evil from the good. Also, whatever effects the beginning or middle of a chant is worthy of consideration. A 'turn' classifies a chant and maintains it within its proper mode; so in the Church, for whatever happens in the beginning or in the middle of human life it is the ultimate intention that condemns or commends and establishes the position of a man as virtuous or evil.

Baltic and became a major territorial power in Eastern Europe. There was no formal Order of Lepers, but lepers were often regarded as individuals singled out by God for special trials, and some leper houses were quasi-collegiate with their own refectories and chapels.

[137] This list encompasses, in ascending order of spiritual merit, the secular clergy, the Augustinian (i.e. regular) canons, the Benedictine monks, the Cistercians (associated here with their greatest spiritual force and teacher, St Bernard), the Dominican friars (The Order of Preachers), the Williamites (a monastic order founded by William of Maleval, spread widely throughout Italy, France, Belgium, Germany and Hungary), and the Franciscan friars.

[138] A very curious list.

[139] I Phil. 23.

2560-65 Again, by its natural power, music gives protection from imminent disease, cures the present [malady], frightens demons and puts them to flight, and all these things can be plainly witnessed in the Church. Since music is comparable to the Church in such, in so many and in such great ways, it is no wonder if the practice of music and a festive conception of it are cultivated in the Church.

A POEM CONCERNING THE SAME

[lines 2566–714]

2566-80 Music is a token of the Church and will be seen to resemble it; I have written at length about the things which are fitting to music. It has many subdivisions but let it be recognised as being one art. 'My dove is one', says Solomon; music is proved to be a unity. Moreover, the World and Man give a double structure to this art; you may add the two Testaments to the remaining part. There is another apparent binary structure in music which incorporates natural and instrumental music; whence you see the Contemplative Life to be the Life of the Church and equally see it redeemed through the Active Life. There is a third binary structure from this line of argument, for truly there must be plagal and authentic chant, providing that the chant is of specific character; so also in the Church we should pour out a twofold love, and [the Church] wishes the first to go to God but our neighbour [demands] the second.

2581-8 Whence there is a ternary structure everywhere in music, for truly *acutus* follows *gravis* and *peracutus* follows on. There is similarly in the Church contrition of the heart which comes first, then the mouth lamenting for sins comes next, and work of penance comes last. These three things – percussion, strings and wind – lend lustre to the art of music, and Faith and Hope are three if you join Love to them. Just as the Psalm has a beginning, middle and end, so the Father, Son and Holy Ghost are three.

2589-96 The Protus has companions, since it is one of four; of a similar number are the books of the Evangelists in the Church. We recognise four notes as exclusive to them; recognise this as also the number of the virtues of good men. Anyone who wishes to be blessed for his virtues should be prudent, just, resolute and moderate. Hence the symbolism of scarlet, blue, purple and fine flax; each one of these was put into the coverings as a colour.

2597-604 Seven little letters denote the connectives; this is also the number of Sacraments in the Church: communion, Baptism, Confirmation, Unction, Ordination, Holy Matrimony, and finally I put 'I confess'. Seven notes suffice for the *acute*, and God gives his seven gifts of salvation to the Church. Acknowledge that there are eight modes – if they are properly enumerated – so I also know that there are eight Beatitudes.

2605-20 Music incorporates nine intervals; this is the number of holy troops of benign spirits. As the line [of the staff] is joined to ten connectives, so the book of Moses serves this number of commandments. Join nine to ten and you will enumerate all the connectives, and you can distinguish as many kinds of persons in the Church. There is the layman, the pilgrim, the Knight of the Sword, the good Host, the Templar, the Teutonic [Knight], the Trinitarian, and after these the grievously ill. You will note that these are like the eight *graves*. Now you will see seven [kinds of men] and liken them to the *acute*. The [secular] cleric goes before Augustine and Benedict follows; Bernard [comes] after him, he who does not wish to yield in rank like one vanquished. The next one preaches and William follows him; here comes Francis with his bare feet and vexed with his knots.[140] The Barbarian lies in his ditch and the Anchorite in the woods; the worst is endured by the captive: the hermit goes before him.

2621-38 Music seeks to delight and so when I sing I feel a new joy; I sweep away sad things. This is what the Church does; in all its strife, it wishes that it may enjoy peace. Annicius[141] says that God is the supreme delight; the Church seeks this reward for itself. There is a note in the middle position which is called the distinguishing note; in that one should recognise Christ separating the evil men from the good. It is this 'turn' in a chant that assigns it to a particular mode; thus the last hour extols or condemns a dying man. Thus it

---

140 A surprisingly facetious reference to the knotted girdle of the Franciscans.
141 The identity of this Annicius is unknown. He is possibly the author of this chapter.

is with the Church, because music more, and further by far than anything else, can purify; it consecrates what is pure and it saves [them] when grief is buried. You can see so many and so great recommendations of chant of this kind that it must please by right, and it is no wonder if the two aforesaid things [i.e. music and the Church], which harmoniously achieve this, agree well together. It is plain that whatever is good in them they derive from God; it is collected here: let praises be given to the Lord.

2639–44 Praise be to you, O supreme Father, strong in supreme power which nothing can exclude with sealed doors;[142] it overcomes all things; there is nothing so strong that it can resist. You accomplished all things with the Word in a time long past, O Son of so great a supreme Father, O wisdom of the Father, lacking substance, inasmuch as it pleased you to become the son of a mother.

2645–56 You had the power to found the heavens on high with the Father; you, whilst in your mother's womb, undertook to conquer the course of sorrow. The begetter knew nothing of a wife or of being a married man; you lack a father and mother; I know of no such fashion elsewhere. However, you are also Son of the Father, and have been so for eternity, and the son of your mother, the man whom you wish to be. It is plain from your deeds that you are the head of Nature. What Nature denies it marvels at and finally fails to comprehend, since contraries [i.e. Humanity and Divinity] are evidently joined in you. These contraries are not seen to produce a mean in you as is the way with things that have been mixed. Christ is proved to be true God and true man; neither this part nor that is diminished.

2657–66 O kindly spirit of the Father and of the Son, you fount of mercy, you the beginning from which Grace freely comes, you the light in the darkness, you the maintainer of the light, consoling the unhappy, you mend those who are broken, you call back those who err and give rest to the weary, you lead and bring in the hungry to the joy of the harvest. Grant, O Father, that we may rebel from vice through your power; thus, O just judge, you will avert punishment from us. Grant, O Son, grant that when the cloud of the dull mind has been put to flight then the servants may know this: that they are of blessed fortune.

---

[142] Much of what follows is difficult in the Latin.

2667-78 Come, O nourishing spirit, fill our hearts with the dew of goodness lest they remain parched in a sterile manner. They whom I believe in, being the same are not the same; they are three persons but not three. Let the royal path hold me and I shall not retreat from it. You will see in the citadel of this Father how these things may be done; believing with humility you will now keep silence in this vale. May you consume whatever remains in fire in the eating of the Paschal lamb; the Law enjoins these things in its warnings. Whatever doubts grow, absorb them into faith; whatever it is beyond one's understanding cannot do harm, and commit to the Holy Spirit whatever presses strongly upon one; believe me, if you trust in it, the mind will grow in faith.

2679-90 Quite often we speak of these things, but we may well believe that in all things He, three and one, gives us such a gift. The port is near at hand, the anchor secures the prow, the boat moves around [at anchor]; as often as the tide rises let Him be called to open. The boat is a frail one because it is the poor boat of John,[143] which, full of cracks, lacking in ribs and plugged with cloths, first served you, O Virgin, blessed parent, and with your help was brought back with success. The load was great, it was unequal to these forces, but you, merciful and prompt, prevent the shipwreck when you were called. In the sea, you force back the last darkness and tide; it is no wonder if the Star of the Sea has dominion amidst the waves.

2691-6 Whatever has been done through your mediation was done by you. Rule me! Save me! I ask for a covenant concerning this for myself. Thus the little boat has carried a lighter burden and a map which, O Lord, the grace of the Lord skilfully contrived. In that matter, writings teach in various ways what the letter and word of mouth require, what the witness knows how to express.

2697-714 This third work[144] concerning music is aimed at friends; not to the false but to those who are honest and to innocent boys, for the false man condemns, biting back by not teaching true things. He who finds all recent things base will scarcely be pleased by what is ancient. Anyone who sees any part of this our work will not be disposed to blame any disposition of our mind. On a

---

[143] I have been unable to identify this legend.
[144] The significance of this remark is obscure.

slender table a well-fed mind can dine on luxurious things; the clear mind of this author illuminates this work. Grant, O God, that the writer and any benign readers may be worthy to sing the heavenly song in your presence. Grant us that we may but live in a just fashion and with a pure spirit; grant that we may afterwards sing praises to you with glad voices in Heaven. Perhaps a detractor will...[*text missing*] to this art, weighing in his mind this work and also the brief space of time. From the beginning, four months gave birth to this work, and they were not the cause of any ceasing of study.[145] Here there are eight hundred and sixty lines of verse; this book – if you turn back to its beginning – demonstrates this from the first folio.

---

[145] A common topos. Compare the *Equivoca* of Johannes de Garlandia: 'considerata etiam brevitate temporis in quo istud perstruxi opusculum, quia vix fuit duorum mensium...' (Hauréau, 'Notice sur les oeuvres...de Jean de Garlande', p. 60).

Summa musice: The text

1^r Amicorum iusta et honesta petitio coactio reputatur. Hac
itaque me stimulante super doctrina musice componenda,
scribenda et docenda, respondi quod fere in qualibet
insigni ecclesia reperiuntur quidam in hac arte competenter
periti, et si nugatorium quidquam de musica docere   5
presumerem idipsum vel arrogantie mee vel temeritati
mihi assuete forte ascriberetur ab ipsis, et quod vel absenti
vel presenti mihi questio posset fieri que stultis et ambitiosis
quandoque solet proponi, an scilicet exigant panem
meliorem quam triticum et potum meliorem quam vinum.   10
Sed cum frequenter animadverterem sociorum et
discipulorum meorum quam plurimos errare graviter in
via, id est in hiis que sunt principia musice – scilicet in
cognitione intervallorum que ab equalitate sonorum vel
secundum arsin et thesin cantantur – succurrendum   15
confesse ignorantie ipsorum fore existimavi et consulendum,
maxime ut regularem cantum cognoscendo cantarent, et
cantando inter imperitos honorem contingerent ut magis
provecti.

De musica tamen, an sit ars liberalis vel non, et quid   20
habeat pro subiecto, et que sit propria passio subiecti
eiusdem, et qualiter secundum proportiones numerorum
fundari et institui habeant intervalla, et circa ipsa
consistentia, dicere supersedebo; super vires etenim
puerorum est hoc negocium et maioris indigens   25
inquisitionis. Illud vero quemadmodum de hiis ac de
propositis et quidam moderni et quidam antiqui, et maxime

139

horum Odo, Guido, Salomon et Hermannus, probabiliter
tractaverunt, scribere attentabo, ab altioribus quidem
questionibus abstinens, simpliciores vero mediocriter   30
coniectans. Plurima tamen omittam que illi dixerunt, et
aliqua illis intacta ex ductu ingenioli mei adiungam
secundum quod mihi visa fuerint expedire. Et pro isto
quantulocumque labore nec a fame susurro nec alieno
quoque marsupio remunerari vel spero vel posco, sed ab   35
illo qui nullum bone intentionis laborem irremuneratum
dimittit, cui nihil preteritum, nihil futurum, sed omnes
actus humanos in suo eterno presenti absque oblivionis
tempusculo comprehendit. Faveat ergo debili mee phaselo
et ad portum usque perducat quia, teste Augustino, quamvis 40
ad malum ex nobis sufficimus, nemo potest bene facere
sine deo, et Salomon, omnis sapientia a domino deo est.

METRUM EIUSDEM

Cogere dicatur dum iusta precatur amicus;
Hic rogat, hortatur quem sermo terret iniquus.   45
Sic sceleris clamor mihi frigida pectora prestat,
Sed virtutis amor pellit quodcumque molestat.
Forsitan audacem faciet; deus ipse iuvabit.
Parvis parva loquor nec me labor iste gravabit.
1ᵛ   Musica subiectum quod habet, que passio fertur,   50
Qualiter ad mathesim tanquam pars quarta refertur,
Maxima quid resonant inter secreta polorum
Corpora, cur discors concordat motus eorum,
Hoc non est facile describere, nam nimis altum
Hoc ultra vires pueris faceret quasi saltum.   55
Qui de proposito non sunt, dormire sinamus;
Qui nimis alti sunt fructus, pendere sinamus.
Intervalla tamen referamus queque sequuntur,
Et que precedunt, et qualiter hec oriuntur;
Sed precedentis candelam cum comitatur   60
Practica theorice, sine qua tenebrosa vagatur,
Hinc erit, et cur sic dicantur singula scire
Vocibus ut notis contingat longius ire.
Assis ergo deus; ad portum duc mea vela

Et mihi quod possim bene dicere posco revela.   65
Nec mihi sit precium scribenti fistula fame,
Non aliud quodvis terrenum poscitur a me.
Tu mihi sis precium, sine quo nihil esse probatur
Usquam quod speciem bonitatis habere sciatur.
Nil mihi preteritum nihil et valet esse futurum;   70
Quolibet in fluctu, deus, eligo te Palinurum.

1ʳ   PREFATIO CAPITULORUM

Cum inter artes omnes musica pre ceteris distinctionibus
multis indigeat, ut facilius inveniatur lectori de quo magis
intenditur multis enim sufficit pars pro toto. Cum ea que   75
postea dicentur per capitula sint distincta, expedire [1ᵛ]
videtur ut nunc tituli capitulorum pariter proponantur
eundem ordinem observantes quem et capitula post in suo
loco disposita videbuntur habere. Quod musica indigeat
signis quibus error possit averti ex hoc manifestum est quia   80
peccatum quanto apertius tanto deterius esse probatur;
cantus autem inter artes ceteras clamore magno perficitur,
et ita peccatum illius longius et citius percipitur et magis
infamat.

CAPITULA SIVE TITULI CAPITULORUM

Quid sit musica et a quibus sit inventa.   I
Ad quid sit utilis musica.   II
Qui primo in ecclesia utebantur musica et quare.   III
De divisione musice in naturalem et
    instrumentalem, mundanam et humanam.   IV
De musica humana.   V
De notulis cantus usualis, que sint et
    ad quid sint invente.   VI
De sex notularum vocibus et sufficientia earumdem.   VII
De palma seu de manu musica et lineis vel
    spaciis eius.   VIII
Quare manus potius est instrumentum musice
    quam aliud membrum.   IX

I   QUID SIT MUSICA ET AD QUID FUIT
INVENTA

Musica, secundum quod de ipsa intendimus, est ars
modulandi sonos discrete de qua primo videndum est unde   125
dicatur et a quibus fuit inventa; postea dicendum est que sit
eius utilitas, postea qualiter musica dividatur et que
antecedunt et que sequuntur ad ipsam. Et sic ob honorem
ternarii per tribus predictis principaliter investigandis in
ternario tractatus iste consistit. Ternarius primus est impar   130
numerus in duo equalia indivisibilis; primus numerus est
qui habet medium in quo unitas consistit, unde et a
philosophis dictis superis consecratur.

Cuius mentione relicta sciendum est quod de hoc nomine
'musica' diversi diversa sentiunt. Quidam dicunt quod   135

musica dicitur quasi *moysica* a *moys*, quod est aqua, eo quod
aqua pluvialis, vel quecumque alia, dum cadit super diversam
materiam, nunc super tecta, nunc super lapides, nunc
super terram, nunc super aquam, nunc super vasa vacua,
nunc super arborum folia, sonos diversos reddere videatur,   140
a quibus adinvicem comparatis antiqui dicuntur musicam
invenisse.

Alii dicunt quod musica dicitur a musa quoddam
instrumento quod excellens et perfectissimum dicunt inter
omnia musica instrumenta, et quod ab ipso per   145
antonomasiam tamquam a digniori musica nominetur; alii
dicunt quod a musis poeticis propter diversos modos
scribendi quos ministrare dicebantur poetis, sed ante usum
poetarum musica fuit inventa. Propter hoc dicatur, et melius,
quod musica dicatur a musa quoddam simplicissimo   150
instrumento quod a pastoribus gregum circa mundi
principium primo fuit inventum, [2ᵛ] et hoc de palustri
harundine vel de calamo segetum erat factum, et pastores
in hac musa propter diversam eius magnitudinem et
longitudinem et foraminum impositionem perpendebant   155
diversitatem tonorum. Etymologice vero bene dicitur musica
quasi 'muniens usu canentem'. De hac inventione muse a
pastoribus dicit Petrus Riga

Ut pastoralis gaudeat inde labor

et quia hoc primum fuit musicum instrumentum merito   160
musica denominatur ab ipso. Huius inventionem fistule
Moyses ascribit ipsi Iubal de quo propter hoc quidem
dicitur quod erat pater canentium in cithara.

Alii dant musice primam inventionem et ascribunt ipsi
Mathusalen aquarum puteos fodienti, qui cum ibidem   165
audiret malleorum sonos multimodos traxit eos in
exercitium cantandi. Boecius ascribit eam Pythagore iuxta
fabricam gradienti et malleorum sonos multiplices audienti;
ipse vero quod in sono differrent notavit et plures malleos
apposuit in quantitate dispares et in pondere differentes, et   170
ita sonorum differentiis multiplicatis traxit eas in exercitium
canoris. Quidam etiam Amphioni Thebano, quidam
Orpheo Trecensi ascribunt inventionem canendi. Ad que
nota   omnia dici potest convenienter, cum Aristotele, quod
principia omnium artium et instrumenta tempore prime   175

inventionis ruda fuerunt et pauca, quibus auctor quicumque
succedens aliquid novi adiecit. In hunc modum etiam de
rivulo supremi fontis fit per collectiones aquarum fluvius
portans naves, et poterat esse quod Iubal primus esset, ut
dicit Moyses, a quo et iubilus et iubilare dicitur, et quod alii   180
subsequentes predicti novum aliquid addiderunt, et sic
usque hodie. Contingit quod sicut dicitur in Predicamentis
licet nomina fingere, sic et dici potest de novo modo
canendi quod aliquid a modernis addicitur quod ab antiquis
non fuit inventum quia, teste Prisciano, quanto iuniores   185
tanto perspicatiores.

METRUM EIUSDEM

Musica dicatur ars que recte modulatur
Discreteque sonos; hoc nomine iure vocatur.
Fistula musa fuit olim pastoribus apta   190
Illiusque sono fuit auris mens quoque capta.
Discant longa brevis maiorque minorque patenter;
Primi pastores hoc audivere libenter
Et concordantes has coniunxere frequenter
Quamvis discordes videantur sintque decenter.   195
Hanc alii dicunt a musis nomen habere,
Corda poetarum consuetis multa docere;
Sive moys, quod aquam signat, caput huius habetur,
Multisono strepitu cuius nova prima docetur.
Iubal, Mathusalen cum Pythagora docuerunt   200
Orpheus, Amphion illam primique fuerunt.
Unus erat primus, non primi tempore cuncti,
Prima sed augendo poterant omnes fore iuncti.
Sic hodie multi vivunt hoc munere functi,
Sic nova protrahitur ab origine linea puncti.   205
Usu cantantes quia munit musica nomen
Hoc habet et faustum dat ab incantantibus omen.
Nomen et auctores per dicta patent manifeste,
Cuius et utilitas post hoc succedit honeste.
Finis enim pigros monet, excitat, approbat artis   210
Totius seriem tantille munere partis.
Tercia pars sequitur que dividit et docet uti,

3ʳ

Et que sint quibus imprudens consuevit abuti.
Sic ternarius hoc tenet, occupat omne volumen,
Felici felix designans omine numen.   215
Hic numerus primus infames deserit ante,
Nec vacat a medio virtutem significante.

2^v   II   AD QUID SIT UTILIS MUSICA

Utilitatem musice investigantes attendant quid dicit Horatius
de bono poeta; nisi commendans eum ait   220
nota   *Omne tulit punctum qui miscuit utile dulci.*
Hec duo reperiuntur in musica. Dulcis est quoniam inter
omnes artes nulla tam velociter oblectat; [3^r] utilis quoniam
eius artifex, qui est musicus, novi et regularis cantus inventor
et eiusdem iudex et irregularis potest esse corrector.   225
nota   Ex iam dictis diligenter intuenti patet differentia inter
musicum et cantorem. Omnis enim musicus est cantor, sed
non e contrario. Cantor enim qui est musicus et theoricus
et practicus est in hac parte; cantor vero qui non est musicus
nec etiam dici debet practicus, nisi nomine usurpato, quia   230
practica tenetur procedere secundum preeuntis theorice
rationem, sicut in Isagogis Johannitii continetur. Cui ergo
cantorem artis expertem comparare potuerimus nisi ebrio
versus locum propositum eunti, vel ceco alicui canem
verberare volenti? Sed cum plurimos tales cantores   235
perceperimus et noscamus, in eis contingere videmus quod
dicit Boecius de minus provectis in libro Consolationis
quod ipsi tales vestem Philosophie lacerant, et cum sibi
rapuerunt ex ea paniculum sibi cedere et se habere vestem
eius integram gloriantur. Sed ad propositum redeuntes,   240
musice utilitatem breviter perstringamus.
     Musica itaque medicinalis est et mirabilia operatur. Per
musicam morbi curantur, precipue per melancholiam et ex
tristicia generati. Per musicam prohibetur ne quis incidat
in desperationis exilium et merorem. Musica viatores   245
confortat, fures et latrones exanimat et in fugam convertit.
[3^v] Per musicam in bello timidi confortantur, dispersi
revocantur et victi, et de Pythagora legitur quod luxuriosum
quemdam per musicam ad continentiam revocabat; est

enim quedam species cantilene qua luxuria effugatur et est   250
alia qua luxuria provocatur, quemadmodum et est quedam
species que sopit vigiles et est alia que excitat dormientes.
Musica mitigat iracundos, tristem letificat, varias cogitationes
dissipat et ab eis dissolvit. Musica et quod maius est spiritus
malignos perterret et fugat, sicut et David citharista in libro   255
Regum legitur a Saule rege obsesso a demone demonium
nota   effugasse. Et nihil mirum est hominem ut pote animal
rationale in musica delectari cum et greges quadrupedum,
quedam aves et quidam pisces musice videantur oblectamine
permulceri.

260

METRUM DE EODEM

Artis presentis frugem si noscere queris,
Flaccum dicentem verbis cognoscito veris:
Utile qui miscet cum dulci laude fruetur.
Ars presens tenet hoc; laudari iure tenetur.   265
Aures demulcet, menti blanditur, et eius
Utilis est usus removetque suo bene peius.
Musicus est cantus iudex, inventor, et harum
Que sint distorte corrector in arte viarum.
Musicus est cantor, quod non convertere debes   270
Subiecto quevis pro signo si tibi prebes.
Cantor non debet laudari qui caret arte;
Decipitur credens totum visa sibi parte.
Cantor ut ebrius est vadens per compita ville;
Musicus at bene scit que cantat per loca mille.   275
Cantorem ceco similem dic arte carentem;
Hunc simul ac illum Fortuna regit gradientem.
Musica quid valeat et quantum qui bene scire
Vult, per synodocen quesita potest reperire.
Egrotum sanat confortans musica sanum;   280
Exhilarat parvum iuvenemque virum quoque canum.
Precipue cerebri morbos mentisque timores
4ͬ   Lenit et alleviat, fugat ac facit esse minores.
Sic et Pythagoras curavit luxuriosum;
Compulit illecebras cantu liquisse lutosum.   285
Carminis id genus est per quod lasciuia crescit;

Est aliud quod eam compescens ludere nescit.
Musica confortat tristem, solatur euntem
Oblicumque vie facit hunc ascendere montem.
Fures exanimat, latrones cogit abire;   290
Curas depellit, facit et quandoque perire.
Adiuvat in bello timidos, revocat fugientes;
Fortes protrudit palmam bellando petentes.
Insuper et Bucephal ad cantum saltat in hostes,
Hos quoque prosternit prius immotos quasi postes.   295
Spiritus immundus etiam fugit hac mediante,
Signans quod discors est nunc velut et fuit ante;
Sic David in Saule sedavit demonis iram,
Ostendens cithare virtutem carmine miram.

3ᵛ   III   QUI PRIMO UTEBANTUR MUSICA   300
               IN ECCLESIA ET QUARE

Cum itaque tot et tanta immo innumerabiliter plura musice
reperiantur preconia, statuerunt primo Ignatius, et post
beatus Ambrosius Mediolanensis archiepiscopus, ut in
ecclesia deo serviretur per cantum propter maiorem eius   305
reverentiam et honorem. Ordinantes igitur quid et quantum
et quando et qualiter cantandum esset in ecclesia,
preceperunt ut non ioculando, ridendo vel saltando sed
humiliter ac devote in divino quoque officio coram domino
in sancta ecclesia cantaretur. Idem Ambrosius cantum fecit   310
cuilibet diei totius anni proprium et specialiter assignatum,
et per sue iurisdictionis omnes ecclesias eum instituit
solemniter observandum. Ab inde sanctus Gregorius
Romane sedis [4ʳ] antistes, super cuius humerum Petrus
diaconus vidit sedere columbam quando idem Gregorius   315
utilitati ecclesie previdendo scribebat, cantum composuit
per totam Romanam ecclesiam promulgandum et primo
eum ad ecclesias cathedrales transmisit. Sed prolixum eum
non fecit quemadmodum sanctus Ambrosius dictus est
cantum suum fecisse, et hoc, ut quidam asserunt, propter   320
fatigationes morborum, fuit enim semper quartanarius et
preterea urgebat eum syncopis et podagra. Alii dicunt, et
melius forte, quidquid scripsit Gregorius, tam in cantu

quam in prosa, et materiam et quantitatem et qualitatem a
Spiritu Sancto accepit.   325

Auctoritatem autem in ecclesia cantandi causa devotionis
traxit a cantu religiosorum antiquorum tam in novo quam
in veteri testamento. Legitur in Daniele de tribus pueris
laudem deo canentibus in fornace. Legitur etiam in Exodo,
postquam Hebrei mare transierant et viderent Egyptios   330
involutos atque submersos, Maria soror Moysi cum fratre
suo in cantico suo laudes deo psallebant cantando narrantes
magnalia salvatoris. Item rex David et citharando cantavit
coram arca et coram domino, et alios cantare monuit in
diversis instrumentis musicis, dicens 'Cantate domino   335
canticum novum', et cetera; et iterum 'Cantate et exultate
et psallite', et iterum, '[Cantate] domino in tympano et
choro, in psalterio et cithara, in cymbalis benesonantibus,
in chordis et organo, in tubis ductilibus et voce tube
cornee'. In novo etiam testamento postquam unus angelus   340
nuntiaverat pastoribus Christi nativitatem, ne parum
videretur unius auctoritas multitudo angelorum simul cum
illo cantavit 'Gloria in excelsis deo' et cetera. Preterea
reperitur canticum Zacharie, scilicet *Benedictus*, canticum
Marie, *Magnificat*, canticum Symeonis, *Nunc dimittis*, que 345
non sine cause cantica nuncupantur. Modus itaque canendi
et ipsius cantoris devotionem ostendit et in audiente, si
bone [4ᵛ] voluntatis est, suscitat devotionis affectum, et
propter hoc in ecclesia merito frequentatur humiliter ac
devote.   350

METRUM DE EODEM

Fructus cantandi magnus perpenditur; usque
Hoc attendentes Ignatius Ambrosiusque
Decrevere deo quod in ecclesia celebretur
Cantu qui mentem devotam concomitetur.   355
Ambrosius dedit officium speciale diei
Cuilibet in cantu prolixe materiei.

N[ota]   Inde Gregorius est Romanus papa secutus,
Cui placuit modus hic quod non stet homo quasi mutus,
Nam decet ut mundi salvator, trinus et unus,   360

Obsequii trinum nostri capiat sibi munus;
Cor cupiat, sonet os et machina tota laboret
Corporis ad dominum quod sic devotius oret.
Qui bene mente, sono, factis orans operatur,
In domini templo merito citharista vocatur.   365
Cantum papa novum distinxit in ordine factum;
Spiritus hunc Sanctus docuit quod in hoc fuit actum,
Nam Petrus aspexit quod pulchra columba sedebat
Auresque pape tangens quandoque monebat.
Morbis ascribunt quidam cantus brevitatem;   370
Quidam pro causa ponunt domini bonitatem,
Nam quamvis brevis est quidam nescire videntur,
Magnos cantores sese tamen esse fatentur.
Est melius quod non crevit confusio multa;
Estimo quod fuit hec domini pietate sepulta.   375
Syncopis et podagra quartana silere iubebant
Hunc quandoque virum nec eum cantare sinebant.
Queritur a tergo quod precantaverat ergo;
Quo decet impleri vacuum quod nescit haberi?
5^r   Traxit in exemplum tres in fornace canentes   380
Et Moysen quando sub aquis periere sequentes.
Rex David omnimodo cantu servire docebat
Ante deum, citharamque tenens hanc percutiebat
Multociens cantare iubens, psallens iterabat
Verbum cantandi, signans quod ab inde vocabat.   385
Nec non et Christo nato sub tempore noctis,
Civibus angelicis hoc in modulamine doctis,
'Gloria' cantatum pastoribus est recitatum
Et nobis per eos dictum scriptumque relatum.
Cantus in ecclesia si sit devotus, honestus   390
Et placet et magnus est illius ilico questus.
Hunc amat auditor mens cuius tollitur orans,
Cantibus angelicis quasi presens esse laborans.
Quod si non bonus est huic displicet estque molestus;
Aut dolet reatus aut conqueritur quia mestus.

4ᵛ   IV   DE DIVISIONE MUSICE IN NATURALEM,   395
            INSTRUMENTALEM, MUNDANAM ET
            HUMANAM

Musica quedam est naturalis, quedam instrumentalis.
Naturalis quedam est humana et quedam mundana. Musica
mundana fit per varietatem et concordiam sonorum a   400
motibus supercelestium corporum causatorum. Sicut enim
testantur philosophi, non fuit possibile tanta corpora tam
velociter moveri et tam continue absque sono. Cum igitur
firmamentum et planete spirituales et differentes motus
habeant a quibus et spirituales et differentes causantur 405
[soni], harmoniam quamdam ex se generant que musica
mundana vocatur.
    Artificialia vero instrumenta musice plurima sunt, que
ternario dividuntur: quedam enim chordalia, quedam
foraminalia, quedam vasalia esse dicuntur. Chordalia sunt 410
ea que per chordas metallinas, intestinales vel sericinas
exerceri videntur; qualia sunt cithare, vielle et phiale,
psalteria, chori, monochordium, [5ʳ] symphonia seu
organistrum, et hiis similia. Foraminalia sunt quorum
diversitas in sonis a foraminum diversitate creatur; qualia 415
sunt muse, syringe, flaiota, tibie, cornua, fistule, tube et
similia. Vasalia sunt que et foraminibus carent et chordis
per modum vasorum concavorum formata; qualia sunt
cymbala, pelves, campane, olle et similia que secundum
materie et forme diversitatem diversos sonos emittunt. Sed 420
inter cetera instrumenta musicalia instrumentum vocis
humane est dignissimum eo quod profert et sonum et
verba, cum cetera de sono tantum serviant, non de voce et
verbis.

METRUM DE EODEM

                                                          425
Ut naturalis, instrumentalis habetur
Musica; sic species binas proferre videtur.
Et naturalem binas genuisse decebit:
Mundanam velut humanam sub se retinebit.
Motu mundanam celestia corpora causant   430

Magno continuo que nullo tempore pausant.
Hec humana parum nos expectando moretur;
Instrumentalis prius inspicienda videtur.
Huic tres dant species tria: chordaque vasque foramen.
Chorda preit, reliquis mage digne suum et notamen.   435
5ᵛ   Intestinales, sericinas atque metalli
Vidi quas credo meliores nec puto falli.
Psalterium, chorus et sistrum cithare socientur,
Impulsu quoniam simili hec resonare videntur.
Arcus dat sonitum phiale, rotule monochorde;   440
Concava dicta quidem sunt sed resonantia chorde.
Multa forata simul sunt instrumenta sonora
Nec solum forma distant maiora minora.
Tibia, flaiotum syringaque, fistula, musa:
Utitur hiis modo plebs et eis quondam fuit usa.   445
Organa sive tube, cornua sonitu vehementi,
Aures percellunt valido sufflamine venti.
Musica sit nobis etiam per vascula nota
Pondere que distant et forti verbere mota.
Cymbala, campane, pelves olleque videntur,   450
Talia que resonant quando pulsata moventur.
Humanum tamen huic videas prestantius esse,
Dum que significant voci dat verba subesse.

5ʳ   V DE MUSICA HUMANA

Dicto de musica instrumentali fiat recursus ad humanam,   455
de qua principaliter intenditur, ut de ipsa dicatur. Cum
itaque musica sit modulatio sonorum discreta, stricte sumi
debet hec dictio *discreta.* Si enim large sumeretur, ut discreta
idem diceret quod distincta, id est 'cum distinctione facta',
sic etiam musica rebus irrationabilibus conveniret sicut   460
avibus quibusdam que sonos diversos in cantu suo satis
distinguunt. Si vero stricte sumatur idem est discreta quod
'cum discretione facta', [5ᵛ] et musica sic accepta tantum
habet homini convenire, homo enim inter animalia cetera
cum discretione cantat et alias operationes exercet. Cantare 465
dicitur philomena, psittacus, laudula, merule, grus, hirundo
et gallus et hiis similia, sed hec sola Natura impellente seu

cogente cantum suum exprimunt; homo vero cum
discretione cantat, sed cantui suo perfecte sententie verba
coniungit.   470

Cantus dicitur quasi 'sonorus actus', canor autem quasi
'cum anhelitu labor'. Inventores itaque cantus et primi
doctores consideraverunt trachiam arteriam, id est organum
vocis humane, secundum triplicem dispositionem triplicem
cantum posse proferre. Quandoque enim dilatatur multum   475
et emittit sonum gravem; quandoque constringitur multum
et reddit sonum peracutum; quandoque medio modo se
habet et reddit sonum acutum. Et huiusmodi triplicem
cantum diatonicum appellabant quasi de proprietate
tonorum. Cantum autem qui est gravi gravior postponebant   480
propter sui molliciem parum et nihil valentem, et hunc
organicum appellabant eo quod organum vocis est deficiens
in illo. Similiter illum qui est acuto acutior non curabant
propter intolerabilem eius laborem – in ipso etiam nulla
dilectio invenitur – et cantum huiusmodi enharmonicum   485
appellabant eo quod extra diatonici cantus harmoniam
positus et cantorem et auditorem fatigat et ledit, per nullam
recreationem delectationis oblectans.

METRUM DE EODEM

Dictis postpositis decet humanam repetamus;   490
Est de proposito magis et magis hanc videamus.
Hec modulare sonos discreta mente docebit
6ʳ   Verbaque subiungit; volucres nil tale decebit
Nam per Naturam volucres cantare docentur;
Nil rationis habent quoscumque sonos modulentur.   495
Sic philomena canit, sic laudula, gallus, hirundo
Et plures alie, quarum nec nomina fundo,
Qui cantare tamen dicantur corde profundo.
Plus valet hiis humana satis quia plus operatur;
Cantum cum verbis docet: hanc ratio comitatur.   500
Qui viciosa canit non curat ut illa sequatur
                    ....
Organicum mutat enharmonicumque rescindit;
Obscurus nimis est hic, alter guttura findit.

Inter utrumque gravis et acutus et est peracutus
Estque tonos proprios proprie modus iste secutus.   505
Est et ab inde diatonicus de iure vocatus;
Iste placere potest cunctis recte modulatus.

VI   DE NOTULIS CANTUS USUALIS, QUE SINT ET AD QUID INVENTE

Cantores antiqui maxime in cantu delectari non solum   510
curaverunt sed ut alios cantare docerent sollicite studuerunt.
Ingeniaverunt ergo figuras quasdam que unicuique syllabe
dictionum deputate singulas vocum impulsiones tamquam
signa propria denotarent, unde et note vel notule
appellantur. Et quia cantus multiformiter procedit, nunc   515
equaliter, nunc ascendens, nunc vero descendens, propter
hoc et differenter sunt note predicte formate et diversa
nomina sortiuntur. Quedam enim notula dicitur punctum,
quedam virga, quedam clivis maior vel minor, quedam plica
maior vel minor, quedam pes vel podatus maior vel minor,   520
quedam quilisma maius vel minus, quedam pressus maior
vel minor.
   Punctus ad modum puncti formatur et adiungitur
quandoque virge, quandoque plice, quandoque podatu,
quandoque unum solum, quandoque plura pariter, precipue   525
in sonorum descensu. Virga est nota simplex ad modum
virge oblonga. Clivis dicitur a cleo, quod est 'inclino', et
componitur ex nota et seminota, et signat quod vox debet
inflecti. Plica dicitur a plicando et continet notas duas,
unam superiorem et aliam inferiorem. Podatus continet   530
notas duas quarum una est inferior et alia superior
ascendendo. Quilisma dicitur 'curvatio', et continet notulas
tres vel plures quandoque ascendens et iterum descendens,
quandoque e contrario. Pressus dicitur a premendo, et
minor continet duas notas, maior vero tres, et semper debet   535
equaliter et cito proferri. Sed cantus adhuc per hec signa
minus perfecte cognoscitur, nec per se quisquam eum
potest addiscere, sed oportet ut aliunde audiatur et longo
usu discatur, et propter hoc huius cantus nomen usus
accepit.

METRUM DE EODEM   540

Olim cantores cantu sic complacuere
Heredesque süos voluerunt scita docere.
6ᵛ Contigit ergo novas hos ingeniare figuras
Ut possent varias vocum figurare tenuras
Quas dixere notas certus quod ab inde vocatur   545
Cursus cantandi qui vocali sociatur.
Clives, plice, virga, quilismata, puncta, podati
Nomina sunt harum; sint pressi consociati.
Pes notulis binis vult sursum tendere crescens;
Deficit illa tamen quam signat acuta liquescens.   550
Vult notulis binis semper descendere clivis
Obscurumque sonum notat illius nota finis.
Precedit pausam vel stat pausantis in ore,
Ac si perfecte notule fungatur honore.
Virgam si tollis numeri pluralis habentur   555
Cetera namque minor vel maior sepe videntur.
Sed tamen hinc oculi nequeunt perpendere cantum
Si non auris adest et voces premodulantum,
Et quia sic tali pro consuetudine crescit,
Usus habet nomen cantus quem musica nescit.   560

VII   DE SEX VOCIBUS NOTULARUM
         ET SUFFICIENTIA EARUM

Cum itaque, sicut dixi, et sicut quotidiana experimenta
ostendunt, quidam sunt cantores qui musici appellari non
debent eo quod musicis rationibus non utuntur, et qui   565
cantum non possunt addiscere nisi a sepe cantante alio, ut
magistro vel socio, propter hoc musice inventores plurima
indagatione ad hoc obtinendum diligentissime studuerunt
ut qui musicam nescit, et scire desiderat, secundum regulas
musice artificialiter procedens, cantum musicum, id est   570
musice scriptum, discat absque docente, examinet
iudicetque, confirmet rationalem, corrigat incorrectum.
    Adinvenerunt ergo primi doctores musici sex syllabas *ut,
re, mi, fa, sol, la* que sunt nomina sex notarum si considerantur
absque alternatione et mutatione ipsarum. Si cogente   575

necessitate alternantur, supra et infra omnes notas usque in
infinitum significant et nomina sunt earum. Hiis nominibus
note, ut dictum est, appellantur a Gallicis, Anglicis,
Teutonicis, Hungariis, Slavis et Dacis, et ceteris Cisalpinis.
Itali autem alias notas et nomina dicuntur habere, quod qui   580
scire voluerit querat ab ipsis.

Sex predicta notarum nomina sufficiunt non solum
propter senarii dignitatem sed etiam ut in arte superfluitas
evitetur. Senarii dignitas est cum sit primus numerus
perfectus, sicut Arithmetici dicunt et probant. Dicit etiam   585
Moyses in Genesi quia deus creavit celum et terram, id est
quatuor elementa, diei prime in spacio, per quinque dies
continue sequentes ipsa ornavit. In die septimo quievit ab
omni opere quod patrarat, et ait Moyses 'igitur perfecti sunt
celi et terra' et cetera. Postquam enim deo placuit non die   590
una sed pluribus opus mundanum perficere, in spacio sex
dierum hoc bene debebat contingere cum senarius numerus
nota   sit et dicatur perfectus ut ex hoc ostenderet opus suum esse
perfectum. Et propter hoc merito subiungitur 'et requievit'.

Necessitas [7ʳ] etiam sive opportunitas pluralitatem   595
nota   notarum avertit cum superfluitas in arte vicium reputetur,
quod sic probatur. Cum ab *ut* incipiendo perveniatur in
musica, de qua postea dicetur, usque *la*, si ulterius ascensus
fuerit ponetur semitonium, de quo postea dicetur. Sed
semitonium habitum fuerit prius; sic ergo idem bis   600
poneretur inutiliter et pro vicio reputatur in arte.

questio   Sed forte queret aliquis quare semitonium sic locatur in
medio sex notarum predictarum, quod nec in principio
solutio   nec in fine. Ad hoc dicendum est, cum Philosopho, quod
ars imitatur naturam. In naturalibus autem sic est quod   605
membra mollia in medio sunt locata et intra reclusa, ut
cerebrum in craneo, intestina et spiritualia in crate costarum,
medulla in osse, et cum semitonium mollem habeat sonum
respectu aliarum notarum, in medio illarum potius quam in
extremitate locatur.   610

questio   Queri etiam potest quare ille syllabe potius quam alie
nomina sint sex predictarum notarum, id est quare littere
solutio   iste in syllabis ponantur? Ad hoc dicendum est secundum
quosdam quod absque ratione fortuito hoc evenit, quod
non estimo verum esse. Dicit enim Perseus quod quidam,   615

imperitie sue solatium querentes, fortuitas estimant partium
orationis positiones et contra ordinem non posse peccare,
quod dicere stultum est et potest probari. Sciendum itaque
cum syllabe predicte signa sint vocum, et vocales multum
de voce habeant a qua nomen acceperunt ut vocales dicantur,   620
recte in hiis syllabis omnes quandoque ponuntur. Sex
autem syllabe sunt, unde oportet quod prima vocalium in
ultima syllabe reputatur. Et non ordinantur hee vocales in
hiis syllabis quemadmodum in Orthographia; ibi enim
ordinantur secundum situm organi vocalis, hic autem   625
secundum quod minus et plus habent de sono et sic ut a
minus aperto sono fiat processus ad magis apertum,
quemadmodum dictum est, quod prius est cantus gravis,
post acutus, ultimo peracutus. Et sic patet inquirenti quod
potius cum sexta syllaba repetitur *a* vocalis quam aliqua   630
reliquarum quia plus habet de sono.

De consonantibus dicendum est quod ibi ponuntur et
mute sed que in syllibando plus habent de sono, scilicet *t* et
f. Continent etiam quatuor semivo[ca]les, et sic omnes
species litterarum ad signandum quod generaliter pro   635
omnibus differentiis vocum accipiantur in cantu. Et sic
patet numerus et sufficientia dictarum notarum. Quod
autem vocales vicine non continue ponuntur, sed mixtim,
hoc factum est ne sonorum vicinia, que a fere simili cantatur,
hiatu cacemphaton ac tedium introducat.   640

METRUM DE EODEM

Artis doctores cui musica nomen habetur
Cantum laudabant qui cum ratione docetur.
Usum spernebant quasi sepe nimisque gravantem,
Dicentem 'quia sic' sed nulla per 'ergo' probantem.   645
Protinus errorem removebat regula talem;
7ᵛ   Cursum cantandi certum dedit et specialem.
Quadrupla cum spaciis fiebat regula certis,
Certis cum notulis certa ratione refertis.
Ut, re, mi, fa, sol, la: notularum nomina sena;   650
Sufficiunt notule per quas fit musica plena.
Nec mirum; numerus idem perfectus habetur.

Machina mundana per eumdem facta docetur.
Quod sex sufficiunt potes hac ratione probare
Ultra *la* notulam si tentas continuare,   655
Nam, magis ascendens, quod erat positum replicabis,
Sive, quod est nimium, quod abundat in arte locabis,
Semitonus; quoniam precessit et hoc sequeretur:
Est ergo melius quod precedens iteretur.
Sex notulas mediumque semitonum posuerunt;   660
Si bene perspicimus usi ratione fuerunt.
Ut decet, in mediis clauduntur mollia duris;
Hoc Natura facit preservans a nocituris.
Mollisonum *mi fa* poterit bene tale videri,
Et mediam sedem notularum iure tueri.   665
Si querat quicumque velit cur hec elementa
In dictis notulis sunt hoc et in ordine tenta,
Primo grammaticus *a* profert *u* que supremo;
Navigat hoc resonans et verso Musica remo.
Organicum notat ille situm speciesque sonorum   670
Ista; gravis prior est et primus ponitur horum.
Quod magis os aperit magis et sonat inde locatur.
Mute vel liquide vocalis consociatur.
U prior hinc alia que plus resonare notatur,
Quartaque vocalis in quinta sede locatur;   675
Conveniens tamen est in sexta quod repetatur

....

8ʳ   Mixtim ponuntur similis ne peccet hiatus;
Euphonia iubet ne sit sonus immediatus.
Tres elementales species hec nomina poscunt,
Nam triplicis cantus gades migrantia noscunt.   680

7ʳ   VIII   DE PALMA ET LINEIS ET SPACIIS EIUS

Dictum est de sex notis que ad significationem cantus
uniuscuiusque sufficiunt et quod in lineis et spaciis habent
poni. Sed que [7ᵛ] et quot sint nomina linearum et spaciorum
interpositorum nondum vel tactum est vel expressum.   685
'Interpositorum' dico, quia infra lineam que est infima
linearum, et supra supremam, spacium notabile non
habetur. Ad cuius rei evidentiam preconsiderandum est

quam solerti animadversione antiqui doctores posteros
suos erudire studebant. Considerabant enim quod artifex   690
quiscumque per instrumentum bene dispositum propositi
sui facilius potest obtinere effectum. Ingeniabant ergo
musice principia ponenda esse in interiori parte manus, et
habilius sinistre quam dextere, sic tamen si Natura effigians
non peccavit in ipsa, id est, si manus eadem in abundantia   695
vel penuria non peccat digitorum. Cum itaque decemnovem
sint articuli digitorum, ut palpe vel frontes vel summitates
eorum, quod pro eodem accipio, articuli esse dicantur.
Dicti doctores decemnovem sedes notarum locaverunt in
ipsis, unicuique nomen proprium assignantes compositum   700
ex littera, que est nomen clavis, et nomine vel nominibus
note vel notularum quam vel quas insinuat ipsa clavis. Et
primum articulum lineam, secundum spacium esse
dixerunt, et sic usque in finem; linea tamen et spacium
ratione pagine alicuius magis differentiam quam manus   705
[ostendunt].

8ʳ   In pulpa itaque sive in fronte pollicis locaverunt sedem
notabilem, id est note convenientem, et eam gammut Γ *ut*
appellabant, quod dicitur compositum a Γ, quod est littera
Greca que apud Latinos dicitur G quod est clavis illius   710
articuli, et a nomine cuiusdam note que dicitur *ut*, que
domestica est illi clavi. Plures etiam notas non habet.

Ulterius in gremio ipsius pollicis posuerunt A *re*, et est A
nomen clavis et *re* nota que debetur eidem. Et clavis ista
plures notas non habet.   715

Item in radice pollicis positum est B *mi*: B nomen clavis,
mi nota que debetur eidem. Et hec sedes, seu iste articulus,
plures notas non habet.

Item in radice indicis posuerunt C *fa ut*: C est nomen
clavis, *fa* et *ut* sunt nomina duarum notarum que illi clavi   720
debentur, *fa* in comparatione ad claves inferiores, *ut* vero
superioribus comparatur.

Item in radice medii D *sol re* locatur, et est D figura et
nomen clavis, *sol* et *re* note que debentur eidem; *sol*
inferioribus, *re* superioribus comparatur.   725

Item in radice medici posuerunt E *la mi*, et est E nomen
clavis, *la* et *mi* note que debentur eidem; *la* inferioribus, *mi*
superioribus comparatur.

Item in radice auricularis vel minimi, quod idem est, locatur F *fa ut,* et est F nomen clavis, *fa* et *ut* note que 730 debentur eidem; *fa* inferioribus, *ut* superioribus deputatur.

Item in gremio ipsius minimi situm est G *sol re ut.* G est nomen clavis; *sol, re* et *ut* nomina sunt notarum que debentur eidem; *sol* inferioribus, *re* superioribus prope, *ut* longe superioribus est affine. 735

Item in sinu minimi ponitur a *la mi re,* a nomen clavis, *la mi re* nomina sunt notarum que ipsi clavi debentur; *la* inferioribus, *mi* prope superioribus, *re* longe superioribus est cognatum.

Item in pulpa vel in fronte minimi situm est b *fa* ♮ *mi;* b et 740 ♮ nomina sunt clavium, diversimode tamen accepte, quia per b rotundum figuratur *fa* et per ♮ quadratum figuratur *mi.*

Item in fronte medici ponitur c *sol fa ut;* c nomen clavis est; *sol, fa* et *ut* sunt note que eidem debentur, *sol* longe 745 inferioribus, *fa* prope inferioribus, *ut* superioribus famulatur.

Item in fronte medii d *la sol re* locatur; d nomen clavis; *la, sol* et *re* nomina sunt notarum; *la* longe inferioribus, *sol* prope inferioribus, *re* superioribus comparatur.

Item in fronte indicis ponitur e *la mi;* e nomen clavis, *la* 750 et *mi* nomina sunt notarum que clavi debentur; *la* inferioribus, *mi* superioribus assignatur.

Item in sinu indicis f *fa ut* collocatur; f nomen clavis, *fa* et *ut* nomina sunt notarum; *fa* inferioribus, *ut* superioribus est additum. 755

Item in gremio indicis g *sol re ut* est impressum; g nomen est clavis; *sol, re* et *ut* nomina sunt notarum que clavi debentur; *sol* inferioribus, *re* prope superioribus, *ut* longe superioribus deputetur.

Item in gremio medii ponitur ♮ *la mi re,* ♮ nomen clavis; *la,* 760 *mi* et *re* nomina sunt notarum; *la* inferioribus, *mi* et *re* superioribus debentur, sed differenter si continue fuerit. Supra b rotundum in dicto ♮ *la mi re* dicetur *mi;* si vero continue post ♮ quadratum fuerit *re* in ♮ *la mi re* dicetur.

Item in gremio medici ponitur ♭ *fa* ♮ *mi;* utrumque ♭ ♮ 765 nomen est clavis unius, sed differenter. Si enim fuerit ♭ rotundum, in eo dicetur *fa;* si vero ♮ quadratum, *mi* solum.

Item in sinu ipsius medici ℭ *sol fa* collocatur; ℭ nomen est

clavis, *sol* et *fa* nomina sunt notarum et utrumque debetur
inferioribus; *sol* prope ponitur, *fa* longe positis condescendit.   770
Ultimum ♪ *la sol* in sinu medii radicatur; ♪ nomen clavis, *la*
et *sol* nomina sunt notarum et comparantur inferioribus
differenter; *la* clavibus longe positis et *sol* vult prope positis
adiungi.

Inter cetera sciendum est quod sedes ipsa sive articulus   775
dicitur in linea, ut est Γ, B, D et cetera; articulus vero pariter
in spacio ut est A *re*, C *fa ut* et similia. Clavis autem cuiusque
articuli dicitur esse in linea eo quod est principium linee
que tota usque ad finem vel usque ad sui mutationem
nomen illius articuli sibi observat. Similiter et clavis ista   780
dicitur esse in spacio que signum est articuli et principium
spacii quod ab ipso articulo denominatur usque ad finem
spacii vel usque ad sensibilem mutationem eius. Spacium
vero dicitur superficies articulum parem designans a Γ *ut*
usque ♪ *la sol*. Ex hoc videndum est quod supra ♪ *la sol* et   785
infra Γ *ut* spacium notabile, ut dictum est, non habetur,
quia spacium in musica nihil aliud est quam superficies
duabus lineis proximis actualiter vel intellectualiter
interclusa. 'Intellectualiter' dico, quia contingit quandoque
lineam supremam vel infimam quatuor linearum actualiter   790
poni, et aliam que potest poni, et non ponitur, subintelligi.
Et spacium tale interpositum notabile, id est notis
assignabile, debet dici.

Sciendum est etiam quod antiqui primo inter claves A *re*
et post B *mi* [cantabant], et sic ascendendo invenerunt   795
secundum cursum litterarum in abecedario. Postquam
vero considerabant cantum aliquem usque ad A *re*
descendere, sicut antiphonam *O sapientia* et similia, sed
non potuit esse notabile spacium nisi certis limitibus
interclusum, et propter hoc adinvenerunt gamut quod ipsi   800
A *re* suppositum removet errorem. Videtur enim errare
quicumque itineris vel cuiusque sui laboris finem vel ignorat
vel non proponit. Amplius considerandum est quod claves
dictis articulis appropriate per tres limites distinguuntur.
Primus limes continet has claves Γ A B C D E F G, et hee   805
graves dicuntur quia sono gravi et respectu aliarum obtuso
utuntur. Secundus limes etiam continet a b c d e f g, et hee
dicuntur acute quia sonum acutum respectu premissarum

reddere consueverunt. Limes tertius continet has claves
ᵃᵇᶜᵈ, et dicuntur peracute quia sunt acutiores acutis. Et hec   810
ₐᵦᵪₔ
de clavibus ad presens sufficiant.

METRUM DE EODEM

Artis principiis non notis nemo scit artem:
Illa sciens immo totum non scit quia partem;
Scire manum cupiens quam musica poscit habere,   815
Doctorum poterit subtilia corda videre.
Articulos denos digitorum iunge novenos
Hii distinxerunt notulis et carmine plenos.
Gamma *ut* in summo posuerunt pollice Grecum;
Γ tibi sit clavis, *ut* sit nota; sic erit equum.   820
Pollicis in gremio statuerunt A *re* priores;
A clavis, nota *re* sit, sic docuere minores.
Radix dat B *mi*; reserat B, *mi* notulabit.
C *fa ut* hinc sequitur sed et indicis in pede stabit.
C clavis tibi sit; *fa* respicit inferiora,   825
Ut nota que sequitur, tantummodo posteriora.
Sic est in reliquis, sit clavis littera prima;
De notulis quedam scandit, quedam petit ima.
Hinc tamen excipias ᵌ *sol fa*, ♮ *la sol* altum,
Supra se quoniam non possent addere saltum.   830
Respiciunt tantum claves gradiendo retrorsum;
Deficiente via non est fuga vertere dorsum.
In b*fa*♮*mi* non sic tamen esse videtur,
Namque duplex ibi b duplici pro clave tenetur.
Molle rotundum b *fa* precipit esse futurum,   835
♮ si quadratur, poscit *mi*, sic quoque durum.
Quodque rotundum sit vel quadrum linea prebet;
b molli spacium duro quoque musica debet.
Articulus cum par fuerit spacium retinebit;
Impar si fuerit tunc linea nomen habebit.   840
Suntque novem spacia sed abundat linea dena
Extra quam spacium non sit tibi querere pena.
Interclusum sit spacium vel mente vel actu
Omni vel careat notularum tegmine tactu.
Cum sapiens fueris finem prenosce viarum,   845

Quo fine si gradieris; confusio ledet earum.
Linea vel spacium currit quasi pagina tota
Ut clavis docuit que non est clave remota.
Queritur in palma cur linea non variatur;
Pagina sepe tamen, cum scribitur, hoc patiatur.   850
Solvitur ad totum quia palma stat integra tantum,
Nec posset facile dare quadrupla linea cantum.
An multi paucis plus possint non dubitatur;
Hinc est in magnis hominum quod turba rogatur.

9ʳ   IX   QUARE MANUS POTIUS SIT INSTRUMENTUM   855
          MUSICE QUAM ALIUD MEMBRUM

Dispositionem manus sive palme musice et utilitatem
considerantes, non est mirum si queritur cur doctores
primi non fundaverunt principia musice in quocumque
instrumento exteriori sed potius in manu que humani   860
corporis organum et pars esse docetur. Sed questio ista
primo per interpretationem, secundo per rationem solvatur.
Non enim est verum quod solum per manum huius principia
cognoscantur, sed etiam per monocordum. Sed id nec
habetur a quolibet nec semper est presto; habilius etiam et   865
promptius per manum habentur ista et etiam exercentur.
Considerabant igitur predicti doctores quia, ut dicit
Aristoteles, inter quinque sensus duo tantum reperiuntur
disciplinares, scilicet visus et auditus, quorum uterque
doctrinam apprehendit que fieri habet per manum; homo   870
enim videns et audiens, et hanc diligenter attendens, multum
in ea capit profectum. Per visum enim discernit figuras [9ᵛ]
et diversitates et distantias articulorum, et per auditum
discernit et comparat diversitatem sonorum. Unde Horatius
in Poetica: 875
    Legitimumque sonum digito callemus et aure.
Notandum est etiam quod musica valet videnti et surdo,
sed parum, ut si ante surditatem participabat auditum et si
tunc non ignorabat. Similiter ceco et audienti valet hoc
artificium, quia tactu preambulo potest manum discere   880
quamvis prius nescivit. Si vero fuerit surdus et numquam
audiv[i]t, nihil ei valet musica neque manus, quia, ut dicit

nota   Aristoteles, cecus non syllogizat de coloribus, et similiter
possumus addere quod nec surdus de sonis. Sonorum enim
proprium est subiectum auditus, quemadmodum coloratum   885
ipsius visus. De instrumentis exterioribus musicis dicendum
est quod surdo non valent, quamvis ante peritus fuerit in
arte exercendi musica instrumenta. Cecus autem et audiens
quibusdam musicis instrumentis uti potest, quibusdam
vero minime, quod facile est cognoscere, non eget exemplis.   890

METRUM EIUSDEM

Utilis ista manus reliquis magis esse docetur;
Quanto plus habilis et presto semper habetur.
Sensus precipui prosunt hac arte iuvante,
Auditus tactu visusque situ mediante.   895
Surdo nil valet hec, cecus tamen hac operatur
Discens atque docens, quoniam cantare notatur.
Pone sonum surdo, ceco propone colorem,
Si libet in vanum consumere forte laborem.
Instrumenta ferunt ceci resonantia multi,   900
At surdi recitent nullo modulamine fulti.

X   DE SPECIEBUS INTERVALLORUM

Dicto de articulis qui et sedes esse notarum dicuntur, habito
etiam de notis que articulis assignate sunt. Sciendum quod
unicuique articulo vel nota una debet ascribi vel due vel tres   905
et non plures, cum nihil aliud sit quam soni unica percussio
seu ictus. Ulterius autem considerandum est quod si melodia
fiat [10ʳ] composita ex duabus notulis quo nomine censeatur
et quot modis habeat variari.

Notandum igitur quod huiusmodi combinatio notarum   910
dicitur generali nomine intervallum.

Intervallorum novem sunt species, scilicet unisonus,
semitonium, tonus, semiditonus, ditonus, diatessaron,
diapente, semitonium cum diapente, tonus cum diapente.
Ad hec ultimo coniungitur diapason. Unisonus autem est   915
quasi principium et fundamentum intervallorum, nec est

unum novem intervallorum quia non cantatur ex ascensu
vel descensu notarum, unde et dicitur unisonus eo quod
plures note uniformiter sonant dum continue in eadem
linea vel in eodem spacio continentur, sicut est *re re, fa fa, sol
sol* et similia. Et dicitur unisonus a soni unitate.   920

   Contra dicendum est de semitonio, sed quia semitonium
minus est quam tonus et sicut ad modum privationis se
habens, tonus autem ad modum habitus, et cum privatio
non cognoscatur nisi per habitum, prius videndum est quid
sit tonus. Sed hoc nomen tonus equivocum est ad multa.   925
Tonus enim in Grammatica est accentus qui ab antiquis
dividebatur in acutum, circumflexum et gravem; moderni
vero in acutum, moderatum et gravem. Tonus in musica
equivoce adhuc dicitur, et dividitur in tonum duarum et in
tonum plurimarum notarum et in tonum minorem et in   930
tonum maiorem.

   Tonus minor nihil aliud est quam consonantia duarum
notarum dissimilium perfecta et prima, et huius consonantia
dicitur intervallum quasi intersticium sive distancia.
Consonantia dicitur tonus quasi simul sonantia, quia si   935
melodia toni scinditur per intersticium diutinum virtutem
et naturam toni amittit, nec tonus est appellanda.
'Consonantia' igitur in hac definitione sumitur ut genus,
'dissimilium notarum' ut unisonus excludatur. Hec
differentia 'perfecta' excludit semitonium, et hec particula   940
'prima' excludit semiditonum et alias species intervallorum
sequentes.

nota   Sciendum itaque quod semitonium non dicitur a semis,
quod est 'dimidium', sed a semus, -ma, -mum, quod est
'imperfectum', eo quod non perfecte est tonus. Est enim   945
plusquam toni medietas. Sic dictum est de Troianis
         Semiviri Phryges
et iterum
         Nos Phryga semivirum et cetera
Vestibus enim utebantur ad modum mulierum unde et   950
semiviri dicebantur. Hiis dictis de tono minori, restat dicere
do tono maiori.

   Tonus maior est melodia plurimarum notarum unius
cantus; proprietas eius maxime attenditur penes finem.
Sed ne tractatus proposili fiat interruptio, mentio huius   955

cesset ad presens quia de ipso postea multa dicentur.
Semiditonus dicitur a semis, quod est 'imperfectum', et
ditonus, quemadmodum *re fa* et e contrario. Ditonus dicitur
quasi duplex tonus, sicut est *mi ut* vel e contrario. Diatessaron
dicitur a dia, quod est 'de', et tessaron, quod est 'quatuor'   960
vel 'quadratum', quia precedit de quarto articulo in quartum,
ut est *la mi, fa ut, mi la, sol re* et e contrario. Diapente dicitur
a dia, quod est 'de', et pentha, quod est 'quinque', quasi de
quinque notis facta, prout in *re la* et similibus apparet.
Semitonium cum diapente dicitur quia semitonium cum   965
diapente adiungitur, quemadmodum si fiat processus a *fa*
quod est in c *sol fa ut* ad *mi* quod est in E *la mi* gravi. Tonus
cum diapente est consonantia constans ex tono et diapente,
quemadmodum si iungitur *la* in a *la mi re* cum *ut* quod est
in C *fa ut* gravi, et sic de aliis.   970

10ᵛ   Nonum et ultimum intervallum est diapason, et dicitur a
dia, quod est 'de', et pan, quod est 'totum', et son, quod est
'sonus', quasi 'continens omnes consonantias' eo quod
transit omnes articulos omnium aliarum consonantiarum.
Alii dicunt quod dicitur a dia, quod est 'de', et pasin, quod   975
est 'simile' vel 'equale', quia procedit de simili ad simile.
Quamvis enim articuli sint diversi, unaqueque littera initialis
articuli, que est clavis illius, habet aliam litteram sibi
consimilem octavam supra vel infra cum qua constituit
diapason, quemadmodum Γ *ut* habet G *sol re ut*; A *re*, a *la mi*   980
re; B *mi*, b*fa♮mi*, et similia; unde sonus transiens de clavi
quaque ad sibi consimilem, seu ascendat seu descendat,
sicut dictum est, constituit dapason.

[METRUM DE EODEM]

Unam vel binas vel tres habet articulorum   985
Quisque notas; plures non continet ullus eorum.
Fit nota, fit totiens quotiens fuerit sonus ictus;
Hoc fine continuus etiam non est nota dictus.
Contingit notulas geminari; si geminantur
Intervalla novem fieri, non plura, sciantur.   990
Unisonus prior est quem semitonus comitatur;
Hunc tonus insequitur, tamen equivoce variatur.

Est tonus accentus, modulatio certa notarum,
Aut minor aut maior; tantum minor esto duarum
Que sint dissimiles, perfecte continueque.   995
Semitonus minor est et ab hiis non discidet eque.
Dum tonus est maior plures notulas retinebit,
Finem pretendens a quo sibi nomen habebit.
Dormiat iste tonus et ad intervalla redire;
Nos predicta monent et eorum nomina scire.   1000
Ditonus esse duplex tonus a lectore sciatur,
Ditonus et preit hunc sed semi tamen sociatur.
Quarta coit quarte diatessaron hinc veniente;
Quintam cum quinta socies, fiet diapente.
11ʳ   Continue sequitur cum semitono diapente.   1005
Est diapente tono iungens octava repente.
Nona subit species diapason, vel quia cunctas
Continet hec alias vel consimiles sibi iunctas.

10ᵛ   XI   QUARE PLURA NON SINT INTERVALLA
             QUAM NOVEM ET ARTICULI QUAM   1010
             DECEMNOVEM

Cum due note combinari habeant novem modis ita ut ex eis
novem intervalla formentur, non absurde queret aliquis,
cum note pluribus modis et supra diapason et infra habeant
coniungi, quare musicus tantum novem contentus est 1015
intervallis. Ad quod dicendum est quod in qualibet arte sic
est. Quidquid impedit finem artis illuminare iure debet ab
arte removeri. Sicut in Grammatica, que finaliter intendit
congruum, errare dicantur barbarismus et soloecismus, et
quod magis mirum est, etiam cacemphaton evitatur, sic et 1020
diale[c]tica, que intendit [11ʳ] facere de re dubia, dum
venatur syllogisticam necessitatem inutiles coniugationes
propositionum extricat, qualis est coniunctio duarum
affirmationum in secunda figura et ceteras huiusmodi
paralogisticas phantasias. Et in singulis artibus est aliquid 1025
huius reperire, sic et in musica. Cum precipue delectationem
intendat, quidquid eidem contrariari videtur abicit et
contempnit. Iuncture autem notarum que non constituunt
aliquod intervallorum quod sint unum ex novem predictis

merito a musico debent vitari cum non sint de genuino 1030
melodie sed odiosam dissonantiam operantur que proposito
musice [contraria] iudicantur. Tale est *fa* in b molli acuto
cum E *la mi* inferiori et superiori, si per modum intervalli
fuerit ei coniunctum. Tale est a *la mi re* cum b *mi* et e
contrario, et de similibus simile iudicium habeatur. Similiter 1035
dicendum est de intervallo quod superat diapason.

Item cum decemnovem articuli seu sedes notarum ab
antiquis doctoribus habeantur, queritur an plures esse
possint an debeant inveniri. Ad quod potest dici quod
decemnovem sufficiunt sed plures bene possent haberi. 1040
Cum enim cantus distinguatur in gravem, acutum et
peracutum, et cum octo claves deserviant gravi, septem vero
acuto et quatuor peracuto, vix continget aliquem habere
vocem tanti vigoris ut sine vocis mutatione istas claves
canendo transcurrat, et plures ascendat, licet essent invente. 1045
Quod si forte cantor aliquis cantum inferius non inceperit
oportune, sed eum incompetenter sublimius incohando
superiores claves ascenderit, in modo clavium se non
conqueratur habere defectum; loco enim superioris clavis
quesite, et non invente, sumat inferiorem proximam eidem 1050
littere servientem et per diapason in ea sonum inveniet
exoptatum, quod patet in instrumentis musicis que non
habent nisi septem vel octo notarum differentias in quibus
quilibet cantus invenitur.

Quidam predictum decem novenarium ascribunt 1055
decemnovem ipsius manus articulis qui dum plures non
reperiuntur in manu dicunt quod plures notarum sedes
non possunt inveniri. Sed estimare talia stultum videtur
quoniam extra manum, sicut et intra, diverse et differentes
figure articulorum habentur. Sciendum est etiam quod 1060
Guido in Musica sua tres articulos notabiles predictis
decemnovem superaddidit, et nostrum c *sol fa* c *sol fa ut*
appellavit, et nostrum d *la sol* d *la sol re* appellavit, et
superadiecit e *la mi*, f *fa* et g *sol.* Et rationem huius assignat.
[11ᵛ] Cum habeamus diapason in gravibus a Γ *ut* usque G 1065
sol re ut, et similiter in acutis a G *sol re ut* quod est finis
gravium usque a g *sol re ut* quod est finis acutarum, in
peracutis dixit Guido tot habendos articulos ut etiam
diapason in eis possit compleri vel quod musica in hac parte

pateretur defectum. Ad quod responderi potest, ut diximus 1070
ante, quod cum tribus articulis predictis carere possumus
quodammodo superflue videntur apponi. Ars enim ut
desiderat supplere diminutum sic et eius est quecumque
superflua resecare.

METRUM DE EODEM

1075

Intervalla novem faciet iunctura duarum
Apte que resonent fuerit si facta notarum.
Extendi numerus poterit tamen amplius horum
Et queri posset cur non placet usus eorum.
Sed que prepediunt finem turbare videntur;   1080
Ars ea secludit fore: talia dicta putentur.
Fa b molle sonans E *la mi* contemnit habere,
C *fa ut* et supra non aspiciens a *la mi re.*
Quodlibet istorum resonabit more luporum;
Hinc excluduntur nec nomen habetur eorum.   1085
Si quid transcendat diapason forsitan edas,
Barritum potius quam cantum promere credas.
Deni iunge novem sunt articuli notularum;
Queritur augeri numerus si possit earum.
Guido refert quod sic; docuit nos addere dictis   1090
Et tres articulos aliis post terga relictis.
Proximus est e *la mi,* post f *fa,* g *sol* que sequatur;
Addidit hos ut eis diapason perficiatur,
Nam sic in gravibus et acutis et peracutis
Hoc reperire potes tribus hiis in fine secutis.   1095
Cum tamen hiis aliqua liceat ratione carere
12ʳ   Non opus est quod eos teneamur in arte docere;
Raro cantorem contingit scandere tantum
Clavibus in reliquis ut non mutet sibi cantum.

11ᵛ   XII   DE SIGNIS INTERVALLORUM A DIVERSIS   1100
           DIVERSIMODE ORDINATIS   RUBRICA

Ex predictis patet quod intervalla que habentur in cantu
secundum arsin et thesin procedunt, quare opportunum

est ut certis limitibus mensurentur; alioquin distantie minoris
ad maiorem nulla differentia videretur. Unde signa sunt 1105
necessaria per que species intervallorum possint agnosci;
de signis igitur musicalibus aliquid dici potest. Sed in
sonoris musice instrumentis diversimode se habent signa
notarum secundum instrumenti proprietates diversas. Nam
foraminalia instrumenta maiora non habent continua quam 1110
tonum et semitonium secundum quod progressive disposita
ordinantur. Talia sunt organa, tibie, [12^r] cornua, muse,
syringe, flaiota et cetera. Chordalia etiam quedam
progressive temperantur, ut cithare et psalteria, organistrum,
monocordium et similia, et hec habent signa propria suarum 1115
notarum. Talia sunt etiam vasa sonora que secundum situm
et ordinem cognoscuntur ut cymbala et similia. Sunt et alia
chordalia que solum auditu discernuntur; temperantur
autem per consonantias diapason, diatessaron et diapente,
et per diversas digitorum interpositiones artifices ipsorum 1120
formant sibi tonos et semitonos, et sic de aliis. Sed qui cantat
in manu ipsos articulos et sonorum differentias habet pro
signis, quibus autem placuerit in pagina vel cantum scribere
vel scriptum addiscere vel cantare. Signis indiget manifeste
que sonorum certificent quantitatem. Antiqui signis diversis 1125
diversimode utebantur, et ad subsequentium evidentiam
notandum est quod primi doctores claves articulorum
omnium diversimode formare solebant. G *ut* enim per Γ
Grecum signabant, postea vero A B C D E F G simplices
litteras pro clavibus posuerunt et has gravibus ascribebant. 1130
Secundum autem claves acutas a b c d e f g litteras capitales
fecerunt. Ultimo peracutas cum duplo ventre $^{abcd}_{abcd}$ claves
quatuor formaverunt, ex quibus manifestum est quod clavis
uniuscuiusque articuli propriam suam formam tenebat.
Exinde quidam antiqui absque lineis cantum sibi potius 1135
quam aliis notulare volentes ipsam figuram clavis pro nota
scripserunt. Qualiter autem cantus super dictiones per
litteras notulatus fuerit ex predictis facile est videre, sed
constat quod iste modus canendi labore utens duplici
nimium difficultatis habebat. 1140
　　De clavium difficultate seu diversitate ab antiquis inventa
dicimus quod non est opus claves omnes adeo diversimode
figurari. Quamvis enim post Γ simplicibus litteris et graves

et acute scribuntur satis hoc operatur differentiam quod
littera vel clavis que in gravibus est in linea in acutis in spacio 1145
invenitur et e contrario. In peracutis autem figure capitales
apte scribuntur ad differentiam gravium ne forte error pro
eorum similitudinem generetur. Post predictos cantores
Hermannus Contractus cantum absque lineis vel aliter
notulabat, nam pro equali sono vel unisono, quod est idem, 1150
e posuit, pro semitonio s, pro tono t, pro semiditono t et s,
scilicet s supra t hoc modo t^s, pro ditono duplex t^t, pro
diatessaron d, pro diapente n, pro semitonio cum diapente
n^s, pro tono cum diapente n^t, pro diapason A capitale. Et
hec signa intervallorum, dum punctis carebant, signabant 1155
ascensum. Sed cantus talis adhuc multum obscuritatis
habebat; propter hoc Salomon, Odo [et] Guido ingeniabant
alias cautelas canendi ut scilicet articulos musicales per
lineas in superficie pagine protractas et per spacia interposita
designarent, [12^v] et per notulas quibus utebantur usualiter 1160
canentes lineis et spaciis iam dictis interpositas intervallorum
differentias demonstrarent. Ponebant igitur in principio
linearum claves ipsos articulos designantes vel usque ad
finem vel usque ad mutationem ipsarum. Item alia discretiva
signa ponebant, notificabant enim per colores: c *sol fa ut* 1165
per citrinum, a *la mi re* per viridem, F *fa ut* per rubeum
ostendentes. Sed decoloratio propter linearum mutationem
et in cantu vel superiori vel inferiori varietatem multociens
fit causa erroris.

METRUM DE EODEM

1170

Est thesis, est arsis, est unisonus; videantur
Signa prius per que species tot certificantur.
Quidam pro notulis claves posuere priores,
Credentes quod eis vellent cantare minores.
Signabant alii post intervalla figuris;   1175
Hermannus per eas voluit prodesse futuris.
Utraque dicta prius parvis obscura fuerunt;
Post alii melius notulis documenta dederunt.
Linea cum spaciis affixis clavibus ante
Certificat notulas nobis Guidone iuvante.   1180

Amplius et voluit varios addendo colores
A suprapositis quod distent inferiores;
Sed quia vel cantus vel linea dum renovatur
Errorem generat, modus hic non semper amatur.

XIII   DE CAUTELIS QUIBUS NOVUS CANTOR   1185
       ET RUDIS CANTUM ADDISCIT

Signis musicalibus visis et intellectis, qui cantum ignorat et
modum cantandi et eum scire in brevi desiderat, consideret
primo claves et utrum prima nota in linea vel spacio teneatur,
et quot note uni vocali debentur. 'Vocali' dico, et non 1190
'consonanti', quia sicut est in Grammatica non consonanti
sed vocali principaliter debetur accentus, sic et in musica
nota vel note.

   Item cantor clausulam sive congeriem notularum per se
canat distincte, et anhelitum recipiendo pausans 1195
nequaquam syllabam incipiat post pausam nisi forte prima
fuerit dictionis; talis enim scissio in cantando faceret
barbarismum et sic incongruam ostensionem.

   Item cantor huiusmodi puerilis circa semitonium caute
procedat ne vel ipsum ponendum postponat vel proferat 1200
negligenter. Et maxime circa b molle et ♮ durum caveat ne
oberret; hec enim figuris propriis debent assignari de iure,
quod si forte per negligentiam signata non fuerint, sepe
inducit errorem in illo qui cantum corde non scivit.

   Item hoc precipue novus cantor attendat ut notam unam 1205
tam diu teneat donec perfecte consideret ubi et qualiter
alia sequens debeat incohari.

   Item rudis cantor cum alio frequenter cantare studeat et
mutationes et intervalla consideret diligenter, et ut melius
per se cantare valeat cantum corde addiscat. Visitet etiam 1210
cantilenam suam extra intervalla vel cuius sit modi, et si
flexibilem vocem non habeat sed dissonus fuerit, et si
favorem forte [13ʳ] vel etiam adiutorium doctoris obiectum
amiserit, curam impendat, instrumenta musica exercet et
sepius eis utatur qualia sunt monocordium [et] symphonia 1215
que dicitur organistrum; in organis etiam cantare laboret.
In huiusmodi etiam instrumentis nota de facili errare non

potest et a sono suo legitimo distorqueri eo quod note per claves certas et signatas facile possunt considerari et prompte proferri absque socio vel magistro cantore.

1220

METRUM DE EODEM

Si rudis est cantor qui vult cantare libenter,
Ut cantum discat solitus cantare patenter
Cum socio cantet vel cum doctore frequenter.
Ut cantans cantor possit cantare decenter   1225
Claves prospiciat, discernat, sit memor harum
Donec mutentur vel duret cantus earum.
Post hoc inspiciat notulam que primo locatur
Linea vel spacium si sit, cui iuncta notatur,
Et discat notulas vocali continuare,   1230
Que debent eius voci de iure vacare.
Congeries notulas fert plures, clausula dicta,
Quas cantet pariter; sit earum nulla relicta.
Distincte cantet nova, non tamen incipietur
Syllaba post pausam nova dictio ni comitetur.   1235
Circa semitonum caveat, ne fiat ineptus,
Artis noticiam rigide dum non sit adeptus,
Optima cantori cuius cautela probatur
Ut notulas teneat donec post visa sciatur.
Intervalla sciat *Ter terni* sepe cavendo,   1240
Non manibus tantum que sit sed corde tenendo.
Scire putans totum vix novit denique partem;
Exerce studium quamvis perceperis artem.
Forsitan est discors et perdit ab inde favorem
Doctoris frustra qui non vult ferre laborem.   1245
13ᵛ   Non tamen hic cesset; colat instrumenta sonora,
Clavibus et tactis iungat concorditer ora.

13ʳ   XIV   DE INVENTIONE TONORUM ET NUMERO
              EORUMDEM

Dictum est supra quod hoc nomen tonus est equivocus ad 1250
tonum maiorem et tonum minorem. De minori dictum est

supra; nunc dicere de maiore sequitur, unde videndum est quid sit et qualiter dividatur. Supra tactum fuit in parte quid sit, quia ut habitum est tonus maior est regularis modulatio cantus plurimarum notularumque maxime attenditur penes 1255 finem. 'Modulatio' ponitur ut genus, 'regularis' additur ad differentiam cantus qui diatonicum vel supra vel infra excedit; 'plurimarum notularum' dicitur ad differentiam toni minoris qui consistit tantum in melodia duarum; 'que maxime attenditur penes finem' additur ad removendam 1260 opinionem illorum qui existimant [13ᵛ] cantum penes principium iudicandum.

Habita definitione toni, restat videre qualiter dividatur. Unde sciendum est quod antiqui musice doctores tonum in partes quatuor dividebant, scilicet in protum, deuterum, 1265 tritum et tetrardum, id est primum, secundum, tertium et *questio* quartum. Sed potest queri qua ratione fuerunt inducti ad ponendum quaternarium in speciebus predictis. Ad quod *solutio* dicendum est quod abundi doctores studiose et sollicite considerabant quod musica in maxima et amicabili 1270 concordia sonorum fundatur. Unde rationaliter est inventa secundum numerum et proportionem eorum que amicabilem et maximam et primam concordiam habere probatur in rebus mundanis, que sunt elementa quorum colligantia et adinvicem concors discordia constituit 1275 *nota* macrocosmum, id est mundum maiorem. Ignis enim est summe calidus, aer humidus, terra sicca, aqua frigida. Hinc rationem numeri sui trahentes, primi doctores musicum tonum per quaternarium diviserunt. Idem quaternarius, etiam ab elementis causatus sed non sic ordinatus, reperitur 1280 *nota* in microcosmo, id est in mundo minori qui est homo. Constat enim ex quatuor humoribus, scilicet cholera, sanguine, phlegmate et melancholia, et hii participant quatuor elementares qualitates predictas sed non disponuntur secundum ordinem qui est supra et infra. 1285 Elementaris autem complexio et etiam ordo reperitur in quatuor quadris anni, mensis, diei.

Statuerunt etiam quod cantus proti finem acciperet in D *sol re*, deuterus in E *la mi*, tritus in F *fa ut*, tetrardus in G *sol* *questio* *re ut*. Sed queri potest quare in hiis articulis et non in aliis 1290 ut superioribus vel inferioribus cantus decentius terminatur, et quare in articulis continuis et non interpolatis. Ad hoc dicendum est quod cantus inventus est propter delectationem principaliter, et propter hoc potius gravibus quam acutis vel peracutis finem suum committit que enim   1295 opus hoc rationaliter ac delectabiliter finire proponit. Sed *obiectio*   contrarium huius videntur intendere quoniam per notam finalem videntur in diapente conscendere. Ad quod dicendum est quod hoc fit per accidens ad ornandum videlicet finem cantus in gravibus qui principaliter est   1300 intentus; in cuius rei evidentiam cum plures cantum firmiter servent in gravibus pauci possunt ascendere diapente, quod si sit e contrario irregulare probatur. Cum itaque in gravibus cantus omnium tonorum regulariter finiantur, potius claves gravium superiores quam inferiores admittunt quoniam,   1305 sicut postea dicetur, cantus persepe infra suum finalem descendit, quod non liceret eidem si finem in infimis gravium aliquatenus attemptaret. Quod autem non in uno articulo sed in quatuor, et non interpolatis sed continuis terminantur, hoc est ideo quoniam elementa, quibus toni   1310 proportionantur, non similia sunt sed quatuor habent loca – terra infimum, aqua secundum, aer tertium, ignis quartum – et sic elementa non interpolate sed continue sociantur, unde et toni.

Post dictos tonorum quatuor inventores alii successerunt,   1315 perspicaciores antiquis, considerantes quod cantus tonorum quatuor predictorum quandoque multum ascendit, quandoque multum descendit. Propter quod, vitantes confusionem, unumquemque ipsorum diviserunt in duos, protum in protum authentum et protum plagalem,   1320 deuterum in deuterum authentum et deuterum plagalem, tritum in tritum authentum et tritum plagalem, tetrardum in tetrardum authentum et tetrardum plagalem. Et dicitur plagalis a plaga, quod est 'positio' vel 'depressio', eo quod in articulis inferioribus plurimum conversatur. [14ʳ] Authentus dicitur quasi 'alte extentus', quia superiores   1325 claves magis ascendit, vel dicitur authentus quasi 'authenticus', quia dignior est plagali et quasi dominus est illius. Et nota quod autentus quilibet est impar, et si fuerit par est plagalis. Protus autem autentus et protus plagalis eandem habent clavem finalem D, qui sunt primus et   1330

secundus; deuterus autem authentus et deuterus plagalis,
id est tertius et quartus, habent E; tritus autem authentus et
tritus plagalis, id est quintus et sextus, F; tetrardus autentus
et tetrardus plagalis, id est septimus et octavus, G.

questio   Et forte queret aliquis que sit ratio istius octonarii, et an   1335
aliud sit in naturalibus in quo numerus iste et proprietas
solutio   eius fundetur. Ad quod dicendum est quod ab eadem causa
extrahitur iste octonarius a qua et quaternarius predictus,
sed aliter considerata. Quamvis enim sint quatuor elementa,
et quatuor tantum elementares qualitates prime, una illarum 1340
uni convenit elemento principaliter, et alia tamen eidem
convenit minus proprie non eque primo. Verbi gratia, ignis
enim principaliter calidus est, secundario siccus; terra
principaliter sicca, per posterius frigida, sed aqua proprie
frigida, per accidens humida invenitur; aer principaliter 1345
humidus, secundario calidus esse dicitur. Et exinde trahitur
octonarius tonorum numerus predictus, et sicut una qualitas
principaliter, et relique secundario, eidem elemento
debentur, sic et duo toni clavi conveniunt uni finali,
principaliter authento, secundario vero plagali.

                                                                          1350
METRUM EIUSDEM

Quatuor antiqui species dixere tonorum;
Queritur unde fuit numerus detractus eorum.
Hoc sunt contenta numero que sunt elementa
Mundi maioris; humores adde minoris   1355
Et partes anni, mensis magneque diei;
Hiis conferre tonos potes eiusdem speciei.
Contiguas partes et habent et in ordine certas;
Quatuor inde toni species perpende repertas.
Supremas gravium claves pro fine tenebunt;   1360
Non alibi proprio finiri iure valebunt.
In numero primos iuvenes peccare notabant
Qui nunc inferius, nunc alta voce tonabant
Authentum quemvis dictorum sive plagalem;
Dicebant unum dictorum non fore talem.   1365
Dicitur authentus tonus hic, alte quasi tentus,
Inde plagalis erit, pressus quia scandere lentus.

14^v Est par et famulus peditat serpitque plagalis;
Est impar dominus authentus prevolat alis.
Sic numerus crescit, sic octonarius exit;   1370
Unus nempe duos quasi sub velamine texit.
Par imparque tonus notulam venantur eandem
Ut possint cantum pariter concludere tandem.
Quamvis ad mensam non combinantur onusque,
Pernoctare solent pariter dominus famulusque.   1375
Dicto cur fuerint duo bis, iam nunc referatur
Cur modo sint octo, quia sic numerus duplicatur.
Arbor producit ramos magnosque priores;
Finditur in geminos magnus quandoque minores.
Ignis cum calidus sit primo, siccus ab inde   1380
Est per posterius, ignem sic in duo finde,
Terraque sicca prius, post frigida iure docetur.
Sic est in reliquis; aqua sic aerque dupletur.
Octonarius hinc solque surgit esse duorum
Primum principium; reliquum famulatur eorum.   1385
Authentis claves finis dantur quasi primo;
Post per posterius paribus debentur ab imo.
Dicit Aristoteles quod non possint fore plura
Sed nec pauca magis elementa per hec sua iura.
Circulus hinc factus, cum sit perfecta figura,   1390
Non plus non minus est quam quod satis est habitura.
Hinc patet et quod sit perfectio musica digna
Que fundatur in hiis et habet certissima signa.

14r   XV   QUE SUNT CLAVES ET VICECLAVES
              TONORUM FINALES
                                                                             1395
Dictum est quod protus finitur in D *sol re*, deuterus in E *la
mi*, tritus in F *fa ut*, tetrardus in G *sol re ut*, et hee claves
proprie et regulariter tonis iam dictis debentur. 'Proprie'
dico, quia cantus quandoque improprie terminatur.
Contingit enim quandoque quod cantus, qui regulariter et 1400
proprie terminari deberet in gravibus, terminetur superius
in acutis, et hoc fit propter necessitatem precipue a semitonio
venientem. Cantus enim huius si locaretur in gravibus vel
semitonio careret [14^v] ubi deberet habere, vel ipsum

haberet ubi deberet carere. Cum itaque cantus talis in 1405
acutis ascensum et descensum inveniat exoptatum, ne
impediatur propter semitonium postpositis gravibus in
acutis locatur. Sed hoc de gratia, non de iure; licentia
quoque ista non datur nisi proto, deutero et trito quia D *sol
re*, quod proprium est proti, causa simillimum vicarium 1410
habet a *la mi re*; E *la mi* etiam, quod proprium est deuteri,
vicarium habet ♮ durum in b*fa*♮*mi*; sic et F *fa ut*, quod
proprium est trito in gravibus, vicarium habet c *sol fa ut* in
acutis. Tetrardus autem finem suum G *sol re ut* non evitat
quia propter vicinitatem semitonii supra et infra non 1415
incumbit ei necessitas que in aliis reperitur et ideo vicarium
non debet habere, unde et proprium suum officium in loco
suo exerceretur. Si ergo cantus tetrardi aliquotiens quantum
ad situm exorbitare videtur, imputetur ignorantie vel primi
eius cantoris vel forte scriptoris, [15^r] et subiacet correctioni 1420
cantoris periti.

Et ne nullum predicte necessitatis habeatur exemplum,
cantus proti fallit in gravibus in hac antiphona secundi toni
Magnum hereditatis mysterium, quam necessitas compellit in
a *la mi re* finiri. Et nota quod si cantus finitur superius, debet 1425
secundum finis exigentiam et superius inchoari huius cantus
translatio. Cum propter defectum semitonii sepe, ut dictum
est, habeat evenire, quidam artifices in instrumentis musicis
locant semitonium inter G *sol re ut* et F *fa ut*, quidam inter
G *sol re ut* et a *la mi re*, et clavem istam clavem falsam 1430
appellant, et in cantu illud commoditatem operatur
precipue in instrumento quod organum appellatur,
verumtamen in musica vocali humana locum non habet.
Guido enim in arte musica peritissimus, qui et in Musica sua
quedam posuit quibus bene caremus dum claves tres novas 1435
addidit peracutis propter diapason habendum in illis, ipse
quidem hanc clavem semitonii facile apposuisset si
necessaria nobis fuisset. Necessitate itaque dum cantus
huiusmodi finiri non potest in gravibus, petamus auxilium
ab acutis. Cantus proti, cum in gravibus D *sol re* non possit 1440
attingere in hoc responsorio *Sancta et immaculata es virgo*,
ascendens ad acutas finem vicarium sibi postulat a *la mi re*.
Item cantus deuteri cursum proprium non observat
communione *Quod dico vobis in tenebris*. Similiter quandoque

et cantus triti, proprium cursum evitans, c *sol fa ut* pro F *fa*   1445
ut sibi adaptat, ut in hoc responsorio *Tua sunt hec Christe.*
Hec omnia si quis in clavibus vicariis seu affinibus inceperit
et cantaverit, ad finem perveniet absque errore. Tetrardus
tamen sedem propriam non mutabit.

METRUM DE EODEM   1450

In gravibus cantus finitur iure tonorum;
Tres in acutis sunt viceclaves clavibus horum.
Protus D sed deuterus E sibi possit habendum;
F trito sed G tetrardo crede colendum.
Sunt tribus hiis primis a ♮ c collaterales;   1455
Forma dissimiles in cantu sunt bene tales.
G solam tetrardus habet solamque teneto;
Cantor qui negat hoc sese peccasse doleto.
Si cantus proti proprio male definit in D,
Ascendas ut in a per acutas definat inde.   1460
Deuterus E perdens ♮ durum querit habere;
F tritus fugiens vult per c fine placere.
Septimus, octavus propriam retinent sibi sedem,
Nam vicinus eos aliam non ducit in edem.
Est melius claves cantus licite variari   1465
. . . .

XVI   QUE SINT CLAVES INICIALES TONORUM ET QUALITER ET QUANTUM ASCENDANT VEL DESCENDANT

Dictum est quod cantus uniuscuiusque toni maxime penes
finem attenditur et etiam iudicatur, et hoc est dicere quamvis   1470
cantus aliquis in principio toni specialis alicuius proprietates
habeat, et in medio magis assimiletur adhuc eidem, in fine
tamen ei precipue adaptatur. Et cum dictum sit de clavibus
que et quot sint finales tonorum, nunc ulterius est dicendum
de clavibus inicialibus cantus eorum et quante note transeant   1475
finalem suum [15ᵛ] supra et infra.

questio   Sed queri potest quare prius dictum est de finalibus *solutio* cantus tonorum clavibus quam de inicialibus eiusdem vel de hiis que circa medium attenduntur. Ad quod dicendum est quod hoc fit propter finis dignitatem maiorem eo quod 1480 per principium cantus vel per medium minus discernitur quam per finem.

Protus itaque authentus quatuor habet proprie claves iniciales, C D F a, nam omnis cantus primi toni aut proprie incipit in C *fa ut,* sicut in hac antiphona *Post excessum* 1485 *beatissimi,* aut in D *sol re,* ut in hac antiphona *Ecce nomen domini,* aut in F *fa ut,* sicut in *Venit lumen,* aut in a *la mi re,* sicut *Exi cito.* In E *la mi* aut in G *sol re ut* non invenit principium huius toni. Et invenitur cantus primi toni descendere usque ad A *re* ad quatuor notas sub suo finali, sicut in principio 1490 responsorii *Letetur omne seculum.* Ascendit in g litteram, scilicet decem claves super suum finalem, ut in eodem responsorio ibi *eternus amor.* A quibusdam autem iudicatur cantus idem irregularis propter nimietatem ascensus, quibus responderi potest quod ascensus iste delectabilis est et ita 1495 finem non excedit musice que propter delectationem precipue fuit inventa.

Protus plagalis quatuor habet inicia seu principia: A C D F. A *re* ut *Ecce advenit;* C ut hic *Fuit ad tempus;* D ut *O sapientia;* F ut *Consolamini.* Et descendit cantus huius toni in Γ, quod 1500 in aliis non reperitur, ut in *Collegerunt* et in principio sequentie *Eya dic nobis;* et invenitur ascendere in d acutum, ut in responsorio *Omnis pulchritudo,* septem claves super suum finalem.

Deuterus authentus tria habet principia propria: E, F, G. 1505 E ut hic *Hec est que nescivit;* F ut *O gloriosum;* G ut *Te semper idem.* Et descendit tantum in C, ut in hoc responsorio *[O] magnum mysterium,* et ascendit in g acutum, ut in hoc responsorio *Virtute magna,* ibi *testimonium.*

Deuterus plagalis quinque habet claves iniciales: C, D, E, 1510 F, G. C ut *Frange esurienti;* D ut *Tuam domine;* E ut *Vigilate animo;* F ut *Tota pulchra;* G ut *Post partum virgo.* Descendit autem in B *mi* ut in hoc responsorio *Tanto tempore.* Ascendit in c acutum ut hic *Exequie Martini.*

Tritus authentus tres habet proprias claves iniciales: F ut 1515 *Paganorum multitudo;* a ut *Solvite templum hoc;* c in linea ut

Sanctus, sanctus, sanctus. Et ascendit in g linea, ut in hoc responsorio *Qui cum audissent.* Sub finali autem suo nihil [vel] rariter descendit, quod in aliis non invenitur.

Tritus plagalis ascendit quandoque in d peracutam 1520 supremam, sed tunc improprie terminatur in c clave vicaria in acutis, ut in sequentia *Verbum dei deo natum.* Habet autem, quando in gravibus terminatur, claves duas iniciales, D et F: D ut *Hodie scietis,* F ut *O admirabile.*

Et notandum est quod toni dicti claves habent proprias 1525 iniciales que dicte sunt quando proprie terminantur; verumtamen si propter necessitatem contingit eos proprias finales mutare et alias etiam iniciales sibi accipere oportebit. Sed huius clavium variatio in septimo et octavo non reperitur, ut dictum est supra.   1530

Tetrardus authentus quatuor habet claves iniciales: G ut *Angelus ad pastores;* ♮ ut *Misit dominus;* c ut *Populus Syon;* d ut *Omnes sitientes.* Et non descendit nisi ad F *fa ut,* ut in predicta antiphona *Angelus ad pastores.* Ascendit autem in [16^r] g acutam, ut in antiphona predicta *Omnes sitientes,* ibi *querite.* 1535

Tetrardus autem plagalis sex habet inicia: C ut *Sapientia clamitat;* D ut *Spiritus domini;* F ut *Alleluia 'Nativitas';* a ut *Quodcumque ligaveris;* g ut *Repleti sunt omnes;* c in linea ut *Erat enim.* Et ascendit in a peracutam ut in graduali *Miserere,* ibi *omnia ossa.* Descendit autem in C in qua incipit predicta 1540 antiphona *Sapientia clamitat,* et semper in eodem terminatur, scilicet in G *sol re ut,* sicut dictum est supra.

METRUM DE EODEM

Finis precessit mage dignus principiique
Sed non precipui modo mentio fit mediique.   1545
Incipit in C D primus tonus F *fa ut* aut a;
Ductus et *Ecce* probant, *Venit; Exi* fit quasi cauda.
g petit ascendens sed descendens petit A *re;*
Cantes *Letetur* potes hic utrumque notare.
A *re* secundus ivit, C D subit F *fa ut* idem;   1550
Quidam gamma volunt iam dictis addere pridem.
Ecce sed introitus hic, *O Genuit* que probabit
Eya dic nobis proti per Γ que notabit.

Natus, Natalis multi per Γ que sonabunt,
Et cum *re* multi quod dixi principiabunt. 1555
Ecclesie mores prudens ad parva sequetur,
Compatiens aliis ne semper lite gravetur.
In *Collegerunt* concedis *gamma ut* isti;
Omnis forte canens in acuta d cecinisti.
Tercius intrat E vult F vult G sociari, 1560
Hoc est *O, Pauli, Te* semper habet comitari.
In C descendit, scandens g tangit acutum,
Quo te cantantem ducit virtute secutum.
Quartus quinque tenet C D post E subit F G

. . . .

16ᵛ In B descendit sed in e bene scandit in altum; 1565
Exemplo careo: cum sit leve do quoque saltum.
Quintus tres habet, F a c quod linea scitur.
Subtus nil graditur; in acuto g reperitur.
Sextus in F capiens finem primum capiet D
Aut F principium, descendens C petit imum. 1570
Hinc sunt introitus *Hodie, Testes, Benedictus.*
Claves mutantur sursum dum sumitur a c;
Sic fit et in dictis fuerit si forte necesse,
Sed non tetrardum propria de sede movebis
In G finitum quem semper ubique videbis. 1575
Septimus intrat G; post ♮ c d quoque iunges;
Hoc *Caput,* hoc *Misit, Populus* testatur et *Omnes.*
F sibi vicinum premit et g scandit acutum;
Angelus ac *Omnes* facient tibi psallere tutum.
Octavus reliquis est ditior incipiendo; 1580
Si petit hospicium sex aspicit in gradiendo.
Intrat C vel D simul F G poscit et a c.
In C descendit sed in ♮ superardua tendit.
Hoc *Sapientia* dat, illud *Miserere* ministrat.

16ʳ **XVII QUANTUM TONI AUTHENTI ASCENDANT ET** 1585
DESCENDANT, ET QUANTUM PLAGALES

Dictum est in speciali de cursu et lege tonorum, sed hoc brevius teneri potest per regulas generales, et appello cursum sive legem in cantu certum ascensum vel descensum

per claves, id est quantum unusquisque tonorum intendi 1590
potest vel remitti, hoc est quantum ascendere vel descendere
possint proprie vel improprie, id est secundum regulam vel
permissionem. Notandum igitur quod cantus authentus
rariter potest ascendere per diapason, id est usque ad octo
notas super suum finalem, de licentia vero usque ad nonam 1595
et tandem usque ad decimam, sed hoc raro. Quod enim
quis de iure possidet, usui suo deputare [16ᵛ] potest
frequenter; concessis autem sapiens utitur caute et raro.
Cantus autem plagalis rariter potest ascendere per diapente
et usque ad clavem sextam, de licentia vero usque ad 1600
septimam et tandem usque ad diapason, sed raro.
Descendunt autem plagales usque ad quatuor notas, id est
per diatessaron, et etiam usque ad quintam, sed raro, infra
suum finalem. Authenti vero descendunt usque ad
diatessaron, quod est plagalium. Excipitur tercius, qui nec 1605
transit infra proximam inferiorem, et quintus, qui nihil
tenetur descendere infra suum finalem. Considerandum
est etiam, quamvis dictum sit quod authenti ascendant per
diapason et quandoque ulterius, et plagales per diapente et
quandoque ulterius, non est intelligendum quod semper 1610
sic fiat, sed quod fieri possit hoc modo, sicut dicimus quod
episcopus in quatuor temporibus celebret ordines et maiores
et minores; non intelligitur quod omnibus quatuor
temporibus hoc faciat, sed quod possit.

METRUM DE EODEM

1615

Legem vel cursum te credas scire tonorum
Dum scis quo quantus cursus precedat eorum.
Authenti poterunt diapason scandere iure;
Una potest addi vel bine forte figure.
Concessis raro sapientem condecet uti,   1620
Sed propriis poteris secure preter abuti.
Iure plagalis habet conscendere per diapente;
Gratia dat notulam vel binas, tres quoque lente.
Bis binas notulas sub fine plagalis habebit;
Additur una magis raro sed quinque videbit.   1625
Quatuor authentis da; tercius excipiatur

17ʳ

Uni se iungens; quintus nulli sociatur.
Sic ascendere sic descendere nemo putabit
Quod semper fiat, fieri sed posset notabit.

16ᵛ   XVIII QUALITER CANTUS AUTHENTUS   1630
              DISCERNITUR A PLAGALI PER CLAVES
              DISCRETIVAS

Cum tamen quatuor sint claves proprie tonorum, scilicet D
E F G, 'proprie' dico quia necessitate urgente [17ʳ] protus,
deuterus et tritus, ut dictum est, collaterales habent sibi 1635
claves vicarias per diapente, quasi ipsius convenientiam
habentes, a ♮ c acutas per quas excusatur defectus qui sit in
dubitatio D E F gravibus prius dictis. Dubitabit aliquis qualiter primus
a secundo possit discerni, quorum uterque finem accipit in
D *sol re.* Similiter queri potest de tertio et quarto, quorum 1640
finis est E gravis, sic et de septimo et octavo, quorum
uterque G sibi finem adoptat. Sed cum scire et posse in
predictis differentiam assignare et bonum sit et difficile,
arte indigere probatur. Dicit etiam Aristoteles quod multum
dissimilium differentiam assignare non est difficile, sed 1645
inter ea que maxime convenire videntur.

nota   Ad quod notandum est quod sicut quatuor sunt claves
finales, sic et quatuor sunt claves discretive tonorum. Quid
sint claves finales supra pluries dictum est. Claves discretive
tonorum in digito minimo continentur, que sunt F *fa ut,* G 1650
sol re ut, a *la mi re,* ♮ durum. Sunt autem quatuor, nec plures
nec pauciores, quia cum toni sint octo, quelibet clavis
discretiva differentiam operatur duorum tonorum: F *fa ut*
enim primum a secundo discernit, G tercium a quarto, a
quintum a sexto, ♮ durum septimum ab octavo.   1655

questio   Forte queret aliquis quare claves discretive iste et non alie
solutio sunt statute. Ad quod dicendum est quod cantus plagalis
magis perambulat claves inferiores et superiores authentus,
et propter hoc merito claves discretive sic ordinantur ut due
ipsarum ultime sint gravium et alie due prime sint acutarum. 1660
Itaque per hanc regulam – cum exemptione quadam que
iam dicetur – intelligendam, cantum authentum a suo
plagali discernes. Si cantus proti plures habet notas super F

fa ut, quantum ad hoc est authentus et primi; si plures infra, quantum ad hoc est plagalis et secundi. Item si cantus 1665 deuteri plures habet notas super G, quantum ad hoc est authentus et tercii; si plures infra, quantum ad hoc est plagalis et quarti. Item si cantus triti plures habet notas super a *la mi re,* quantum ad hoc est authentus et quinti; si plures infra, quantum ad hoc est plagalis et sexti. Item si 1670 cantus tetrardi plures habet notas super ♮ durum, quantum ad hoc est authentus et septimi; si vero plures infra, quantum ad hoc est plagalis et octavi. Et nota quod hec determinatio 'quantum ad hoc' additur idcirco quia pluralitas notarum predicta super clavem discretivam quantum in se est ipsum 1675 cantum trahit in proprietatem toni authenti; pluralitas vero notarum, si reperitur sub clave discretiva, quantum in se est ipsum cantum trahit in proprietatem toni plagalis. 'Quantum in se est' dico, quia sicut dictum est continget si tropus cum cursu cantus concordat; si vero tropus et cursus 1680 cantus discordant, [17ᵛ] postposito cursu tropo cedere nos oportet. Sed quia nondum dictum est quid sit tropus, de quo postea satis dicetur, quantum ad presens notandum est quod cantus authentus curialiter et paulatim declinat ad finem. Finis autem denominat actum, et propter hoc 1685 huiusmodi antiphone iudicantur primi toni et non secundi: *Volo pater, Reges Tharsis, Circumdantes,* cum tamen plures notas habeant sub F *fa ut* quam supra. Cantus vero plagalis cadendo sive precipitando magis tendit ad finem, sicut per semiditonum vel per maius aliud intervallum, et ideo 1690 derogando authento tantum trahit inde proprietatem toni plagalis, sicut contingit in communione *Tu puer propheta.* Dicunt etiam Odo et Guido quoddam notabile de differentia et distinctione tonorum, quod si cantus quinquies vel pluries clavem super suum finalem percutit per diapente, 1695 authento et non plagali debet ascribi quamvis currat per legem plagalis. Et hoc manifestum est in hac antiphona *Ecce tu pulchra es,* et in hoc responsorio *Deus omnium exauditor,* et in aliis quampluribus ita se habet. Et hec regula non invenitur per omnia generalis; mentionem tamen eius 1700 fecimus ut sciatur quod cantus plagalis raro debet attingere diapente, quod ideo fit ut prerogative ascensus in clavibus authentis quasi dominis plagalium attribui videantur.

Notandum est etiam quod cantus qui a quibusdam dubius
appellatur, de quo minus bene cognoscitur utrum sit 1705
authentus vel plagalis, semper authentus dicetur; a digniori
enim denominatio fit de iure, quod patet in hac antiphona
Circumdantes et in similibus, et in hoc introitu *Deus in*
adiutorium, quod septimi potius quam octavi esse dicatur.
Maior enim honor et prior attribuendus est domino et non 1710
servo.

METRUM DE EODEM

Quatuor ut claves finales esse feruntur,
Sic discretive bene quatuor inveniuntur
Suntque graves F G, sed acutas dicimus a ♮.   1715
Sufficit hic numerus quia clavis queque duorum
Quatuor istarum fit discretiva tonorum.
Primus vult notulas plures super F *fa ut* esse
Atque secundus ei vult plures rite subesse.
Tercius a quarto distat sed G mediante;   1720
Quintus et a sexto differt a clave iuvante.
Septimus octavo per ♮ differre docetur.
Impar stat supra sed par depressus habetur.
Si numeras recte, satis est data regula certa
18ʳ Si fuerit concors finalis neuma reperta.   1725
Si forsan prope finem principiatur,
Lex perit authenti prior et plagis inde vocatur.
Evenit econtra; locus ille morosius exit
Lexque plagalis obit quam neuma subultima texit.
Sic *Nisi, Dominus* primus tonus intitulatur,   1730
Sic a fine tonum concedere neuma probatur.
Odo tamen Guidoque refert, si forte canatur
Et sub lege plagis cantus currendo gravatur,
Si tamen hic sursum quater in diapente trahatur
Pluribus aut vicibus authentus iure vocatur.   1735
Regula ne fallat, sic tandem verificatur
Concors authento si finis neuma sciatur.
Si cantus dubius fuerit – si noscere quis sit
Non potes in notulis – hic authentus fore gliscit,
Nam decet interpres ut in ambiguis meliorem   1740

Partem confirmet, contempnens deteriorem.
Sic volo; sit primi quamvis sub lege plagalis.
Hoc et neuma facit cantus fini socialis.
Et breviter, finis si non a lege recedit,
Scire tonum facile poteris cui cantus obedit.   1745
At si discordant, fini credatur honeste;
Lex fini cedit quod nescit ferre moleste.

17ᵛ   XIX   DE TROPO, TENORE ET CAUDA QUE
               ATTENDUNTUR IN CANTU

Habita consideratione tonorum in eo quod omnes proprie 1750
terminantur in gravibus, per accidens autem in acutis
(preter septimum et octavum, qui non variant locum suum)
notande sunt alie tres proprietates in cantu secundum
quod in ecclesia solet cantari, quarum nomina sunt hec:
tropus, tenor et cauda quam quidem a fine appellant.   1755
    Tropus enim equivoce multa signat. Grammaticus et
Rhetoricus [18ʳ] tropum figuram appellant modum seu
quamdam figurationem loquendi. Tropus vero in musica
est proclamatio quedam vocis que speciali tono cantatur.
Adaptatur maxime circa finem; qualecumque etenim 1760
principium cantus fuerit aut medium, intentio tamen
artificiose cantantis retorquet semper cantilenam ad finem
proprium toni alicuius specialis specialiterque intenti. Et
huiusmodi retorsio sive proclamatio tropus appellatur in
cantu quasi conversio ad tonum a cantore intentum. Tropus 1765
iste quandoque incipit in principio cantus et nusquam
discordat cum lege vel cursu sic in antiphonis omnibus de
Trinitate, et ibi vel nulli vel stulti de tonis dubitare videntur.
Quandoque tropus oritur in cantus medio, quandoque
ante finem non longe a fine, sicut patet in hoc responsorio 1770
Preparate corda vestra domino quod in principio videtur
authenti proti, id est primi, in fine autem desinit in E *la mi*
et proto deutero, id est tercio, deputatur; responsorium
etiam *Gaude Maria*, quod in principio et in medio est
deuteri authenti, id est tercii, in fine autem datur plagi 1775
tertio, id est sexto. Nam sicut dicit Aristoteles, 'Finis est
optimum in re', et item 'Finis est cuius gratia' sic igitur

merito contingit in cantu ut per finem optime cognoscatur.
Caveat ergo velociter iudicare qui non vult penitere post
iudicium. Unde Salomon 'Fili esto velox [18ᵛ] ad 1780
audiendum, tardus autem ad iudicandum'.

Notandum est etiam quod cantus quidam non ex ratione
sed quadam consuetudine detorquentur a quibusdam ad
proprietatem toni unius et ab aliis aliter et per clavem aliam
finiuntur; et tunc, ut dictum est, propter controversiam 1785
litigantium evitandam sequi vel ad minus pati debemus
consuetudines ecclesiarum. Et hoc ideo habet fieri quia in
cantu tali diversi diversis tropis utuntur in comparatione ad
tonos diversos; verbi gratia hec antiphona *Et respicientes* a
quibusdam ita finitur ut sit tercii et a quibusdam ut sit 1790
octavi. Similiter aliquibus finalis antiphone ut *Bene fac*
itaque quandoque finitur ut sit quarti, quandoque ita ut sit
octavi. Similiter hec antiphona *Germinavit* quandoque ita
finitur ut sit primi, quandoque ita ut sit quarti, quandoque
ita ut sit octavi. Exempla horum, quia invenire etiam cantori 1795
sunt facilia, in littera non ponuntur.

Ex predictis diligenter animadvertenti manifestum est
quod dubitatio de cantu quantum ad diversitatem tonorum
duobus modis contingit. Quandoque enim utreque parti
dubitationis eadem est littera finalis in cantu et tunc 1800
dubitatur utrum cantus contineatur sub tono authento vel
sub suo plagali. Et in hiis pluralitas notarum plerumque
discernit. Quandoque autem dubitatur de cantu qui apud
quosdam habet clavem unam finalem et reducitur ad tonum
proprium tali fini; apud alios idem cantus alia utens clave 1805
finali, immo et iniciali, iudicatur per tonum qui est
domesticus illi fini. Verbi gratia ut de hac antiphona *Gloriosi*
principes dubitatur utrum sexti vel octavi secundum quod
incipitur et finitur in F *fa ut* vel in G *sol re ut,* sed magis tamen
proprie est sexti. Similiter contingit de hac antiphona *Nemo* 1810
te condemnavit mulier. Si enim incipitur et finitur in F *fa ut*
sexti sit toni; si autem incipitur et finitur in G *sol re ut* sit
octavi, et magis proprie est octavi. Similiter hoc
responsorium *Gentipeccatrici* dubius cantus est, unde quidam
cantant versum sicut istum: 1815

      Esto placabilis
Alii cantant sic:

Esto placabilis
et in hiis consuetudini ecclesie consentiendum est et libro
inspecto.   1820

Tenor etiam equivocum est ad multa. Dicitur tenor
alicuius orationis summa vel significatio principalis. Tenor
autem in musica est aptitudo quedam modulationis tenens
cantum infra terminos toni sui. Tenor cantus observatur
per has duas dictiones *seculorum amen*, et maxime per has et 1825
non per alias, quia sunt finis versiculi qui frequentissime
solet proferri. Differentia est inter tropum [et] tenorem
quia ipse tropus incipit quandoque in principio cantus,
quandoque in medio, quandoque prope finem; etiam patet
quod neuma finalis, de qua supra dictum fuit, et tropus sunt 1830
idem, et quilibet tonus proprium habet tropum prope
finem. ['Prope finem'] dixi, et non 'in fine', quia plagalis
et suus authentus notam habent unam finalem; non igitur
distingui possunt per eam. Et quamvis tot sunt tenores quot
toni, principium tamen unius tenoris est pluribus continue 1835
quandoque, quandoque non, verbi gratia secundum
principium tenoris secundi cum dico:

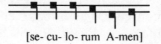

[se- cu- lo- rum A-men]

a vero acuta est principium tenoris primi, quarti et sexti; c
acuta tercii, quinti et octavi; d acuta septimi.   1840

Sed queret aliquis quare secundus et septimus pre ceteris
tonis litteras habeant speciales iniciales suorum tenorum?
Ad quod dicendum est quod hoc fieri potest ad
significandum quod hii duo toni [19ʳ] longe aliter se
habent quam ceteri, secundus enim pre ceteris magis 1845
descendit et septimus secundum se totum magis ceteris
ascendit. 'Secundum se totum' dico, quia sextus alicubi,
sed raro, supremam d tangere invenitur ut dictum est
supra, sed septimo inferior sepe invenitur.

Cauda vel finis in cantu est modulatio quedam que ad sui 1850
toni discretionem et ad commendationem tenoris eius fieri
solet cantu finito, et quia cauda finis est animalis, et finis ex
re nomen habere videatur, propter hoc finali antiphone
finis vel cauda huiusmodi solet adiungi. Et hac de causa in

Completorio, cum unica sit antiphona super psalmos, 1855
caudam habere non debet, et si quod magis videtur non est,
neque quod minus, et propter hoc, quia caudata non debet
esse antiphona in Completorio super psalmos, neque super
Nunc dimittis, similiter, et eadem de causa, in horis antiphone
non debent esse caudate. 1860

METRUM DE EODEM

Dicto quid tonus est et quorsum possit abire,
Cantor ad hec alia sapiens debet tria scire.
Quid tropus aut tenor est, quid cauda novissima noscit;
Dividat equivocum, videat quid musica poscit. 1865
In cantu tropus est vocis conversio quedam,
Intentum finem qua cantum tangere credam.
Nunc prius exoritur, prope finem nunc habet ortum;
Hoc mediante solet sibi cantus querere portum.
Posterior tropus hic finalis neuma sciatur, 1870
Que predicta toni sibi ius pro fine lucratur.
Quidquid precedit quod pristina pondera portet,
Dum tropus accedit tropus et dare nomen oportet.
Verborum tenor est, vocum tenor esse docetur,
Intra rara toni cantus per eum retinetur. 1875
Secula dant illi nomen, si nunc genitivo
Amen iungatur, sed eumdem carmine privo.
Sepius hec reliquis vox est cantoris in ore;
Debet et ergo frui bene nominis huius honore.
Fine prior tropus est finemque tenor comitatur; 1880
Approbat ipse tonum, quasi legitimum veneratur,
Cuique tono proprius tropus atque tenor tribuatur
Caudaque, finalis modulatio, rite sequatur.
Non pungit retro fallacis acumine teli

   ....

Quidquid agat coramque retro fidelis amicus 1885
Inventus fuerit; non est dicendus iniquus.
Cauda malum quandoque notat fraudis quoque cladem;
Pavo, capo, volucris rapax ornatur eadem.
Sic fit in cantu quia nescit cauda nocere;
Hunc probat, hunc ornat; sic debet iure placere.

19ᵛ

XX   QUALITER ET UBI *GLORIA* INCOHATUR   1890
        ET DE HEMITONIIS ET DIFFERENTIIS
        TONORUM

Cum tenor cuiuslibet toni, qui et *seculorum amen,* sit finis
versiculi qui est *Gloria patri,* ex predictis patet qualiter
finitur predictus versiculus. Unde ergo videndum est qualiter 1895
debet incohari et precipue secundum quod psalmo debetur.
Psalmodia enim ecclesia frequentissime debet uti, et hoc
est investigare qualiter psalmus secundum tenorem
uniuscuiusque toni habeat modulari.

Sciendum est ergo *Gloria* primi, quinti et sexti incipit in 1900
F *fa ut;* secundi in C gravi; quarti in E gravi; tercii et octavi
in G *sol re ut;* septimi in ♮ duro. Et notandum est quamvis
tamen unum *seculorum* uni tono assignavimus [19ᵛ] pro
tenore, tenor tamen uniuscuiusque toni vel unam habet
differentiam vel plures preter secundum, cui absque 1905
differentia sufficit ipse tenor. Quod autem unus tenor
plures habeat differentias quam reliquus hoc est immo quia
antiphonarum principia unius plus diversificantur quam
alterius et ideo pluribus indigent differentiis et habilius fiat
accessus ad principium antiphone, psalmodia sita secundum 1910
tenorem vel differentiam talem vel talem. Secundum
consuetudines tamen ecclesiarum diversarum diversas
plures vel pauciores differentie tenoribus assignantur, unde
et tu

versus   *Si fueris Rome Romano concinne more;*   1915
            Si fueris alibi concinne sicut ibi.

Et notandum quod sicut sunt octo toni et octo tenores
tonorum, sic et octo sunt hemitonia que dicuntur ab hemis,
quod est 'dimidium', et tonus. Sicut enim consideratur
modulatio tonalis circa principium et circa finem, sic et 1920
penes medietatem ipsius. Magis tamen ab usu quam a
ratione duo principia et duo hemitonia dantur octavo,
quoniam differentie huius antiphone *Nos qui vivimus* et
consimilibus assignatur hemitonium speciale differens ab
hemitonio sui tenoris et aliarum differentiarum ipsius. 1925
Differenter etiam modulantur hemitonia secundi, septimi
et octavi secundum diversarum ecclesias regionum, quod
non videtur mirum cum vestium quoque et conversationum

commercia varientur. In universis autem tolerabilibus cui
talibus commorari placuerit placeat et converti, nam   1930
    Temporibus mores sapiens sine crimine mutat.
Considerandum est etiam quod in *Benedictus* et in *Magnificat*
hemitonia differunt a psalmorum hemitoniis in primo
tono, quarto, sexto et octavo; in reliquis concordant cum
hemitoniis psalmodie, quorum exempla ponerentur in   1935
littera si non fastidiosum esset cantum prose misceri,
             sed tu
  ingenio verbis concipe plura meis.
Horum tamen si experientiam habere volueris, transferas
te ad libellum tonorum, et ibi   1940
    Exerce studium quamvis perceperis artem
donec dispositio in habitum convertatur. Diligenti etiam
animadversione considerandum est quod quemadmodum
secundum varietatem tonorum variantur modulationes
psalmorum, sic et versus responsoriorum. Similiter et   1945
psalmus et *Gloria* introituum variantur secundum tonos
diversos. Sed quia talia fere in qualibet ecclesia fere
demonstrantur ad oculum per libellum tonalem, decet ut
supersedeamus quidquid diffusius determinare de ipsis,
quia dicit Horatius   1950
  Nec circa patulum vilemque moraberis orbem.

20^r   METRUM DE EODEM

Dicto quid tenor est, quid finis dicitur esse,
Gloria principium merito non debet abesse.
Quod semel aut multis vicibus tenor est variandus   1955
Cuiuscumque toni, tamen exit ab inde secundus,
Gloria finiri variata voce docetur,
Antiphone capiti quod eo magis assimiletur.
Nec solum primum cantor distinguat et imum,
Pausam quo prebet medium distinguere debet.   1960
A reliquis distant primus, quartus quoque sextus,
Additur octavus in *Magnificat, Benedictus.*
Responsoria dant versus dant *Gloria* queque,
Claves finales non aspiciunt tamen eque;
Hoc fit post versum quia cantus pars iteratur   1965

Cuius principio finis versus famulatur.
Introitus et habent versus et *Gloria* cuncti
Cum quibus in clavi finali sunt bene iuncti.
Tertius excipitur, quarto quinto sociatis,
Propter principium claves mutare paratis.　　　　1970
Quem versum cantus quod *Gloria* debet habere
[20ᵛ]　Absque notis facile nequeo per metra docere.
Hoc licet ecclesie satis edocet atque patenter;
Quod qui scire volet, querat cantetque libenter.
Si tibi scire placet, breviter differe tenorum　　　1975
Qualiter et quantum varietur quivis eorum,
Plenius hoc notulis liber hic docet ipse tonalis;
Sepius ille tibi, tibi consulo, sit manualis.

20ʳ　　XXI　QUALITER ET QUOT MODIS FIAT ERROR IN
　　　　　　　CANTU　　　　　　　　　　　　　　　1980

Cum sepe cantus proprietas non observetur ab omnibus,
videndum est quot et quibus modis error fiat in cantu. Fit
enim error quandoque ex impotentia, quandoque ex
negligentia, quandoque ex obstinatia, quandoque ex
incuria. Ex impotentia male cantatur a senibus, pueris et 1985
infirmis, et hoc est veniale quoniam tales excusat impotentia
naturalis, propter quod Perseus docet
　　　Naturale vicium
　　　　Non est deridendum.
Ex negligentia male cantatur ab ebriis et ab illis qui 1990
pigritantur vel contempnunt cantum diligentius usitare, et
etiam ab illis excusantur qui totum a parte iudicant
improvise; et isti autem vix excusantur aut omnino venia
non sunt digni. De primis horum dicit Aristoteles 'ebrius
duplici pena punietur'; de aliis bene dicitur quod 'ignorans 1995
ignorabitur'. Contra ultimos dicitur
　　　　　careat successibus, opto,
　　　Quisquis ab eventu facta notanda putat!
Contingit enim diversos cantus modo eodem incohari et
diversimode terminari, sicut has duas antiphonas *Benedicta* 2000
sit creatrix et *Gloriosi principes*, et hanc *Cantabant sancti* et

hanc *Sub trono dei*. Similiter et has *Iste puer*, *In odore*. Tamen
[20ᵛ] hec omnia differunt secundum tropos tonorum quod
ex fine cognoscitur evidenter.

Ex obstinatia male cantatur ab illis qui, cantus propria 2005
lege relicta, propter motum animi sui excurrunt et recte
composita pervertunt, et sic perversa docent alios et in
usum incorrigibilem deducunt ea adeo ut non usus eorum
sed potius abusio pro auctoritate videatur teneri. Contra
tales dicitur   2010
    Qui peccat peccare docens bis peccat: et in se
    Qui reus est, et in hos quos facit esse reos.
De talibus dicit Aristoteles quod 'quidam nati sunt ad
contradicendum', et hii tales tunc primum exultant quando
sinistram opinionem suam cum clamore defendunt.   2015

Ex incuria male cantant qui sive tedio affecti sunt, in
labore quoque defessi. Que in cantu levanda sunt deprimunt,
non cantui sed sibi parcentes, vel petulantia quadam inducti
que deprimenda sunt levant et inepte, et cantum in
comparatione ad premissa perficiunt inconcinne. 2020
Exemplum primi graduale *Qui sedes domine*, ibi *super cherubim*;
cum superius dicendum sit inferius dicunt et errant. Item
aliud communio *Principes persecuti* ibi *concupivit*; altius enim
in c acuta dicere deberent quod dicunt in b molli. Item
aliud graduale *Probasti domine*, ibi *igne me* et cetera, cum 2025
enim in c acuta incipere deberent incipiunt in F gravi. Eque
quedam que deprimenda sunt levant, ut in antiphona *Cum*
appropinquaret dominus Ierusalem, ibi *si cognovisses et tu*.
Similiter in *Terribilis* ibi *et porta celi*; in gravibus enim
canendum est quod levant inepte.   2030

Item per incuriam peccant qui voce insulsa et rudi
cantum incipiendo a cursu legitimo eum detorquent, quod
solet contingere in hiis antiphonis: *Cum inducerent puerum*,
Cum audisset Iob. Cum enim sint primi, si nota nimis inflectitur
videntur concordare cum hiis: *Qui de* [21ʳ] *terra est*, *Quando* 2035
natus es que sunt tercii. Item per incuriam plurimum
damnose peccant et alios quam plurimos faciunt peccare
scriptores qui, claves iniciales et finales cantus non
observantes, dum cantum inepte incipiunt dum ad finem
legitimum pervenire non possunt, vel in cursu corrumpunt 2040
eum vel a fine suo proprio ipsum distorquent et quandoque

ad alium tonum eum procurvant. Pro exemplo huius peccati
revocetur in memoriam cantus aliquis qui necessitatis causa
transfertur a gravibus ad acutas, quem si quis aliter inciperet,
nota   oberraret ante scribendo et post cantando.   2045

Item per incuriam peccant in causam qui credunt et
dicunt quod nota non peccat. Tales autem omnibus
attribuunt unum tonum et hii tales potius cum equis
hinniunt, cum bobus mugiunt, quam cantare aliquid
videantur. De talibus in Poesi dicit Horatius quod   2050
    Ridetur chorda qui semper oberrat eadem.
Tales ignorant quod, inter cetera, nota idem operatur in
cantu quod figura in metro. Est enim intentio actoris in
cantu et actoris in metro una in genere, scilicet ut vox cum
materia dictaminis sui [concordet]. Si enim materia   2055
dictaminis in cantu fuerit gaudiosa, notam decet esse levem
et letam, sicut est cantus de Sancta Maria, de Sancto Iohanne
Baptista, de Epiphania, de Resurrectione et de similibus. Si
vero dictamen rem laboriosam vel secundum virtutem vel
secundum apparentiam significat, nota debet esse gravis et   2060
transire de b molli in ♮ durum et e contrario. Hoc satis patet
in *Fabrice* et in *Collegerunt,* et in prolixitate versuum
responsoriorum Sancti Stephani et hiis similibus. Dum vero
materia medio modo se habet et cantus medio modo se
debet habere, quod stulti putant ratione carere.   2065

METRUM DE EODEM

Errant in cantu nec sunt cantare potentes
Infirmi graviter, pueri senioque trementes.
Hoc nemo culpet quia naturale videtur;
Nature vicium nemo ridere tenetur.   2070
Sic dum negligitur cantus sit durus, ineptus;
Plus aloes quam mellis habens est aure receptus.
Ebrius ac studium qui non exercet in arte
Ac totum qui scire putat visa sibi parte
Cantant et cantus maculant errore decorem;   2075
Sic cantans cantor cantoris perdet honorem.
Sunt obstinati quidam cantare volentes;
21ᵛ   Cantum depravant rationis iure carentes

Erroremque suum valido sermone tuentur.
Nec cessant moniti; bene se cantare fatentur   2080
Et credunt multi; sic talis abusio crescit.
Scribitur et scriptam ratio deponere nescit.
Per tales in G *Deus, Misit* suscipit ortum,
Et tunc inferius dant enormem sibi portum.
Quod male cantatur facit hoc incuria quando   2085
Tedia precedunt aut cura labore gravando.
Sepius illa premunt que debent iure levari,
Sed levat hoc petulans quod debet rite gravari.
Sunt et qui mutare tropum dum turpiter audent;
Qualicumque modo finem contingere gaudent.   2090
Quod nota non peccet quidam dixisse feruntur,
Sic et nunc dicunt etiam, sed falsa loquuntur.
Namque figura dei decet ut similis videatur,
Sic nota materie quantumlibet assimilatur.
Leta notat letam non difficilemque laborem;   2095
Signabis medii mediam mediante colorem.

21ʳ XXII QUALITER NOVUS CANTUS HABET FIERI
         ET DIVERSIFCARI

Cognita cantus proprietate, non satis videbitur alicui quod
potest ea cantare que sunt ab aliis et prius inventa, sed forte 2100
vel proprie virtutis alacritate vel precibus aliorum inductus,
cantus dictamen cum notis condecentibus curabit
componere vel ad minus, dictamini aliunde accepto, cantum
adiungere competentem.

21ᵛ   Considerandum est igitur huius cantori qualiter cantum 2105
proprium suo tono precognito adaptet, quia sicut homines
non omnes delectantur in cibis eisdem sed quidam in
dulcibus, quidam in amaris, quidam vero in hiis que medio
modo se habent, sic et in cantu quosdam in morosas et
curiales vagationes primi toni audire delectat, alios vero 2110
precipites et obscuras gravitates secundi toni. Quosdam
vero quasi severa et indignans presultatio tercii magis iuvat;
alios quosdam sonus quarti quasi mulcens et adulatorius
trahit. Alii petulanti lascivia quinti mulcentur; alii voce sexti
veluti quadam dulci amantum querimonia vel sicut a cantu 2115

philomene moventur. Aliis quoque lib[e]ri saltus toni
septimi iocundi videntur; alii seriositatem octavi quasi
magistralem vel paternam doctrinam pre ceteris libenter
attendunt. Unde et Terentius, diversas diversorum
intentiones considerans, ait: 2120

Quot capita, tot sententie; suus cuique mos est.

Igitur si musicus ad preces alicuius cantum componat, si
voluerit satisfacere intentioni petentis ab eodem scrutabitur
in qua specie cantus precipue delectetur et secundum hoc
proposito tono cantum adaptet. Si vero mores petentis non 2125
tantum advertit quantum proprietatem ipsius materie,
consideret quid dicit Horatius in Poetria quia cuilibet
materie non convenit modus unus metrificandi unde dicit
quod
          Fortia meonio gaudent pede bella referri.   2130
Et iterum:
          Peccat in Andromachen Thaida si quis agit.
Sic et in cantu componendo cautela consimilis debet apponi
ut materie dictaminis tali vel tali suus cantus proprius
adiungatur.   2135

Si enim materia tristis fuerit, cantus erit proprie humilis
[22ʳ] et depressus ut in responsorio *Libera me domine*, et in
antiphona que planctum David insinuat, *Doleo super te*;
similiter et in planctu Didonis *O decus, O Libie regnum*.
Quare tractus missarum secundi toni sunt et octavi. Tractus 2140
vel in missa vel pro animabus vel in die ieiunii debent
cantari, et in hiis vel cantus proprie erit lugubris vel seriosus
ad minus, et propter hoc isti toni pre ceteris tractibus de
iure debentur. Si autem materia leta fuerit, cantus etiam se
conformet in acutis eidem. Sic fit in pascha, dum cantatur 2145
Alleluia 'Surrexit pastor bonus', Cum rex glorie, et similia. Si vero
materia fuerit leta et iocosa, cantus cum saltu convenit,
sicut in Epiphania *Veterem hominem*, et de Sancto Ioanne
Propter insuperabilem, et de Sancta Maria *Gaude mater*. Si
autem materia medio modo se habet, eidem et cantus 2150
proprie se conformet. Contingit enim cantum a quibusdam
fieri talem ut singulos tonos percurrat ita quod prima eius
particula primo, secunda secundo reddatur, et sic de aliis.
Et hoc fit ut ipse musicus peritiam sui magisterii ostendat in
cantu, vel quia considerant idempnitatem esse matrem 2155

fastidii cum diversitas incitet appetitum.

Secunda huius diversitatis causa potest accidere habita consideratione ad materiam in qua sunt quedam prospera et quedam adversa, sicut patet in cantu de Sancta Katerina, de Sancto Gregorio, de transfiguratione domini, et similibus. 2160

Notandum etiam quod quidam cantus inventores cantui suo signum aliquod speciale apponunt; unde quidam repetitionibus responsoriorum notam specialem concedunt quam responsorium non habuit quod precessit, quemadmodum in responsorio *Descendit de celis.* Talis est 2165 cantus Sancti Lamberti per totum. Alii structuram sui cantus erigere volunt nisi super bases rithmi vel metri, quorum exempla facile occurrunt querenti. Alii tenorem toni antiphone per versiculum, qui antiphonam comitatur, declarant. Sic videtur in cantu Sancti Laurentii, Sancti 2170 Pauli, Sancte Trinitatis. Opportunum est etiam cantus compositori, si delectabilem cantum componere et ordinare voluerit, [ut] pausas in cantu ordinet ubi pausandi tempus exigit ipsum dictamen. Hec doctrina bene observatur in hac antiphona *Cum esset desponsata,* similiter in illa *Cum* 2175 *inducerent puerum Iesum,* et de similibus similiter iudicetur. Alioquin dum sensus dictaminis notam impedire videtur et e contrario, tedium non solum subinfertur cantori sed etiam auditori. Notet etiam cantus inventor delectabilia esse cantus intervalla diatessaron et diapente, quod patet 2180 per *Alleluia 'Vox exultationis'.* Et hec sepius possunt poni; diapason etiam, si extrema eius firmiter observantur, cum delectatione interseritur, sed propter eius difficultatem raro ponatur.

METRUM DE EODEM   2185

Est aliquis cantare sciens cantatque libenter,
Et satis est illi quod scit cantare decenter.
Non satis est alii certo procedere calle
Vultque sub umbrosa tempus deducere valle.
Qui cantare cupit que non prius audiit ullus,   2190
22ᵛ   Si non arte canit mihi cantor erit quasi nullus.
Musicus attendat, qui cantum fingere curat,

Cantum propositum que formula iure figurat.
Materie docet hoc virtus dictaminis ante,
Qui sequitur cantus hac prodeat insinuante.   2195
Tristis dat tristem submissum, letaque letum;
Qui manet in medio cantum iubet esse quietum.
Cum planctum signet vel saltem seria Tractus,
Iure secundus erit, huic octavus quoque tactus.
Vox exultantis cum *Rex* vult sextus habere;   2200
Maxima per cantum vult gaudia nempe docere.
Sed tamen os quodvis non laudat quemque saporem;
Vocem quam fugit hic probat et docet hic meliorem.
Est aliquid speciale tono quem diligit unus;
Alter amans aliud cantum rogat hoc dare munus.   2205
Musicus idcirco faciens quodcumque rogatur,
Materiam cantans non semper concomitatur.
Excusat sese precibus fortasse petentis,
Sed plus laudo modum quidquam peccare timentis.
Est cantor quandoque novus, dum carmina fingit,   2210
Congregat ipse tonos omnesque per omnia pingit
Sic tamen ut sedem primus teneat sibi primam
Et reliquas reliqui, donec veniatur ad imam.
Forsitan ostendunt quia sunt hac arte valentes,
Aut aliter quia multa placent: probo per comedentes.   2215
Pontica sic dulci iunguntur, tristia letis;
Stat rosa cum spinis, abies corilique rubetis.

23ʳ   Laude suum cantum credunt quidam fore dignum
Ac in eo proprium gaudent ostendere signum;
Scriptores etiam libris quandoque metrorum   2220
Affigunt etenim signum speciale decorum.
Perseus et Petrus hoc observare docentur,
Qui versus ornare suos per signa videntur.

22ᵛ   ## XXIII QUE SINT VICIA IN NOVO CANTU CAVENDA

Ex iam dictis patet qualiter novus cantus habeat inveniri, et   2225
qualiter proprie materie sue debeat intendere nisi forte
propter causam quamque extrinsecam aliter informetur.
Sed teste Aristotele in Topicis, eiusdem moris est diligere
amicos et odio habere inimicos; similiter et intendere

proprietatibus que cantui iure debentur et evitare vicia que   2230
cantum depravando corrumpunt. Sed cum non facile
caveatur nisi cognitum, opportunum est ut ea que in cantu
viciosa sunt a magistro novi cantus caute et studiose vitentur.

Caveat itaque novus magister in cantu ne cursu cuiusque
toni tropus contrarius adiungatur, id est ne in principio et   2235
medio cantus uni tono appropriatus in fine alii tono positus
deputetur. Hec doctrina bene observata est in cantu de
Trinitate; male autem in communione *Principes persecuti
sunt me*, que legem et cursum habet quandoque tercii,
quandoque sexti, ultimo tropum habet primi et sic manet   2240
primi toni. Vicium illud in musica [23^r] proportionaliter
assimilatur solœcismo in grammatica qui causatur ex
discoherentia accentuum dict[i]onum.

Item aliud vicium in cantu novo debet caveri ne inveniatur
in eo intervallum irregulare et aliud a novem superius   2245
assignatis, quemadmodum si transitus fieret ab E *la mi* ad b
molle vel e contrario. Et assimilatur hoc vicium propositioni
false que a diale[c]tico multum vitatur. Musica irregularis
et talis iure musica falsa vocatur et multum vitetur.

Item in formatione cantus novi non apponitur inutiliter   2250
repetitio invervalli eiusdem, quemadmodum invenitur in
hoc tractu *Qui habitat* ibi *refugium meum deus meus*, et similiter
in hoc introitu *Miserere mihi domine*. Sciendum tamen quod
intervallum vel clausula repetitione una cum delectatione
auditur; semel igitur potest repeti, sed raro, sicut in *Alleluia*   2255
'*Surrexit pastor bonus*', ibi *pro ovibus*, et in cantu de Sancto
Nicholao [*Qui cum audissent* ibi] *clementiam*. Et considera
quod hoc vicium est simile nugationi, quam rhetor
plurimum detestatur.

Item cantor novus et mutilatam brevitatem et fastidiosam   2260
prolixitatem diligenter evitet, et hec duo vicia cum ellipsi et
macrologia similitudinem habere videntur. Hec duo
removet Horatius a bono poeta ubi dicit

    brevius esse laboro,
    obscurus fio; sectantem levia nervi   2265
    deficiunt...

Quod si quedam predictorum viciorum vel omnia in libris
ecclesiasticis quotidie videantur, talis excessus primis eorum
cantoribus imputetur qui etiam auctoritate ipsorum potest

aliquatenus excusari. Sciendum tamen est modernis quod   2270
eis non licet quidquid antiquis licebat, quod patet in libris
nota   veterum tam in constructione prosarum quam in figuris
metrorum.

METRUM DE EODEM

Dicto quid deceat dum cantus principiatur,   2275
Quid maculet cantum lateraliter hoc habeatur
Nam foveam saltem prudens vult scire viator,
Hanc ut transiliat directi callis amator.
Non de sede tropus cursum detrudat inique;
Est melius concors quod ei sit semper ubique.   2280
Est aliud vicium saltus quem regula spernit;
Hic modus est falsus, dicat qui talia cernit,
Et nota plusquam bis eadem numquam repetatur,
Unisonum demas quia sepius hic iteratur.
23ᵛ   Et brevis et longus nimium sine laude recedit;   2285
Cantus nil movet hic, alius per tedia ledit.
In medio virtus viciorum visa placere,
Nos docet in cantu medium quoque iure tenere.
Est alius querens cur talia nunc prohibentur,
Cum satis antiquis prius observata notentur.   2290
Audiat hic, licita quia non sunt multa modernis
Que prius antiqui posuerunt scripta quaternis.
Multos nempe modos posuerunt sepe loquendi
Qui modo sunt vicium quia sunt viciosa canendi.

XXIV DE POLIPHONIA   2295

Hactenus de cantu simplici dictum est, qui simplex dicitur
quia vel cantatur ab uno vel a pluribus uno modo. Nunc
autem huic operi finem proponentes imponere, ne
poliphonie videamur penitus ignari, de ipsa quid sit et
qualiter dividatur aliquid parvum dicemus.   2300
Poliphonia dicitur a polis [23ʳ] quod est 'pluralitas', et
phonos quod est 'sonus', que nihil aliud est quam modus
canendi a pluribus diversam observantibus melodiam.

Dividitur autem in tres species, scilicet diaphoniam, triphoniam et tetraphoniam, id est in cantum duplicem, 2305 triplicem et quadruplicem.

Diaphonia est modus canendi duobus modis, et dividitur in basilicam et organicam. Basilica est canendi duobus modis melodia ita quod unus teneat continue notam unam que est quasi basis cantus alterius concinentis; alter vero 2310 socius cantum incipit vel in diapente vel in diapason, quandoque ascendens, quandoque descendens, ita quod in pausa concordet aliquo modo cum eo qui basim observat.

Organica diaphonia est melodia duorum vel plurimum canentium duobus modis ita quod unus ascendat, reliquus 2315 vero descendat et e contrario; pausando tamen conveniunt maxime vel in eodem vel in diapente vel in diapason. Dicitur autem organica ab organo, quod est instrumentum canendi, quia in tali specie cantus multum laborat.

Triphonia est melodia sive modus canendi a tribus vel a 2320 pluribus, et modis tribus ita scilicet ut ab uno vel pluribus teneatur pro basi continue nota una, et ab alio uno vel pluribus idem cantus incipiatur in diapente et in eodem cursu cantetur usque in finem; a tertio uno vel pluribus idem cantus in diapason continue incipiatur. Et in prima 2325 voce cursus eiusdem cantus legitime finiatur. Et hic modus triphonie similiter basilica triphonia nuncupatur.

Organica triphonia est melodia vel modus canendi a tribus vel pluribus, modis tribus diversis ita ut unus vel plures basim teneant in gravibus notis pausatis; ab alio uno 2330 vel pluribus cantus distortius organicus incipiatur in diapente vel forte in diatessaron, et a tercio uno vel pluribus cantus incipiatur organicus difformis in diapason. Et pars tercia, secunde organice obviando, cum ea et cum prima utatur aliqua pausatione concordi vel in diapente vel in 2335 diapason. Potest etiam esse ut organica et dissimilis triplex nota simul ab hiis tribus partibus decante[tur] [24^r] et hic modus bene dicitur organica triphonia.

Similis est doctrina de tetraphonia, in qua diverse partes quatuor variantur. Pars enim inferius incipit in gravibus; 2340 secunda pars cantum eiusdem incipit in diapente; tercia respectu prime incipit in diapason, et quarta respectu secunde incipit in diapason similiter. Et sic partes quatuor

cantum pariter percurrendo pariter pausent et pariter
cantum finiant ita ut pars quelibet modo suo predicto.   2345

Organica, ut dictum est, ab organo vocali nomen accepit
eo quod diversa organa diversimode resonent quemadmodum et singuli homines singulas habent formas diversas.
Organica nihil aliud est quam dispar concordia cantus
diversimode sibi occurens. Dum enim in tali specie cantus 2350
pars una multum ascendit, reliqua vero multum descendit
et e contrario, et pausant pariter, ut dictum est, vel in eadem
clave vel in diapente vel in diapason. Si autem eos alibi
pausare contingerit, quod raro videtur, non debet vocem
diu tenere sed raptim resilire a pausa. Sepe tamen contingit 2355
in organica quod pars inferior paucas habet notas et superior
multas; tunc vero pauce tractim sunt, multe canende
velociter. Donec tandem in fine concurrant vel in eodem,
ut dictum est, vel in diapente vel in diatessaron.

METRUM DE EODEM   2360

Est cantus simplex qui per predicta notatur,
Nec duplici, triplici, nec quadruplici sociatur.
Si modus est unus, simplex de voce vocatur
Qui propter plures cantantes non variatur,
Estque duplex, non quod duo sint hoc more canentes;   2365
Immo duplex modus est quem servant arte fruentes.
Pars tenet una notam, pars altera circuit apte,
Et placet hoc auri multa dulcedine capte.
Vel canit utraque pars discors concorsque sodali;
Organicum genus hoc dicas modulamine tali.   2370
Inde triplex cantus triplici modulamine crescit,
Non quia tres cantent: numero maiore tumescit.
Vel pars prima notam retinet bineque sequentes
Concinnunt varie sed prime convenientes,
Vel canit organice prior et, cantum triplicando,   2375
Non differt nisi per claves cantumque gravando.
Est pro quadruplici cantus modulamine quartus,
Nec premissorum quisquam sit in ordine tantus
(Attamen in triplici magis est cautela canoris,
Dum canit organice pars queque magisque laboris.)   2380

24ᵛ

Pars prior in gravibus canit, altera cum diapente;
Tercia, quarta duplex diapason addit neque lente.
Tercia respondet prime sed quarta sequenti,
Talia non cantet nisi cantans mente libenti.
Et pausent pariter, pariter finire notati.   2385
Et nos hunc librum sumus hic finire parati.

24ʳ   ## XXV   INTEGUMENTUM MUSICE

Teste Philosopho, simile congaudet suo simili et aspernatur
contrarium. Cum itaque de musica dictum sit a quibus et
qualiter fuit inventa, quid sit et que sit eius proprietas et 2390
quis finis, non videtur inconveniens quod predictis
adiungatur si aliud est in rebus exemplum cui similis
videatur.

Musica etenim, ut tropologice loquamur, ecclesie similis
esse videtur, quod patet per ea que utrobique [24ᵛ] in 2395
eisdem speciebus numeri radicantur.

Musica scientia est una quamvis in diversis partibus sit
fundata; similiter et cum ecclesie multa sint membra, ecclesia
tamen una est in unitate fidei catholice radicata. Unde
Salomon in Canticis 'Una est columba mea, formosa mea' 2400
et cetera. Sic enim figurative de Sancto Spiritu, de
simplicitate et unitate ecclesie fuit locutus. In musica binarius
reperitur in quantum dividitur in mundanam et humanam;
similiter et in ecclesia binarius esse probatur in quantum
possidet duo testamenta que legit et considerat comparando, 2405
per que operatur et coniungit eorum parietes per lapidem
angularem, qui Christus est, innuendo.

Item alius binarius est in musica in quantum dividitur in
naturalem et instrumentalem; similiter et in ecclesia
reperitur et alius binarius in quantum vita contemplativa 2410
utitur et activa. Naturalis contemplative similatur, et
instrumentalis active. Musica etiam contemplative
assimilatur quam quidam traxit in habitum ut corde et
absque libris eam valeat exercere; similiter et active
assimilatur musica quam sine instrumentis exterioribus, ut 2415
libris, cantor exercere non potest. De hoc tamen dicitur
quod optimam partem elegit sibi qui non aufertur ab ea, sic

nec usus musice ab eo qui habitudinaliter servat eam. Et
sicut vita Marthe, que activam signat, periculosior est quam
Marie, quia maiori periculo subiacere videtur, sic et illi qui   2420
cantum nesciunt absque libris velociori subiacent
detrimento in eo quod libris vel non presentibus vel
inpromptis obmutescere videantur et quasi nihil scire de
cantu. Sed quia

    non cuivis homini contingit adire Corinthum   2425

consulo ut qui Maria non potest esse in cantu saltem et
affectum ipsius Marthe sibi studeat obtinere.

Item binarius adhuc reperitur in musica secundum quod
in ea cantus vel authentus vel plagalis; similiter et huic
similis in ecclesia est binarius amor, scilicet dei, qui similis   2430
est authento, et proximi, qui similis est plagali, quoniam
amor [dei] et cantus authentus aspiciunt ea que sursum
esse videantur; amor vero proximi et cantus plagalis in
inferioribus assignantur.

Amplius ternarius invenitur in musica, dividitur enim   2435
cantus in gravem, acutum et superacutum; similiter et in
ecclesia reperitur ternaria [25^r] cordis contritio que gravibus,
oris confessio que acutis et operis satisfactio que peracutis
comparatur, quia sicut hec tria sic et ista secundum gradus
comparationem se habent.   2440

Item est alius ternarius in musica secundum quod musica
instrumentalis vel consistit in vasalibus vel in foraminalibus
instrumentis vel in chordalibus. Similiter est et in ecclesia
alter ternarius, scilicet fides, spes et caritas in quibus debite
concordantibus ecclesia solemnisat et per modum   2445
citharizantis festive letatur.

Item et in musica est tertium ternarium reperire prout
principium, finis et medium considerantur in illa; similiter
contingit in illa ecclesia invenire ternarium in quo Pater ut
primus, Filius ut secundus, Spiritus Sanctus ut tertius esse   2450
creditur et probatur, quorum nullus absque alio vel est vel
erit vel fuit; et sicut ista tria cantum unum constituunt,
similiter et hii tres unam substantiam dei solius.

Amplius in musica est quaternarius in quantum toni
dividuntur in protum, deuterum, tritum et tetrardum. Sic   2455
et in ecclesia quaternarius est numerus virtutum, scilicet
prudentia, temperantia, fortitudo et iustitia, in quarum

significatione in tabernaculo extra ornando fecit Moyses
vela et saga quatuor colorum que sunt purpura, byssus,
hyacinthus et coccus.   2460

Item in musica ut plurimum solet fieri quod in superiori
parte dictaminis cantus quatuor linee protrahantur sine
quibus note cantorem certificare non possent, sic et in
ecclesia quaternarius precipuorum est Evangeliorum, per
que operationes fidelium ad beatitudinem diriguntur.   2465

Item in musica sunt septem claves finales; similiter et in
ecclesia sunt septem hore officiate.

Amplius in musica sunt septem littere iniciales omnium
articulorum, scilicet A B C D E F G; sic et in ecclesia septem
sunt sacramenta, que nominantur hoc modo vel ab effectu 2470
vel quia sacrant ecclesiam vel rei sacre sunt signa. Res enim
una corporeo sensu percipitur et res alia sacra sub ipsa
intelligitur; hec sunt corpus domini, baptismus, confirmatio,
inunctio, ordo, coniugium et confessio.

Item alter est in musica septenarius in quantum in 2475
septem articulis cantus acutus fundatur. Similiter in ecclesia
septem dona Spiritus Sancti septenario continentur; est
enim spiritus timoris, pietatis, scientie, fortitudinis, consilii,
intellectus et sapientie.

Amplius in musica octonarius reperitur in tonis qui 2480
fundatur super quaternarium tonorum predictum. Similiter
et in ecclesia octo sunt beatitudines que radicantur in
quatuor virtutibus paulo ante dictis; diligenter enim
consideranti etiam manifestum est quod unaqueque
beatitudinum a domino predicatarum ad aliquam quatuor 2485
dictarum virtutum potest reduci.

Amplius in musica distinguuntur intervalla novem
sonorum de quibus competenter dictum est supra et que
sint et qualiter abinvicem distinguuntur; similiter etiam ab
ecclesia novem ordines angelorum considerantur et qualiter 2490
abinvicem sunt distincti qui sunt angeli, archangeli, throni,
dominationes, principatus, potestates, virtutes celorum,
cherubim et seraphim. Item in musica novem sunt spatia;
similiter et [25ᵛ] in ecclesia, quantum ad id quod frequentius
et generalius invenitur, novem sunt lectiones, novem 2495
responsoria et novem psalmi; 'quod frequentius invenitur'

dixi propter consuetudines monachorum, qui pristinam
consuetudinem in maiorem convertunt.

nota   Amplius in musica decem linee possunt videri; similiter
10   et in ecclesia decalogus, id est decem legis preceptorum 2500
precepta continentia reperitur que propter imperitiam minus
decalogi provectorum hic scripta sunt et leguntur; peritis enim
lectoribus multa preter necessaria, immo superflua esse
videntur que utilia sunt minus provectis. Non habebis deos
alienos coram me, id est me solum habebis deum. Non 2505
assumas nomen dei tui in vanum, id est, nec false nec
superflue iurabis. Memento ut diem sabbati sanctifices, id
est eum pro sancto habeas nec opus servile in eo facias.
Honora patrem tuum et matrem tuam, scilicet reverendo
eis et necessaria attribuendo. Non occidas. Supple 'tuo 2510
arbitrio'; vel manu vel consilio vel consensu summi enim
iudicis hoc potest [fieri]. Non mecaberis, id est nullam
mulierem carnaliter vel affectionaliter cognosces nisi
legitimam. Non furtum facies. Supple 'voluntate vel opere
aliena latenter et indebite subtrahas'. Non feres falsum 2515
testimonium contra proximum; unde non licet fratre
quandoque. Non concupisces uxorem proximi tui – si non
licet concupiscere non licet habere – non servum, non
ancillam, non bovem, non asinum vel quidquid illius est,
mobile vel immobile, scilicet offendas.   2520
Amplius in musica sunt articuli decemnovem: octo in
gravibus, septem in acutis et quatuor in peracutis. Similiter
in ecclesia sunt gradus quidam inferiores, quidam
superiores, quidam vero medii predictorum in quibus ab
orthodoxis deo iugiter ministratur. Primus gradus est 2525
fidelium et in caritate manentium laicorum. Secundus
gradus est itinerantium peregrinorum. Tertius est Ordo
Fratrum cum Gladio, quartus Templariorum, quintus
Hospitalariorum, sextus Ordinis Sancte Trinitatis, septimus
Domus Teutonicorum, octavus Ordinis Leprosorum, et hii 2530
octo articuli[s] in gravibus comparabiles esse videntur.
Item sunt septem ordines in ecclesia unde articulis
consimiles in acutis. Primus est ordo secularium clericorum,
secundus Sancti Augustini, tertius Sancti Benedicti, quartus
Sancti Bernardi, quintus Predicatorum, sextus ordo Sancti 2535
Guillelmi, septimus Sancti Francisci; hii iam dicti acutis

merito comparantur quia sunt gravibus altiores. Item gradus
sunt comparabiles in ecclesia quatuor peracutis articulis.
Primus est barbarorum, secundus anachoritarum, tertius
heremitarum, quartus christianorum a paganis vel hereticis 2540
captivatorum. Hii habent similitudinem cum peracutis
quia superexcellunt predictos in tribulatione et in austeritate
penarum. Claves in musica sunt signa specialium suorum
articulorum; sic et in ecclesia sunt habitus dictorum ordinum
speciales per quos ipsi ordines predicti abinvicem 2545
discernuntur.

Item musica finaliter delectationem intendit; similiter in
ecclesia singulis diebus ad delectationem que in sola
beatitudine [26ʳ] reperitur; anhelat cum dicit 'Adveniat
regnum tuum', de qua delectatione Paulus adiecit 'Opto 2550
dissolvi et esse cum Christo'. In musica est clavis media
discreta cantum plagalem dividens ab authento; similiter et
in ecclesia Christus mediator dividet edos ab agnis, malos a
bonis. Est etiam consideratione dignum in musica quidquid
principium vel medium operetur in cantu. Tropus cantum 2555
denominat et in toni sui proprietate conservat; similiter et
in ecclesia quomodocumque se habeat principium vel
medium vite humane ultima intentio vituperat vel
commendat et homini statum bonum vel malum confirmat.

Item musica naturali sua virtute preservat ab egritudine 2560
imminente, curat presentem, demonia terrens in fugam
convertit, et hec omnia in ecclesia manifeste possunt videri.
Cum igitur musica in talibus in tot et in tantis habeat
similitudinem cum ecclesia, nihil mirum si usus musice et
solemnis eius memoratio in ecclesia observetur. 2565

METRUM DE EODEM

Ecclesiam signat similisque videbitur ipsi
Musica; que deceant hanc illam plurima scripsi.
Partibus in multis est, ars tamen una sciatur;
'Una columba mea' Salomon ait; ista probatur. 2570
Mundus, homo duplicem speciem dant insuper arti;
Testamenta duo relique potes addere parti.
Alter in hac arte binarius esse videtur,

Quo naturalis, instrumentalis habetur;
Contemplativam donec ecclesie fore vitam,   2575
Atque per activam pariter videas redimitam.
Tertius hinc binarius est, sit namque plagalis
Cantus et authentus, dum forsitan est specialis;
Sic et in ecclesia duplicem solvamus amorem
Vultque deo primum sed proximus ulteriorem.   2580
Hinc ternarius est utrobique repertus, acutus
26ᵛ Namque gravem sequitur que consequitur peracutus.
Est et in ecclesia cordis contritio primum,
Os peccasse dolens venit hinc, opus exit ad imum.
Hec tria dant arti, vas, chorda, foramen, honorem;   2585
Sed tria sunt spes atque fides si iungis amorem.
Sicut habet primum, medium finem quoque psalmus,
Sic tres sunt Genitor, Natus quoque Spiritus almus.
Protus habet socios, cum quartus sit sociorum;
Ecclesie libri tot sunt Evangeliorum.   2590
Quatuor ut claves proprias cognoscimus horum;
Tot quoque virtutes hominum cognosce bonorum.
Sit prudens, iustus, sit fortis, sit moderatus
Qui per virtutes desiderat esse beatus.
Hinc signant coccus, hyacinthus, purpura, byssus,   2595
Quodlibet istorum fuerat color ad saga missus.
Septem litterule claves sunt articulorum;
Hunc et in ecclesia numerum dic esse sacrorum:
Corpus, baptismus, 'confirmat', 'inunguit' et ordo,
Coniugiumque sacrum, postremum 'confiteor' do.   2600
Septem sunt claves que sufficiunt in acutis;
Dat deus ecclesie septem sua dona salutis.
Disce tonos octo bene si fuerint numerati:
Sic et in ecclesia scio quod sint octo beati.
Musica dicta novem tenet intervalla sonorum;   2605
Tot quoque spirituum sunt agmina sancta bonorum.
27ʳ Articulis denis ut linea consociatur
Qui liber est Moysi tot precepta famulatur.
Iunge novem denis sic articulos numerabis
Totque modis homines nunc ecclesie variabis.   2610
Est laicus, peregrinus, Eques Gladii, bonus Hospes,
Templus, Teutonicus, Trinus, post hos male sospes.
Hos similes gravibus predictis octo notabis.

Nunc septem videas et acutis assimilabis.
Augustum clerus preit et sequitur Benedictus;   2615
Bernardus post hunc qui non vult cedere victus.
Predicat alter et hunc Guillelmus concomitatur;
Hinc pede Franciscus nudo nodisque gravatur.
Barbarus in fovea silvis iacet anachorita.
Ultima captivus patitur; preit hunc heremita.   2620
Est delectari quod musica queritat, ergo
Sentio dum canto nova gaudia, tristia tergo.
Sic facit ecclesia; quocumque labore prematur
Hoccine proponit quod leta pace fruatur.
Annicius dicit quod delectabile summum   2625
Est deus, ecclesia precium petit hunc sibi nummum.
Est clavis media que discretiva vocatur;
Christus discernens pravosque bonosque sciatur.
Hoc tropus in cantu tribuit quod sit tonus unus;
27ᵛ   Laudat seu viciat sic hora novissima funus.   2630
Hoc facit ecclesia, quod musica plus quoque multo
Mundat, munda sacrat, salvat merore sepulto.
Talia, tanta potes preconia totque videre
In cantu per que debet de iure placere
Estque nichil mirum si se bene compatiantur   2635
Que predicta duo concorditer hoc operantur.
A domino quidquid bonitatis habere sciantur;
Est hiis collatum. Domino laudes referantur.

Laus tibi summe pater tua summa potentia fortis
Quamque nichil poterit clausis excludere portis.   2640
Cuncta domat; nichil est quod forte resistat eidem.
Omnia fecisti verbo cum tempore pridem,
Nate patris tanti summi, sapientia patris,
Materie carens, quod sis natus placuit tibi matris.
Tu cum patre polos potuisti condere sursum;   2645
Tu sub matre doloris voluisti subdere cursum.
Uxorem Genitor nescit virumque maritum.
Tu patre matre cares; talem nusquam scio ritum.
Filius et tamen es patris eternumque fuisti,
Filius et matris hominem fore quem voluisti.   2650
Quod sis nature princeps per facta patescit.
Quod natura negat miratur, denique nescit,

In te coniungi contraria cum videantur.
Non ut mixta solent; medium causare notantur.
Christus verus homo verus deus esse probatur;   2655

28ʳ   Sic non diminui pars hec aut illa sciatur.
Spiritus alme patris ac nati, tu pietatis
Fons, tu principium per quod sit gratia gratis,
Tu lux in tenebris, tu lucis continuator,
Consolans miseros, confractis es reparator,   2660
Errantes revocas et das requiescere fessis,
Ducis et inducis inopes in gaudia messis.
Da pater ut simus vicio virtute rebelles;
A nobis penam sic, iudex iuste, repelles.
Da fili stolide quod mentis nube fugata   2665
Hoc sapiant famuli quod sint de forte beata.
Spiritus alme veni, bonitatis complue rore
Pectora ne sterili maneant arentia more.
Non iidem sunt idem, sunt quos tres non tria credo.
Regia sic via me teneat nec ab inde recedo.   2670
Qualiter hec fiant patris huius in arce videbis;
Simpliciter credens hac nunc in valle tacebis.
Quodque superfuerit agni paschalis edendo
Igni comburas, lex precipit ista monendo.
Committas fidei quidquid dubitabile crescit;   2675
Quod supra vires fuerit sic ledere nescit,
Spirituique sacro da quidquid fortiter urget:
Crede mihi si credis ei mens credula surget.

28ᵛ   Sepius hec loquimur sed tale per omnia munus,
Ut bene credamus, det nobis trinus et unus.   2680
Portus adest, proram tenet anchora, cimba movetur,
Sed quotiens adiit fluctus, aperire rogetur.
Cimba quidem fragilis pauper quia cimba Iohannis,
Que rimosa carens costis obstructaque pannis
Primo servivit tibi virgo parensque beata,   2685
Teque iuvante fuit cum prosperitate relata.
Pondus erat magnum, fuit impar viribus istis,
Sed tu naufragio pia prompta rogata resistis.
Tu mare postremas tenebras fluctusque retundis;
Nec mirum si stella maris dominatur in undis.   2690
Te mediante fuit quidquid de te fuit actum;
Me rege, me salva: super hoc mihi postulo pactum.

Hinc onus et levius cartam navicula vexit,
Quam docte domine domini quoque gratia texit;
Illic scripta docent varie quod epistola poscit,   2695
Et quid dictamen, quod testis promere noscit.
Tertius iste labor de cantu servit amicis,
Non reprobis sed simplicibus puerisque pudicis
Nam reprobus reprobat; non iusta docente remordent.
Vix antiqua placent cui cuncta recentia sordent.   2700
Quodlibet hoc operum nostrorum quando videbit,
Affectum mentis numquam culpare valebit.
In tenui mensa mens pinguis pinguia cenat;
Hoc opus auctoris mens ipsa serena serenat.
Da deus ut scriptor lectores quique benigni   2705
Coram te fiant celesti carmine digni.
Da nobis iuste modo vivere menteque munda;
Da post in celis tibi psallere voce iocunda.
Detractor dabit isti […] forsitan arti,
Perpendens opus hoc spacium quoque temporis arcti.   2710
Quatuor hoc menses a principio genuerunt
Nec tamen a studio cessandi causa fuerunt.
Hoc octingenti sunt sexagintaque versus;
A primo folio liber hoc docet ipse reversus.

29ʳ

Textual notes and rejected readings

28   Salomon] Qalamon

60   comitatur] commitatur

71   Palinurum] palinnrum

79–80 Quod musica indigeat signis] Quod musica pre ceteris distinctionibus multis indigeat et signis. *Dittography (compare line 73).*

95   seu de manu musica] *Possibly with mark of deletion.*

111   non plures articuli quam novemdecim] *The scribe took* novemdecim, *written* 19, *to be a chapter number and he numbered all the following chapters accordingly.*

193   libenter] labenter

207   ab incantantibus] abin i.in cantantibus. *The scribe seems to be recording a variant of this line, and one which he copies elsewhere in the manuscript on a folio (30v) that incorporates a few scraps of* SM, *as* abinde canentibus omen.

223   nulla tam velociter oblectat] nulla tam velociter nulla tam oblectat. *Either an uncharacteristic ellipsis or another instance (as I have assumed) of dittography. This line appears at the end of f.2v and the scribe was sometimes prone to make mistakes at a page turn.*

246   exanimat] examinat

281   iuvenemque] *The end of the word is smudged but the reading seems secure.*

285   Compulit illecebras cantu liquisse lutosum] Cum fuit illecebras cantu liquisse lucosum. *A very difficult line, since the MS text does not construe in a satisfactory way, a difficulty intensified by the possibly meaningless* lucosum. *The emendation*

213

of Cum fuit *to* Compulit *may be recommended on three grounds: (1) it produces a line that can at least be construed; (2) it is just possible to imagine, given the contractions of medieval handwriting, how* Compulit *could have become* Cum fuit, *and (3)* Compulit *and* Cum fuit *are similar in sound, and the importance of such phonic similarity in the generation of variants should not be underestimated.* Compulit *poses no metrical difficulty. The emendation of* lucosum *to* lutosum *(literally 'muddied, besmirched') involves a transferred sense of* lutosum *that I have not been able to trace; but the emendation nonetheless gives satisfactory sense, and it may be doubted whether anything can be made of the scribe's* lucosum

290   exanimat] examinat
360   mundi salvator] mundo salvator
373   hec] hoc
444   Tibia, flaiotum syringaque, fistula, musa] Tibia, flaiotum et fistula musa. *The line as it stands is metrically incomplete. It has been reconstructed here on the basis of its prose equivalent.*
482   organicum] organic/nicum
532–3 continet notulas tres] continet notulas est tres
579   Slavis] flavis
617   peccare] peccari
675   Quartaque vocalis in quinta sede locatur] Quintaque vocalis in quarta sede locatur. *It is difficult to see how the MS reading can be correct. The authors are comparing the sequence of the vowels as they are arranged by grammarians (a e i o u) and by musicians in the solmisation syllables (u e i a o a). Since the* sedes *must be the solmisation syllable, the MS text would translate 'the fifth vowel [u] is placed in the fourth solmisation syllable [fa]', which is manifestly incorrect. The difficulty is removed by transposing the numbers so that the sense becomes: 'the fourth vowel [o] is placed in the fifth solmisation syllable [sol]'. The error may have arisen from the use of contracted forms.*
750   clavis] clalis
850   Pagina sepe tamen, cum scribitur hoc patiatur] *After this line the scribe has copied an alternative:* pagina cum tamen hoc vicium crebro patiatur
1001   Ditonus esse duplex] Dytonus duplex esse
1051   in ea sonum] in sonum ea

1086   transcendat] transcendas
1181   voluit] noluit
1184   non semper] semper non
1194   sive] fine
1231   iure vacare] iure d. vacare
1487   sicut in *Venit lumen*] sicut invenit lumen
1514   Exequie Martini] Exequie m'tum
1516   multitudo] militum
1553   per Γ] per g
1773   responsorium] in responsorio
1835   tenoris est] est tenoris
1838   seculorum Amen] *Deleted.*
1952f   *At various places in this Metrum the scribe copies what are
        undoubtedly interpolations. The first lies between lines 1954 and
        1955:* 'F dat principium primo quinto quoque sexto/C que
        secundus habet grave quartus in e capit ortum/Tertius
        octavus G septimus inchoat in ♮'. *The next lies between lines
        1972 and 1973:* 'D grave principium primus dabit a quoque
        sursum /C D vel f aut a subit alter et a sit acuta/G quoque
        dat pro c clavis mutata necesse/Tercius intrat c sursum
        quartus tamen a G/A cum c quintus dat sursum c quoque
        sextus/Octavus per c sed septimus incipit in d'. *The third
        interpolation lies between lines 1976 and 1977:* 'Primus ut ecce
        leva. ductus spe. vel lazar exi/Estque secundus ut O nunc
        cum tibi plus variabo/Tercius est quando quoniam
        dominus Symeonem/Quartus post rubum pete beate
        fidelia Syon/Quintus vox alma. sextus notum
        benedictus/Septimus afferte Joseph omnes stelat
        caputque/Octavus petrus hoc hodie veniet quoque nos in'.
1984   obstinatia] abstinatia
2045   oberraret ante scribendo et post cantando] oberraret
        scribendo et ante post cantando
2070   tenetur] videtur vel tenetur
2552   ibi] et
2405   possidet duo testamenta] possidet habens duo testamenta
2411   utitur et] utitur *(illegible deletion)* et
2480   in musica] in ecclesia
2581   ternarius] binarius
2583   contritio] confessio

2620   captivus] captivis

At end of text: Explicit Summa Jo. de muris ut credo *with* ut credo *deleted.*

Sources, parallels, citations and allusions

In practice a source, a parallel, a citation and an allusion are not always easy to distinguish in the *Summa musice*. The passages from the *De musica* by John 'of Affligem' (hereafter referred to simply as John) were undoubtedly known to Perseus and Petrus, either through John's own text or through some intermediary, and can be regarded as sources. Virtually all of the other passages from music theorists given here should be regarded as parallels. The references to the Bible, to Horace, Virgil, Statius, Ovid, Boethius, Priscian, Aristotle and some other authors arise from explicit pointers in the text and are therefore citations. The category of allusions is the most difficult to define since it encompasses material taken verbatim, but without acknowledgement, from earlier writers (e.g. the passages from Cato), but also includes what may only be distant echoes of other authors, usually Christian Latin poets such as Prudentius and Juvencus.

1   *Disticha Catonis*, I:31 'Quod iustum est petito vel quod videatur honestum,/Nam stultum petere est quod possit iure negari.'

1–42   Compare Quintilian, *Institutio oratoria* (*Prefatio*).

11–19   Much of this passage is taken almost verbatim from the *Disticha Catonis* (*Prologus*) 'Cum animadverterem quam plurimos graviter in via morum errare, succurrendum opinioni eorum et consulendum fore existimavi, maxime ut gloriose viverent et honorem contigerent.'

20–31   Much of this passage is taken almost verbatim from the translation of Porphyry's *Isagoge* by Boethius, p. 5 'altioribus quidem questionibus abstinens, simpliciores vero mediocriter coniectans. Mox de generibus et speciebus illud quidem sive subsistunt sive in solis nudis purisque intellectibus posita sunt sive subsistentia corporalia sunt an incorporalia...dicere recusabo (altissimum enim est huiusmodi negotium et maioris egens inquisitionis); illud vero quemadmodum de his ac de propositis probabiliter antiqui tractaverint, et horum maxime Peripatetici, tibi nunc temptabo monstrare.'

29–33   John, *De musica*, pp. 44–6 'de ipsa me arte compellare coepisti suadens uti ad doctrinam et illuminationem minus eruditorum aliquam ingenioli mei curarem emittere scintillulam.... Puerili quidem stilo usum me profiteor, verumtamen quae utiliora videbantur ac magis necessaria, ex aliorum codicellis compendiose collegi de meo etiam interdum addens igniculo.'

34   Ovid, *Metamorphoses*, XII:61 'Seditioque recens dubioque auctore Susurri.'

40–42   Augustine, *Liber de predestinatione sanctorum* 'Quocirca, sicut nemo sibi sufficit ad incipiendum vel perficiendum quodcunque opus bonum...in omni opere bono et incipiendo et perficiendo sufficientia nostra ex Deo est' (PL 44, column 963).

42   Ecclesiaticus 1:1.

46   Ovid, *Fasti*, II:754 'me subit, et gelidum pectora frigus habet.'

49   Compare Lucan, *Pharsalia*, IX:783, and Statius, *Silvae*, V: 1, line 127.

71   Virgil, *Aeneid*, III:202.

73–9   John, *De musica*, p. 46 'Placuit autem aliquantis libellum capitulis distinguere, ut si quid lector inter cetera avidius quaesierit, citius hoc atque facilius per praemissas annotationes recipere valeat.'

124f   Isidore, *Etymologiae*, III:15–16; John, *De musica*, chapter 3; Aegidius of Zamora, *Ars musica*, chapters 1 and 3.

136   Aegidius of Zamora, *Ars musica*, pp. 40–42.

143–55   John, *De musica*, p. 54 'Dicitur autem musica, ut quidam volunt, a musa, quae est instrumentum quoddam musicae decenter satis et iocunde clangens. Sed videamus, qua ratione, qua auctoritate a musa traxerit nomen musica. Musa, ut diximus instrumentum quoddam est omnia musicae superexcellens instrumenta, quippe quae omnium vim atque modum in se continet: humano siquidem inflatur spiritu ut tibia, manu temperatur ut phiala, folle excitatur ut organa.' Compare Regino Prumensis, *De harmonica institutione*, pp. 236–7.

152–3   Aegidius of Zamora, *Ars musica*, p. 112 'tibia dicitur a tibia quod est scirpus, vel calamus, quia a quibusdam calamis tale instrumentum antiquitus fiebat.'

159   Petrus Riga, *Aurora*, lines 465–8 'Iste Iubal cantu gaudens pater extitit horum/Qui citharis psallunt organicisque modis;/Musica dulce canens fuit ars inventa per illum/Ut pastoralis gaudeat inde labor.' Compare Petrus Comestor, *Historia scholastica*, '[Tubal] inventor fuit musicae, id est consonantiarum, ut labor pastoralis quasi in delitias verteretur' (PL 198, column 1079); also Aegidius of Zamora, *Ars musica*, p. 38 and Johannes, *Metrologus*, p. 67.

161–3   Genesis 4:21.

167–72   Boethius, *De institutione musica*, I:1.

174–7   *De sophisticis elenchis* (trans. Boethius), p. 59 'quae autem ex principio inveniuntur parvum in primis augmentum sumere solent...Hoc autem invento facile est addere at augere reliquum...'. *Commentarius Anonymus in Micrologum Guidonis Aretini*, p. 155 'Erant antiquitus instrumenta musica incerta, quia nulla ratione erant facta, seu cymbala seu organa vel aliquid tale...'.

182–3   Aristotle, *Categories* (trans. Boethius), p. 72 'Licentia fingendi nomina. Aliquotiens autem forte et nomina fingere necesse erit.'

185–6   *Institutio grammaticarum*, I:1. Compare John, *De musica*, p. 59; Aegidius of Zamora, *Ars musica*, p. 42; Wolf Anonymous, p. 209; *Adelboldi episcopi...Epistola cum Tractatu*, pp. 64–5.

204   Ovid, *Metamorphoses*, X:273 'turaque fumabant, cum munere functus ad aras/constitit...'.

218f   Compare John, *De musica*, chapter 2.

221   *Ars poetica*, line 343.

223–5   Schneider Anonymous, p. 113 'Inter ceteras musice artis utilitates quattuor proposuimus, scilicet ignotum cantum cognosere et de eius qualitate iudicare, falsum corrigere et novum componere.' Compare *Commentarius Anonymus in Micrologum Guidonis Aretini*, p. 99.

232   Despite the explicit reference, the text in question does not appear to be the *Isagoge ad artem Galieni* of Johannitius. Compare Boethius, *In Isagogen Porphyrii commenta*, pp. 7–12.

232–4   John, *De musica*, p. 52 'Cui ergo cantorem melius comparaverim quam ebrio, qui domum quidem repetit, sed quo calle revertatur penitus ignorat?'

235–40   *De consolatione philosophiae*, I, Prosa 3 'Cuius hereditatem cum deinceps Epicureum vulgus ac Stoicum ceterique pro sua quisque parte raptum ire molirentur meque reclamantem renitentemque velut in partem praedae traherent, vestem quam meis texueram manibus disciderunt abreptisque ab ea panniculis totam me sibi cessisse credentes abiere.'

242f   John, *De musica*, p. 114 'Sed nec hoc reticeri oportet, quod magnam vim commovendi auditorum animos musicus cantus habet, siquidem aures mulcet, mentem erigit, praeliatores ad bella incitat, lapsos et desperantes revocat, viatores confortat, latrones exarmat, iracundos mitigat, tristes et anxios laetificat, discordes pacificat, vanas cogitationes eliminat, phreneticorum rabiem temperat. Unde et de Rege Saul in libro Regum legitur, quod a daemonio correptus David in cithara canente mitigabatur, cessante vero nihilominus vexabatur.' Compare Isidore, *Etymologiae*, III:17; Aegidius of Zamora, *Ars musica*, chapters 2 and 17.

255–7   I Samuel 16:23.

257–60   Compare Macrobius, *In somnium Scipionis*, p. 105.

272   Horace, *Ars poetica*, line 31 'in vitium ducit culpae fuga, si caret arte.'

291   Horace, *Carmina*, I:7, line 31 'nunc vino pellite curas'; Statius, *Silvae*, V:3, line 34 'tacitisque situm depellere curis'; Boethius, *De consolatione philosophiae*, III, Metrum 5:8 'Tamen atras pellere curas.'

302f   John, *De musica*, p. 115 'Cum igitur in commovendis mentibus hominum tanta sit musicae potentia, merito usus eius acceptus est in sancta Ecclesia. Primum autem a S. Ignatio martyre nec non et a beato Ambrosio Mediolanensium antistite usus musicae in Romana ecclesia haberi coepit. Post hos beatissimus Papa Gregorius Spiritu Sancto ei, ut fertur, assidente et dictante cantum modulatus est, cantumque Romanae Ecclesiae, quo per anni circulum Divinum celebratur officium, dedit. Quod autem canendo laudandus sit Deus non parvam in veteri pagina auctoritatem habemus; legimus namque in libro Exodi, quod submerso Pharaone Moyses et cum eo filii Israel canticum cecinerunt Domino. Sed et Psalmista, artis huius haud ignarus, in decachordo, quod est musicum instrumentum, laudes Domino cecinit, nosque ad concinendum hortatur dicens: *Cantate Domino canticum novum. Laus eius in Ecclesia Sanctorum.*' Compare *Instituta patrum de modo psallendi*, pp. 5–8, and Pseudo-Odo, *De musica*, pp. 275–6.

314–16   Petrus Diaconus, *Vita sancti Gregorii magni* (PL 75, columns 57–8).

321–2   Petrus Diaconus, *Vita sancti Gregorii magni* 'Sustinebat praeterea assiduas corporis infirmitates, et maxime ea pulsabatur molestia, quam Graeco eloquio medici syncopin vocant' (PL 75, column 43).

328–9   Daniel 3:51–90.

329–33   Exodus 15:1–21.

333–40   II Samuel 6:5; Psalms 32:3, 95:1, 97:1, 149:1 and 150:3–5.

340–43   Luke 1:14.

343–6   Luke 1:68–79, 46–55 and 2:29–32.

361   Juvencus, *Evangeliorum libri quattuor*, I, lines 249–51
              'tum munera trina/Tus, aurum, murram regique
              hominique Deoque/Dona dabant.'

378   Psalm 67:26 (iuxta Hebr.) 'praecesserunt cantores eos
              qui post tergum psallebant...'.

395f   John, *De musica*, chapter 3; Aegidius of Zamora, *Ars
              musica*, chapter 4.

401–3   Boethius, *De institutione musica*, I:2.

420–24   Aribo, *De musica*, p. 36.

460f   Regino Prumensis, *De harmonica institutione*, p. 236
              'Nunc restat, ut tertium genus musicae naturalis
              videamus, quod supra meminimus in irrationali
              creatura esse. De hoc itaque talis philisophorum
              opinio est. Et non mirum, inquiunt, si inter homines
              musicae tanta dominatio est; cum aves quoque, ut
              lusciniae, ut cygni, aliaeque cantum veluti quadam
              disciplina musicae artis exerceant...'.

465–70   Aegidius of Zamora, *Ars musica*, p. 40 'Alii ab
              philosopho [dicunt musicam invenisse] ex cantu
              avium   seu   per   cantum,   et   praecipue
              philomelae...Siquidem solo instinctu naturae novit
              ipsa punctum...'.

480–88   Compare Macrobius, *In somnium Scipionis*, p. 109. John,
              De musica, p. 58 'Hoc quoque adiicendum est, quod
              cum tria sint musicae melodiae genera, enharmonium,
              diatonicum, chromaticum, primo propter nimiam
              difficultatem, tertio propter nimiam mollitiem abiecto,
              medium usus retinuit.'

577–81   John, *De musica*, p. 49 'Verum Angli, Francigenae,
              Alemanni, utuntur his: ut, re, mi, fa, sol, la. Itali autem

alias habent, quas qui nosse desiderant, stipulentur ab ipsis.'

584–5   Boethius, *De institutione arithmetica*, I:19.

585–94   Genesis 1:1–31 and 2:1–2.

604–5   *Physica*, II:2. Compare Guido, *Micrologus*, p. 92 'Sed quia voces quae huius artis prima sunt fundamenta, in monochordo melius intuemur, quomodo eas ibidem ars naturam imitata discrevit, primitus videamus.' Compare also *Cuiusdam carthusiensis monachi Tractatus de musica plana*, p. 435.

653   Lucretius, *De rerum natura*, V:96 'sustentata ruet moles et machina mundi'; Prudentius, *Hamartigenia*, lines 248–9 'Si vitiis agitata suis mundana laborat/Machina...'.

662   Theodulfus, *Carmina*, II:125 'Mollibus in pratis miscentur mollia duris...'.

867–70   *Parva naturalia* 'Multas enim et multimodas differentias visus annunciat virtus quia omnia copora colore participant quare et communia magis per huic magis sentiuntur. Dico autem "communia" magnitudinem, figuram, numerum, motum. Auditus [anunciat] autem sonitum differencias, in paucis animalibus et vocis, sed vero per accidens. Ad sapienciam multum confert sermo audibilis existens causa discipline' (Cambridge, Gonville and Caius College, MS 379/452, f. 260r).

876   *Ars poetica*, line 274.

882–3   *Physica* (*Translatio Vaticana*), p. 24 'Sillogizet enim aliquis a nativitate cecus de coloribus.'

902f   John, *De musica*, chapter 8, *passim*.

912–15   John, *De musica*, p. 67 'Inter cetera hoc quoque scire convenit, quod novem omnino sunt modi, quibus melodia contexitur: unisonus, semitonium, tonus, diatonus, semiditonus, diatessaron, diapente, semitonium cum diapente, tonus cum diapente.'

926–8   John, *De musica*, p. 78 'Cum ergo Latini antiqui consonantiam quandam in musica tantummodo tonum vocarent, grammatici etiam accentus orationis, vel distinctiones tonos appellare usurpato nomine coeperunt...Sicut enim toni id est accentus in tres dividuntur species, scilicet gravem, circumflexum, acutum, ita in cantu tres distinguuntur varietates.' Compare Aegidius of Zamora, *Ars musica*, p. 96.

947   Virgil, *Aeneid*, XII:99. Compare John, *De musica*, p. 69 'Virgilius semiviri phryges, id est non pleni viri, quia more feminarum se vestiunt.'

949   Statius, *Achilleidos*, II:78–9 'nos Phryga semivirum portus et litora circum/Argolica incesta volitantem puppe feremus?'

1020–25   Aristotle, *Analytica priora, passim*; Petrus Hispanus, *Summule logicales*, IV:7 'In secunda figura ex puris affirmativis nichil sequitur.'

1049–54   *Commentarius Anonymus in Micrologum Guidonis Aretini*, p. 122 'Sciendum vero est quod affinitas vocum, quam ponit, maxime utilis est in instrumentis musicis constantibus ex octo vocibus vel VII, ut in cymbalis reperimus aut organis. Cum enim non sint ibi tam multae variationes vocum depositione vel elevatione per ordinem, quod non possumus post illas octo voces deponere vel elevare in acutis, quod ibi non sunt sicut ordo exigebat, per affines suas idem prosequamur in gravibus...'.

1060   Compare *Micrologus*, pp. 93–4.

1072–4   Aristotle, *Ethica Nicomachea* (*Translatio antiquissima sive Ethica vetus*), p. 13 'Sic utique et omnis sciens superfluitatem quidem et deficienciam fugit medium autem querit et hoc vult.'

1100f   Compare John, *De musica*, chapter 21.

1141f   Gui d'Eu, *Regulae de arte musica*, p. 151 'Non tamen esset necessarium quod superacute aliter formarentur quam acute, quia per linee et spatii variationem posset inter eas differentia sufficienter ostendi.'

1148–56   Compare John, *De musica*, p. 140 and Wolf Anonymous, p. 196.

1164–7   Guido, *Regulae musicae de ignoto cantu*, pp. 35–6.

1178   Walahfrid Strabo, *Carmina*, III:385 'cui nulla patrum hoc documenta dederunt.'

1185f   John, *De musica*, p. 141 'Per hunc itaque modum quisquis celeriter et proficue ad canendum musice introduci desiderat, tribus insudandum laboris esse sciat. Primus quippe labor est, et quae vel quot syllabae cuique voci attributae sint, diligenter consideretur. Deinde nihilominus studendum est, ut quae voces in linea vel spatio constitutae sint, recte perpendatur. Tertius autem labor cantionis est, ne cantorem vocum varia dispositio ducat in errorem, qui hoc modo facile evitari poterit, si diligentius animadvertatur, quod F unaquaeque minio, et C unaquaeque croco signatur. Secundum quinque semitonia in quinque locis colores disponuntur. Quidam tamen si color desit, pro minio punctum in principio lineae ponunt. Idcirco autem has duas, scilicet F et C, vel etiam colores quibus signantur, tantopere observari praecipimus, quoniam per eas aliae notae reguntur, eisque de loco motis caeterae pariter moventur. Sed si his neumis colores vel notae non aderunt, tales sunt neumae qualis puteus sine fune.'

1243   *Disticha Catonis*, IV:21.

1248f   Aegidius of Zamora, *Ars musica*, chapter 15.

1271f   Aegidius of Zamora, *Ars musica*, p. 56.

1315–18   John, *De musica*, p. 80 'Qui primitus de musica scripserunt, natura vocum diligenter considerata, prout tunc vires ingenium praebuit, omnem modulandi varietatem in quattuor distinxerunt modos, unde et quattuor tantum finales habentur. Moderni autem priorum inventa subtilius examinantes, considerabant harmoniam modorum confusam esse ac dissonam.'

1369   *Cuiusdam carthusiensis monachi Tractatus de musica plana*, p. 444 'Cantus non tangens quintam vult esse plagalis./Qui tangit nec sub cadit autenti volat alis.'

1427–33   *Cuiusdam carthusiensis monachi Tractatus de musica plana*, p. 44 'Verum tamen est quod organiste illa ficta musica bene indigent, maxime quando ipsi sentiunt sua organa ad voces humanas chori commode non concordare, ut tunc sciant hujusmodi organa ad chorum ut oportet proportionare.'

1469f   Compare *Cuiusdam carthusiensis monachi Tractatus de musica plana*, chapter IV.

1491f   Compare *Cuiusdam carthusiensis monachi Tractatus de musica plana*, p. 445.

1587–93   John, *De musica*, p. 91 'Cursum modorum sive tonorum dicimus legem, qua sub certa regula coercentur, scilicet quantum quisque ascendere vel descendere, quantumque intendi ac remitti debeat.'

1596–8   John, *De musica*, p. 92 'Quod enim quis per regulam habet, quasi ex debito habet, ideoque liberius eo frui potest; quae autem per licentiam possidentur, ea tamquam per gratiam possessa humilius atque prudentius sunt tractanda.' Compare *Cuiusdam carthusiensis monachi Tractatus de musica plana*, p. 438.

1682–5   John, *De musica*, p. 119 'Sciendum etiam quod in principalibus ad finem cantum paulatim ducere laus est, in collateralibus vero ad finem cantum praecipitare decet.'

1693–7   John, *De musica*, pp. 92–3 'Nam et Odo huius artis experientissimus, et a Guidone in fine tractatus sui comprobatus, cantum qui a finali ascendens quintam ter vel quater repercutit autento deputat. Unde et haec antiphona: *Ecce tu pulchra es* quamquam in cursum secundi toni decidat, tamen quia superius quintam a finali saepius reverberat, primo tono deputatur. Item R *Deus omnium exauditor est…*'. Compare Schneider Anonymous, p. 111.

1699–703   Compare John, *De musica*, p. 93 'Dominus namque sive magister non tantum in propria potestatem habet, sed etiam in ea quae sunt subditi eius.'

1707–11   *Tractatus Guidonis correctorius multorum errorum qui fiunt in cantu Gregoriano*, p. 53.

1750f   John, *De musica*, chapter 11.

1756f   John, *De musica*, p. 77 'Tropi a convenienti conversione dicti; quomodocumque enim cantus in medio varietur, ad finalem semper per tropos id est tonos convenienter convertitur.' Aegidius of Zamora, *Ars musica*, p. 94 'Tropi vero vocantur a conversione, qiua ubicumque cantus incipiat et quomodocumque varietur in cursu, semper ad finalem suum convenienti conversione per tropos convertitur.' *Cuiusdam carthusiensis monachi Tractatus de musica plana*, p. 434 'Nam Tropus, prout est figura transferens dictionem vel orationem a propria sua significatione ad impropriam seu alienam significationem, pertinet ad grammaticam; prout vero est modum sive regula canendi pertinent ad musicam. Et dicitur Tropus a "Tropos" grece, quod est "conversio" latine: qua quodmodocumque cantus varietur in medio, semper tamen eum tropus ad finem convertit et reducit regularem et legitimum.'

1769–76   John, *De musica*, pp. 110–11 'Nam aliquando cantus non tantum in initio, sed etiam in medio alicuius toni cursu utitur, cui tamen in fine contradicit; quod liquet in hoc R *Gaude Maria Virgo*, cum enim et in principio et in medio autento deutero subserviat, in fine tamen se plagi trito dicat.'

1776–7   *Ethica Nicomachea* (*Translatio antiquior sive Ethica nova*), pp. 65–6 'In omnibus utique architectoricarum fines omnibus sunt desiderabiliores...horum enim gracia et illa secuntur...Si utique quis finis est operatorum quem per se volumus, alia vero propter illum, et non omnia propter aliud optamus...Manifestum quod hic utique erit bonus et optimus.'

1780–81   Epistle of James 1:19.

1813–18   Compare John, *De musica*, pp. 111–12.

1821–4   John, *De musica*, p. 82 'tenores quidem in musica vocamus, ubi prima syllaba *saeculorum amen* cuiuslibet toni incipitur. Quasi enim claves modulationes tenent, et ad cantum cognoscendum nobis aditum dant.' Seay Anonymous, p. 27 'Nullus cantus debet inchoari supra litteram illam in qua suum *seculorum* habet incipere, infra autem vel in eadem littera sivi in finali vel subfinali debet habere principium, prout ratio dictaverit.' *Commentarius Anonymus in Micrologum*

> *Guidonis Aretini*, p. 142 'Ibi enim, id est in illis formulis, sicut in *Saeculorum amen*, videmus in quibus vocibus singulorum modorum cantus saepius rariusve incipiant, et in quibus id, scilicet inceptio, minime fiat.' *Cuiusdam carthusiensis monachi Tractatus de musica plana*, p. 434.

1915–16   Walther, 28521.

1931   *Disticha Catonis*, I:7.

1937–8   Ovid, *Remedia amoris*, line 360.

1941   *Disticha Catonis*, IV:21.

1951   *Ars poetica*, line 132.

1981f   Compare John, *De musica*, chapters 15 and 22.

1988–9   Compare Walther, 15936a 'Naturalia non sunt turpia'; Propertius, *Elegiarum*, II:xxii, line 17 'uni cuique dedit vitium natura creato.'

1994–6   *Ethica Nicomachea* (*Translatio antiquissima sive Ethica vetus*), pp. 33–4 'Et enim in ipso ignorando, puniunt, si causa esse videtur ignorancie. Verbi gracia, ebriis duplices maledictiones...'.

1997–8   Ovid, *Heroides*, II:85–6.

1999f   John, *De musica*, p. 107 'Similiter et hae antiphonae *Ascendente Iesu, Benedicta sit, Gloriosi*, cum sint hypomixolydii, a nonnullis phrygio adaptantur'; compare also p. 106: 'Falluntur etiam persaepe indocti cantores in iudicandis tonis ex similibus cantuum principiis; verbi gratia multi hanc ant. *Iste puer* plagi deutero adiudicant, quia in inceptione convenit cum ista ant. *In odore*, est autem *Iste puer* autenti proti, *In odore* plagis deuteri.'

2005f   John, *De musica*, pp. 104–5. Compare *Tractatus Guidonis correctorius multorum errorum qui fiunt in cantu Gregoriano*, p. 51.

2011–12   Walther, 21061c.

2013–15   *Tractatus Guidonis correctorius multorum errorum qui fiunt in cantu Gregoriano*, p. 51 'Sunt autem plerique clerici vel monachi...veritati adquiescere volunt, suumque errorem suo conamine defendunt.'

2031–6   John, *De musica*, pp. 107–8 'Non solum autem quidam ex similibus principiis seducuntur, sed ipsi ultro pravis vocibus suis quosdam a suo cursu detorquent cantus, quemadmodum istas antiphonas *Quid retribuam, Cum inducerent, Cum audisset Iob*, cum enim istae sint dorii et leniter sint incipiendae, ipsi eas voce acriter suspensiva ad acutas sustollunt, ita ut cum istis in principio conveniant: *Qui de terra est, Quando natus est.*'

2051   *Ars poetica*, line 356.

2097f   Compare John, *De musica*, chapter 18 and Guido, *Micrologus*, chapter 15.

2105f   John, *De musica*, pp. 109–10 'Sicut enim non omnium ora eodem cibo capiuntur, sed ille quidem acrioribus, iste vero lenioribus escis iuvatur: ita profecto non omnium aures eiusdem modi sono oblectantur. Alios namque morosa et curialis vagatio primi delectat, alios rauca secundi gravitas capit, alios severa et quasi indignans tertii persultatio iuvat, alios adulatorius quarti sonus attrahit, alii modesta quinti petulantia ac subitaneo ad finalem casu moventur, alii lacrimosa sexti voce mulcentur, alii mimicos septimi saltus libenter audiunt, alii decentem et quasi matronalem octavi canorem diligunt. Quapropter in componendis cantibus bene cautus musicus ita sibi providere debet, ut eo modo quam decentissime utatur, quo eos maximime delectari videt quibus cantum suum placere desiderat. Nec mirum alicui videri debet quod diversos deversis delectari dicimus, quia ex ipsa natura hominibus est inditum, ut non omnium sensus eundem habeant appetitum. Unde plerumque evenit, ut dum quod canitur isti videatur dulcissimum, ab alio dissonum iudicetur atque emmino incompositu. Certe ego ipse memini, me cantiones aliquot coram quibusdam cecinisse, et quod unus summopere extollebat alii penitus displicuisse.' Compare Guido, *Micrologus*, p. 159; Aegidius of Zamora, *Ars musica*, chapter 15; Schneider Anonymous, pp. 109–10; *Cuiusdam carthusiensis monachi Tractatus de musica plana*, pp. 448–9.

2121   *Phormio*, line 454. Compare Gui d'Eu, *Regulae de arte musica*, p. 150 'Sed quia tot scientia quot homines, quia uni consonum, alii dissonum multotiens videbatur.'

2127   *Cuiusdam carthusiensis monachi Tractatus de musica plana*, p. 444 'sicut dicit Horatius in poetria sua, quod quelibet materia suo proprio gaudet metro...'.

2130   Ovid, *Remedia amoris*, line 373.

2132   Ovid, *Remedia amoris*, line 384.

2136f   John, *De musica*, p. 118 'Providendum igitur est musico, ut ita cantum moderetur, ut in adversis deprimatur et in prosperis exaltetur.'

2144–6   John, *De musica*, p. 118 'Habemus tamen de his quae diximus aliqua exempla. Siquidem antiphonae in Resurrectione Domini exultationem in ipso sono praetendere videntur, ut sunt hae: *Sedit Angelus, Cum rex gloria, Christus resurgens.*'

2148   Compare John, *De musica*, p. 79, and Schneider Anonymous, p. 107.

2151f   Compare *Cuiusdam carthusiensis monachi Tractatus de musica plana*, pp. 444–5.

2171–5   John, *De musica*, p. 120 'Optima autem modulandi forma haec est, si ibi cantus pausationem finalis recipit, ubi sensus verborum distinctionem facit. Quod considerare potes in hac ant. *Cum esset desponsata.*'

2179–84   John, *De musica*, p. 123 'Animadvertendum praeterea quod maximam in cantu iocunditatem faciunt istae duae consonantiae diatessaron et diapente, si convenienter in suis locis disponantur; pulchrum namque sonum reddunt si remissa aliquotiens statim in eisdem vocibus elevantur; quemadmodum patet in *Alleluia Vox exultationis.*'

2228–9   *Topica* (trans. Boethius), p. 41 'id quod est amicis bene facere ei quod est inimicis male non est contrarium; utraque enim eligenda et eiusdem moris.'

2250–57   John, *De musica*, pp. 118–19 'Illud praeterea laudis cupido modulatori iniungimus, ne in una neuma nimium eam inculcando oberret...Similiter in Tracto illo *Qui habitat* vitiosa est unius podati crebra repercussio in eo loco ubi est *et refugium meum Deus meus*. Si autem interdum aliquae decentes neumae semel repetantur, non vituperamus, ut in fine R *Qui cum audissent*, ubi est *laudantes clementiam...*'.

2264–6   *Ars poetica*, lines 25–7.

2287–8   Aristotle, *Ethica Nicomachea* (*Translatio antiquissima sive Ethica vetus*), p. 14 'Est igitur virtus, habitus voluntarius in medietate existens...'.

2400   Song of Songs 6:8.

2406–7   Matthew 21:42.

2417   Luke 10:42. Compare PL 114, column 287 (*Glossa ordinaria*).

2458–60   Exodus 26:31.

2550–51   I Phil. 23.

2588   Prosper of Aquitaine, *Epigrammata*, I:lxv, line 1 'Omnipotens Genitor, Natusque, et Spiritus almus.'

2595   Venantius Fortunatus, *Carmina*, VIII:iii, line 275 'Veste superposita bis corto purpura bysso.'

2606   Venantius Fortunatus, *Carmina*, VIII:iii, line 2 'Laetanturque piis agmina sancta choris.'

2624   Prosper of Aquitaine, *Epigrammata*, I:xc, line 6 'Vera ut securus pace fruatur homo.'

Appendix

The supposed reference to unheightened neumes

Since at least 1905, when the second volume of Wagner's *Einführung in die Gregorianischen Melodien* was published, it has been widely assumed that a passage of the *Summa musice* refers to the continuing use of unheighted neumes. Following the indication in Gerbert's edition, Wagner accepted the *Summa musice* as a work of Johannes de Muris and he therefore interpreted the apparent reference to unheighted neumes as a sign that the treatise was written in Germany since the use of staff notation was fully established in Italy and France in the lifetime of Johannes de Muris.[1] In 1926 Besseler alluded to this argument and tacitly approved it.[2] Smits van Waesberghe rejected this interpretation in his edition of the *De musica* by John 'of Affligem',[3] but in recent years it has surfaced again. In his survey of the music treatises by Johannes de Muris, Ulrich Michels states that in the milieu of the *Summa musice* there were two systems of musical notation in use, one (with staves) that could be relied upon and another imperfect system (without staves) which could not.[4] Michels also repeats Wagner's contention that on these grounds the *Summa musice* would appear to have been written in an area of German speech.[5]

---

[1] Wagner, *Neumenkunde,* p. 172, n. 2.
[2] 'Studien zur Musik des Mittelalters', II, p. 207.
[3] Smits van Waesberghe, *Johannis...De musica,* p. 33, and *idem,* 'Some Music Treatises and their Interrelation', p. 107.
[4] *Die Musiktraktate des Johannes de Muris,* pp. 16–17.
[5] *Ibid.*

This is not quite correct. Having discussed the various forms of neumes, the authors of the *Summa musice* have this to say: 'But to this point (*sed adhuc*), a chant can only be imperfectly (*minus perfecte*) recognised by these signs, nor can anyone learn a chant from it in solitude' (536–8). For *minus perfecte* in the manuscript Gerbert's text reads *minus perfecta*, a crucial difference since this false reading turns an adverbial construction into an adjectival one and we suddenly seem to be dealing with a system of notation which is 'less perfect' than some other – whence, we may suppose, the common misconception that the *Summa musice* refers to two systems of musical notation being in current use. (Wagner, it should be noted, silently emended Gerbert's text correctly.)[6]

Given the revised dating for the *Summa musice* proposed in this edition, it is quite possible that the authors of the treatise had direct experience of two types of notation. Be that as it may, the key point is that when Perseus and Petrus describe the neumes in use and then say 'But, to this point (*sed adhuc*), a chant can only be imperfectly recognised by these signs', they are making a historical observation. 'Adhuc', in other words, has the meaning 'up to this point [in the history of notation]'. We find exactly the same usage at 1156. The authors then go on to describe the invention of the staff which brings the story up to date and closes it with a system which – as far as the precise indication of pitch is concerned – lacks nothing

---

[6] Wagner, *Neumenkunde*, p. 172; so also Smits van Waesberghe, *Johannis...De musica*, p. 33.

Bibliography

Primary sources

Bauer, A. (ed.) *Heinrici Chronicon Livoniae* (Darmstadt, 1959)

Beichner, P. (ed.) *Aurora Petri Rigae biblia versificata* (Notre Dame, Indiana 1965)

Boas, M. (ed.) *Disticha Catonis* (Amsterdam, 1952)

Bieler, L. (ed.) *Anicii Manlii Severini Boethii Philosophiae Consolatio* (Turnhout, 1967)

Bragard, R. (ed.) *Jacobi Leodiensis Speculum musicae*, 7 vols., CSM, III (1955–73)

Brandt, S. (ed.) *Boethius In Isagogen Porphyrii commenta* (Vienna and Leipzig, 1906)

Brundage, J. A. (trans.) *The Chronicle of Henry of Livonia* (Madison, 1961)

Coussemaker, E. (ed.) *Scriptorum de musica medii aevi nova series*, 4 vols. (Paris, 1864–76) [includes *Cuiusdam carthusiensis monachi Tractatus de musica plana* (II) and Gui d'Eu, *Regulae de arte musica* (II)]

de Rijk, L. M. (ed.) *Petrus Hispanus Tractatus* (Assen, 1972)

Dod, B. G. (ed.) *Aristoteles De sophisticis elenchis*, Aristoteles Latinus, VI/1–3 (Leiden and Brussels, 1975)

Dümmler, E. (ed.) *Poetae latini aevi Carolini*, Monumenta Germaniae Historica, Poetarum Latinorum Medii Aevi I (Berlin, 1881) and II (Berlin, 1884) [containing the *Carmina* of Theodulfus (I) and the *Carmina* of Walahfrid Strabo (II)]

Faral, E. (ed.) *Les arts poétiques du XIIe et du XIIIe siècle* (Paris, 1924)

Friedlein, G. (ed.) *Anicii Manlii Torquati Severini Boetii...De institutione musica libri quinque* (Leipzig, 1867)

Gallo, E. (ed.) *The 'Poetria nova' and its Sources in Early Rhetorical Doctrine* (Paris, 1971)

Gautier, R. A. (ed.) *Aristoteles Ethica Nicomachea*, Aristoteles Latinus, XXVI/1–3 (Leiden and Brussels, 1972)

Gerbert, M. (ed.) *Scriptores ecclesiastici de musica*, 3 vols. (St Blaise, 1784) [includes *Instituta patrum de modo psallendi* (I); Regino Prumensis, *De harmonica institutione* (I); the *Dialogus* (I); Berno, *De varia psalmorum atque cantuum modulatione* (II); Guido, *Regulae musicae rhythmicae* (II); *Regulae musicae de ignoto cantu* (II); *Correctorius multorum errorum qui fiunt in cantu Gregoriano* (II); Hermannus Contractus, *Opuscula musica* (II); Elias Salomon, *Scientia artis musice* (III)]

Ghisalberti, F. (ed.) *Integumentum Ovidii* (Milan, 1933)

Godman, P. (ed.) *Alcuin: the Bishops, Kings and Saints of York* (Oxford, 1982)

Hilka, A. and Schumann, O. (eds.) *Carmina Burana*, 3 vols. (Heidelberg, 1930–70)

Hirsch, T., Toppen, M. and Strehlke, E. (eds.) *Scriptores Rerum Prussicarum*, 5 vols. (Leipzig, 1861–74)

Huemer, I. (ed.) *Juvencus: Evangeliorum libri quattuor* (Vienna, 1891)

King, J. C. (ed.) *Boethius's Bearbeitung der 'Categoriae' des Aristoteles* (Tübingen, 1972)

Leo, F. (ed.) *Venanti Honori Clementiani Fortunati presbyteri Italici Opera poetica*, Monumenta Germaniae Historica, Auctorum Antiquissimorum IV/1 (Berlin, 1881)

Lindsay, W. M. (ed.) *Isidori Etymologiarum sive Originum libri XX*, 2 vols. (Oxford, 1910)

Mansion, A. (ed.) *Aristoteles Physica, translatio Vaticana*, Aristoteles Latinus, VII/2 (Bruges and Paris, 1957)

Maurach, G. 'Johannitius *Ysagoge ad artem Galieni*', *Sudhoffs Archiv*, LXII (1978), pp. 148–88

Mettenleiter, D. *Musikgeschichte der Stadt Regensburg* (Regensburg, 1866) [includes Mettenleiter Anonymous II]

Michels, U. (ed.) *Johannes de Muris Notitia artis musicae*, CSM, XVII (1972)

Minio-Paluello, L. and Dod, B. G. (eds.) *Aristoteles Topica, translatio Boethii*, Aristoteles Latinus, V/1–3 (Brussels, 1969)
Porphyrii Isagoge, translatio Boethii, Aristoteles Latinus, I/6 and 7 (Bruges, 1966)
Monumenta Boica, I– (Munich, 1763–)
Petrus Comestor, *Historia scholastica*, PL 198
Petrus Diaconus, *Vita sancti Gregorii magni*, PL 75
Prosper of Aquitaine, *Epigrammata*, PL 51
Reichling, D. (ed.) *Das Doctrinale des Alexander de Villa Dei* (Berlin, 1893)
Robert-Tissot, M. (ed.) *Johannes Aegidius de Zamora Ars musica*, CSM, XX (1974)
Schneider, M. *Geschichte der Mehrstimmigkeit*, 2 vols. (Leipzig, 1934 and 1935) [contains Schneider Anonymous]
Seay, A. (ed.) *Alexander de Villa Dei (?) Carmen de musica cum glossis* (Colorado Springs, 1977)
'An Anonymous Treatise from St Martial', *Annales Musicologiques*, V (1957), pp. 7–42
Smith, J. C. and Urban, W. (trans.), *The Livonian Rhymed Chronicle* (Bloomington, 1977)
Smits van Waesberghe, J. (ed.) *Adelboldi episcopi Ultraiectensis Epistola cum Tractatu*, DMA. A. II (Buren, 1981)
Aribonis De musica, CSM, II (1955)
Expositiones in Micrologum Guidonis Aretini (Amsterdam, 1957) [contains Johannes, *Metrologus*, and *Commentarius Anonymus in Micrologum Guidonis Aretini*]
Guidonis Aretini Micrologus, CSM, IV (1955)
Johannis Affligemensis De musica cum tonario, CSM, I (1950)
Steglich, R. (ed.) *Die Quaestiones in Musica* (Leipzig, 1911)
Sweeney, C. (ed.) *Johannis Wylde Musica manualis cum Tonale*, CSM, XXVIII (1982)
Thomason, H. J. (ed.) *Prudentius*, 2 vols. (London, 1961 and 1962) [includes *Hamartigenia*]
Willis, J. (ed.) *Macrobius*, 2 vols. (Leipzig, 1970)
Wolf, J. 'Ein anonymer Musiktraktat des elften bis zwölften Jahrhunderts', *Vierteljahrsschrift für Musikwissenschaft*, IX (1893), pp. 186–234
Wrobel, J. (ed.) *Eberhardi Bethuniensis Grecismus* (Bratislava, 1887)

Yudkin, J. (ed.) *De musica mensurata: the Anonymous of St Emmeram* (Bloomington and Indianapolis, 1990)

Secondary sources

Altfranzösisches Wörterbuch, ed. A. Tobler and E. Lommatzsch (Berlin and Wiesbaden, 1925–)

Amrhein, A. 'Reihenfolge der Mitglieder des adeligen Domstifts zu Wurzburg, St Kilians-Bruder gennant, von seiner Grundung bis zur Säkularisation 742–1803', *Archiv des Historischen Vereins von Unterfranken und Aschaffenburg*, XXXII (1889)

Auda, A. 'L'école musicale liégeoise au Xe siècle: Etienne de Liège', *Académie royale de Belgique, classe des beaux arts, Mémoires*, II/1 (Brussels, 1923)

Bachmann, W. *The Origins of Bowing*, trans. N. Deane, (Oxford, 1969)

Benninghoven, F. *Der Orden der Schwertbrüder* (Cologne, 1965)

Besseler, H. 'Studien zur Musik des Mittelalters, II: Die Motette von Franko von Köln bis Philipp von Vitry', *Archiv für Musikwissenschaft*, VIII (1926), pp. 137–258

Bischoff, B. *Latin Palaeography: Antiquity and the Middle Ages* (Cambridge, 1990)

Botschuyver, J. *Scholia in Horatium*, I, III and IV (Amsterdam, 1935 and 1942)

Brown, M. P. *A Guide to Western Historical Scripts from Antiquity to 1600* (London, 1990)

Christiansen, E. *The Northern Crusades* (London, 1980)

Dictionary of Medieval Latin from British Sources, ed. R. H. Latham and subsequently ed. D. R. Howlett (Oxford, 1975–)

Dictionnaire de l'ancienne langue Française, ed. F. Godefroy (Paris, 1880–1902)

Dyer, J. 'A Thirteenth-Century Choirmaster: the *Scientia artis musicae* of Elias Salomon', *Musical Quarterly*, LXVI (1980), pp. 83–111

Elias, N. *The Court Society* (Oxford, 1983)

Floros, C. *Universale Neumenkunde*, 3 vols. (Kassel, 1970)

Fleischer, O. *Die germanischen Neumen* (Frankfurt, 1923)

Friis-Jensen, K. 'Horatius liricus et ethicus: Two Twelfth-Century School Texts on Horace's Poems', *Cahiers de l'Institut du Moyen Age Grec et Latin*, LVII (1988), pp. 81–147

Gerson-Kiwi, E. 'Drone and *Dyaphonia Basilica*', *Yearbook of the International Folk Music Council*, IV (1972), pp. 9–22

Haggh, R. H. (trans.), *History of Music Theory, Books I and II* (Lincoln, Nebraska, 1962); see Riemann

Hauréau, M. 'Notice sur les oeuvres authentiques ou supposés de Jean de Garlande', *Notices et Extraits des manuscrits de la Bibliothèque Nationale et autres Bibliothèques*, XXVII/2 (Paris, 1885) pp. 1–86

Hexter, R. J. *Ovid and Medieval Schooling* (Munich, 1986)

Hibberd, L. '*Musica Ficta* and Instrumental Music, *c.* 1250–*c.* 1350', *Musical Quarterly*, XXVIII (1942), pp. 216–26

Huglo, M. 'L'auteur du *Dialogue sur la musique* attribué à Odon', *Revue de Musicologie*, LV (1969), pp. 119–71
'L'auteur du traité de Musique dédié à Fulgence d'Affligem', *Revue Belge de Musicologie*, XXXI (1977), pp. 5–19.
Les tonaires (Paris, 1971)

Hunt, R. W. *The Schools and the Cloister: the Life and Writings of Alexander Nequam (1157–1217)* (Oxford, 1984)

Kelly, D. 'The Scope and Treatment of Composition in Twelfth- and Thirteenth-Century Arts of Poetry', *Speculum*, LVI (1966), pp. 261–78
'Theory of Composition in Medieval Narrative Poetry and Geoffrey de Vinsauf's *Poetria nova*', *Medieval Studies*, XXXI (1969), pp. 117–48

Koller, O. 'Aus dem Archive des Benediktinerstiftes St Paul im Lavantthal im Kärnten', *Monatshefte für Musikgeschichte*, XXII (1890), pp. 22–9 and 34–45

Lapidge, M. 'The Study of Latin Texts in Late Anglo-Saxon England, I: the Evidence of Latin Glosses', in *Latin and the Vernacular Languages in Early Medieval Britain*, ed. N. Brooks (Leicester, 1982), pp. 99–140

La Rue, H. 'The Problem of the *Cymbala*', *Galpin Society Journal*, XXXV (1982), pp. 86–99

Lawrence, C. H. *Medieval Monasticism* (Harlow, 1984)

Leclercq, J. *The Love of Learning and the Desire for God* (New York, 1961)

Le Grand, L. *Statuts d'Hôtels Dieu et de Léproseries* (Paris, 1901)

Martin, J. 'Classicism and Style in Latin Literature', in *Renaissance and Renewal in the Twelfth Century*, ed. R. L. Benson and G. Constable (Oxford, 1982), pp. 537–68

McKinnon, J. 'The Emergence of Gregorian Chant in the Carolingian Era', in *Antiquity and the Middle Ages*, ed. J. McKinnon (London, 1990)

Michels, U. *Die Musiktraktate des Johannes de Muris* (Wiesbaden, 1970)

Olsen, B. M. *L'étude des auteurs classiques latins au XIe et au XIIe siècles*, I–II (Paris, 1982 and 1985)

Orme, N. *From Childhood to Chivalry* (London, 1984)

Paetow, J. J. *The Arts Course at Medieval Universities with Special Reference to Grammar and Rhetoric* (Champagne, 1910)

Page, C. 'Early Fifteenth-Century Instruments in Jean de Gerson's *Tractatus de Canticis*', *Early Music*, VI (1978), pp. 339–45
'Jerome of Moravia on the *Rubeba* and *Viella*', *Galpin Society Journal*, XXXII (1979), pp. 77–95
'The Medieval *Organistrum* and *Symphonia* I: a Legacy from the East?' *Galpin Society Journal*, XXXV (1982), pp. 37–44
'The Medieval *Organistrum* and *Symphonia* II: Terminology', *Galpin Society Journal*, XXXVI (1983), pp. 71–87
Voices and Instruments of the Middle Ages (London, 1987)
The Owl and the Nightingale: Musical Life and Ideas in France 1100–1300 (London, 1989)
'*Musicus* and *Cantor*', in *The Everyman Companion to Early Music*, I, ed. T. Knighton and D. Fallows, (forthcoming)

Palisca, C. and Babb, W. *Hucbald, Guido and John on Music* (New Haven, 1978)

Pesce, D. *The Affinities and Medieval Transposition* (Bloomington and Indianapolis, 1987)

Riemann, H. *Geschichte der Musiktheorie im IX–XIX Jahrhundert* (Leipzig, 1898); see Haggh

Samaran, C. and Marichal, R. *Catalogue des manuscrits en écriture latine*, I, Publications de l'Institut de Recherche et d'Histoire des Textes, VII (Paris, 1959)

Schlager, K. *Alleluia-Melodien*, 2 vols., Monumenta Monodica Medii Aevi (Basel, Paris, London and New York, 1968 and 1987)

Sedgewick, W. B. 'The Style and Vocabulary of the Latin Arts of Poetry of the Twelfth and Thirteenth Centuries', *Speculum*, III (1928), pp. 349–81

Smits van Waesberghe, J. 'Some Music Treatises and their Interrelation: a School of Liège c. 1050–1200?', *Musica Disciplina*, III (1949), pp. 25–31, and 95–118
  Cymbala, MSD, I (1951)
  Musikerziehung: Lehre und Theorie der Musik im Mittelalter, Musikgeschichte in Bildern, III/3 (Leipzig, 1969)

Steer, G. '*Carmina Burana* in Südtirol', *Zeitschrift für deutsches Altertum*, CXII (1983), pp. 1–37

Stevens, J. *Words and Music in the Middle Ages: Song, Narrative, Dance and Drama 1050–1350* (Cambridge, 1986)

Swerdlow, N. 'Musica dicatur a Moys, quod est aqua', *Journal of the American Musicological Society*, XX (1967), pp. 3–9

Thurot, C. *Extraits de divers manuscrits latins pour servir à l'histoire des doctrines grammaticales au Moyen Age* (Paris, 1869)

Urban, W. *The Baltic Crusade* (Dekalb, 1975)

von Bunge, F. *Der Orden der Schwertbrüder* (Leipzig, 1875)

Wagner, P. *Einführung in die Gregorianischen Melodien*, I (Fribourg, 1895, rev.1911), II (Neumenkunde) (Leipzig, 1905, rev.1912) and III (Leipzig, 1921)

Waite, W. 'Two Musical Poems of the Middle Ages', in *Musik und Geschichte* (Cologne, 1963), pp. 13–34

Walther, H. *Proverbia sententiaeque latinitatis medii aevi*, 6 vols. (Göttingen, 1963–9)

Warren, C. W. 'Punctus Organi and Cantus Coronatus in the Music of Dufay', in *Papers read at the Dufay Quincentenary Conference*, ed. A. Atlas (Brooklyn, 1976), pp. 128–43

Wegner, G. *Kirchenjahr und Messfeier in der Würzburger Domliturgie des späten Mittelalters* (Würzburg, 1970)

Annotated catalogue of chants

This catalogue lists every chant whose incipit is given in the text (i.e. unspecific references to 'the chant for St Catherine' etc have not been pursued and listed). Each entry gives the incipit, expanded in square brackets if the treatise gives only a single word, or if there is a risk of confusion with another chant that begins in the same way. Beneath the incipit the catalogue gives:
- the numbers of the lines in the text where the chant is mentioned
- the category to which the chant belongs, placed in square brackets if the authors do not specify it
- the mode of the chant if it is mentioned
- a paraphrase of what the authors say about the chant
- a list of published sources, editions or facsimiles where (unless some indication is given to the contrary) the chant may be found in a form corresponding to the version known to Perseus and Petrus in at least the particular which they describe. When a chant is also cited in John's *De musica*, its occurrence there is noted by page references to the edition of John's treatise by Smits van Waesberghe, and to the translation of John's work in Palisca and Babb, *Hucbald, Guido and John on Music* (abbreviated HGJ).

Alleluia 'Nativitas'
    1537
    [Alleluia]
    VIII
    Cited for beginning on *F*, thus illustrating an initial note of its
    mode.
    GS, pl. u; compare Schlager, *Alleluia–Melodien*, I, pp. 277–8

Alleluia 'Surrexit pastor bonus'
    2146; 2255–6
    [Alleluia]
    Cited for matching the joyful material of its text with a setting *in
    acutis*, and because at the words *pro ovibus* there is a pleasing
    repetition of a melodic phrase.
    Schlager, *Alleluia–Melodien*, II, p. 514

Alleluia 'Vox exultationis'
    2181
    [Alleluia]
    Cited to illustrate the delightfulness of the intervals of fourth and
    fifth. [The passage in question occurs at the words *in taberna*.]
    Compare John, *De musica*, p. 123; HGJ, p. 143 (with transcription of
    the relevant passage from **GS** 215).
    Schlager, *Alleluia–Melodien*, II, p. 573 (where the notated pitch
    differs from the one employed by John).

Angelus ad pastores
    1532–4; 1579
    Antiphon
    VII
    Cited for beginning on *G*, thus illustrating an initial note of its
    mode, and for descending to *F*, the lowest pitch of its mode.
    AM 241, **AS** 53, **LA** 37, **LU** 397, **WA** 32

Benedicta sit creatrix
2000–2001
Antiphon
Cited as a chant that is begun in the same way by various singers but ended differently. Compare John, *De musica*, p. 107; HGJ, p. 132.
AM 538, **AR** 520, **AS** 293–4, **LU** 908, **WA** 162

Benedictus
1571
[Antiphon]
VI
Cited as one of several chants of the plagal Tritus that take either *D* or *F* as their initial note. Could be either *Benedictus dominus deus meus* or *Benedictus dominus in eternum*. Compare John, *De musica*, p. 186 (Tonary); HGJ, p. 179.
AM 155 and 156, **AS** 101, **LA** 102, **WA** 70 (*Benedictus dominus deus meus*); **LA** 100, **WA** 69 (*Benedictus dominus in eternum*)

Bene fac
1791
Antiphon
IV and VIII
Cited as a chant of mode IV when sung by some singers and of mode VIII when sung by others.
AS 115–16, **LA** 102 (both mode VIII)

Cantabant sancti
2001
Antiphon
Cited as a chant that is begun in the same way by various singers but ended differently.
AS 72, **LA** 61, **WA** 46–7 (all mode VIII)

Caput [draconis salvator]
1577
[Antiphon]
VII
AS 95, **LA** 78, **VP** 96, **WA** 59

Circumdantes [circumdederunt me]
>1687; 1708
>Antiphon
>I
>Cited as a chant that is of mode I, despite other indications, because
>it proceeds to its final *curialiter et paulatim*, as authentic modes do.
>Compare *Nisi ego abiero*, *Reges Tharsis* and *Volo pater*.
>**AM** 400, **AR** 422, **AS** 206, **LA** 181, **WA** 113

Collegerunt [pontifices]
>1501; 1558; 2062
>[Responsory]
>II
>Cited as descending to Γ, as its mode uniquely can, and as an
>example of a chant which is *gravis*, matching the *res laboriosa* of its
>text. Compare John, *De musica*, p. 136 (with music); HGJ, p. 147–8
>(with transcription of John's example).
>**GB** 105v, **GR** 66, **GS** 84 (with upward transposition)

Consolamini [consolamini populi]
>1500
>[Antiphon]
>II
>Cited for beginning on *F*, thus illustrating an initial note of its
>mode. Compare John, *De musica*, p. 95; HGJ, p. 124.
>**AM** 231, **AR** 254, **AS** 41, **LA** 17, **WA** 18

Cum appropinquaret dominus Ierusalem [videns]
>2027–8
>Antiphon
>Cited because bad singers raise what should be kept low at the words
>*si cognovisses et tu*.
>**AM** 599, **AR** 560, **AS** 336, **LA** 314, **LU** 1104–5, **WA** 188

Cum audisset Iob
2034
Antiphon
I
Cited as a chant which can be twisted from its legitimate course
(compare *Cum inducerent*) if the melody is distorted in performance,
whence it becomes like *Qui de terra est* and *Quando natus es*, which
are of mode III. Compare John, *De musica*, pp. 107–8; HGJ, p. 132.
AM 582, **AR** 546, **AS** 312, **LA** 286 (with upward transposition), **LU**
991–2, **WA** 171

Cum esset desponsata [...antequam...quod]
2175
Antiphon
Cited as a chant whose melody has pauses where the text requires.
Compare John, *De musica*, p. 120; HGJ, p. 139 (with transcription of
AS 44).
AS 44, **LA** 31, **WA** 26

Cum inducerent puerum Iesum
2033; 2175–6
Antiphon
I
Cited as a chant which can be twisted from its legitimate course
(compare *Cum audisset Iob*) if the melody is distorted in
performance, whence it becomes like *Qui de terra est* and *Quando
natus es*, which are of mode III. Also praised for having melodic
pauses where the text requires. Compare John, *De musica*, pp. 107–8;
HGJ, p. 132.
AM 803, **AR** 621, **AS** 405, **LA** 347 (with upward transposition), **WA**
268

Cum rex glorie
2146
[Antiphon]
Matches the joyful matter of its text with a melody *in acutis*.
Compare John, *De musica*, p. 118; HGJ, p. 138.
SYG 148, **WA** 225 (with different melodies)

Descendit de celis
    2165
    Responsory
    Cited as a chant to which some add a special *nota* that the previous
    statement of the responsory does not have, as in the *cantus Sancti
    Lamberti* (i.e. the Office of St Lambert by Etienne de Liège).
    PM 27–8, **WA** 31

Deus
    2083
    See *Deus in adiutorium.*

Deus in adiutorium
    1708–9; ?2083
    Introit
    More VII than VIII
    Cited as a chant which is classified as authentic for the sake of
    conferring the more prestigious name.
    GB 78v, **GR** 350, **GS** 51 and 154, **LU** 1027–8, **SYG** 89

Deus omnium exauditor
    1698
    Responsory
    Cited to illustrate the doctrine that a chant which touches the fifth
    above its final five times or more is authentic. Compare *Ecce tu
    pulchra es,* and John, *De musica,* p. 93; HGJ, p. 122 (with transcription
    of **LA** 267).
    AS 298, **LA** 267, **WA** 165

Doleo super te
    2138
    Antiphon
    A chant which is *humilis et depressus* and which therefore
    complements its text, the lament of David for Jonathan. Compare
    Libera me domine.
    AS 296–7, **LA** 274, **WA** 165

Dominus [quidem Iesus]
1730
[Antiphon]
I
Compare John, *De musica*, p. 166 (Tonary); HGJ, p. 164.
AS 274–5, **LA** 253

Ductus [est Iesus...cum]
1547
[Antiphon]
I
Illustrates one of the initial notes of the Protus. Compare John, *De musica*, p. 84 and 105; HGJ, p. 118.
AM 342, **AR** 369, **AS** 156, **LA** 133, **WA** 88 (all beginning on *C*)

Ecce
1547
See *Ecce nomen domini.*

Ecce
1552
See *Ecce advenit.*

Ecce advenit [dominator dominus]
1499; 1552
Introit
II
Cited as a chant that begins on *A re*, thus illustrating an initial note of its mode. Compare John, *De musica*, p. 170 (Tonary); HGJ, p. 169.
GB 32, **GR** 57, **SYG** 30

Ecce nomen domini
1486–7; 1547
Antiphon
I
Cited as a chant that begins on *D*, thus illustrating an initial note of its mode. Compare John, *De musica*, p. 163 (Tonary); HGJ, p. 162.
AM 186, **AR** 211, **LA** 1, **LU** 317

Ecce tu pulchra es
>   1697–8
>   Antiphon
>   Cited to illustrate the doctrine that a chant which touches the fifth above its final five times or more is authentic. Compare *Deus omnium exauditor*. Compare John, *De musica*, p. 92; HGJ, p. 122.
>   **AS** 493, **LA** 455, **WA** 354

Erat enim [in sermone]
>   1538–9
>   [Antiphon]
>   VII
>   Cited as a chant that begins on *c in linea*, thus illustrating an initial note of its mode.
>   **AS** 365, **LA** 324

Et respicientes
>   1789
>   Antiphon
>   III and VIII
>   Cited as a chant of mode III when sung by some singers, and of mode VIII when sung by others. Compare John, *De musica*, p. 113 (with musical example); HGJ, p. 135 (with transcription).
>   **AM** 460, **AR** 446, **AS** 239, **LA** 214, **LU** 783 (all mode III), **WA** 130 (mode VIII)

Exequie Martini
>   1514
>   [Antiphon]
>   IV
>   Cited as a chant that shows how mode IV can ascend to *c acutum*.
>   **WA** 404–5 (ascending to *c* at the words *greges suos*, but ascending to *e* in another passage).

Exi
>   1547
>   See *Exi cito*.

Exi cito
>1488; 1547
>[Antiphon]
>I
>Cited as a chant that begins on *a la mi re*, thus illustrating an inital note of its mode.
>**AM** 558, **AR** 538, **AS** 333, **LA** 310, **LU** 964, **WA** 187

Eya dic nobis
>1502; 1553
>Sequence
>II
>Cited as a chant whose beginning descends to Γ, as only mode II can do. Chevalier, 5285. Also appears with the incipit *Dic nobis* but manuscript sources I have consulted do not show the descent to Γ (e.g. British Library MS Harley 622, ff. 97v–8 and Add. MS 17001, f. 74).

Fabrice
>2062
>Cited as an example of a chant which is *gravis*, matching the *res laboriosa* of its text, and which moves between *b fa* and *b mi*.

Frange esurienti
>1511
>[Antiphon]
>IV
>Cited as a chant that begins on *C*, thus illustrating an initial note of its mode. Compare John, *De musica*, p. 179 (Tonary); HGJ, p. 175.

Fuit ad tempus
>1499
>II
>Cited as a chant that begins on *C*, thus illustrating an initial note of its mode.
>Untraced

Gaude Maria
   1774
   Responsory
   III and VI
   Cited as a chant that begins and continues with the characteristics of
   mode III, but ends in mode VI. Compare John, *De musica*, p. 111;
   HGJ, p. 134.
   AM 1195, **AS** 402, **LA** 354, **VP** 130, **WA** 271

Gaude mater
   2149
   Unidentified.

Genti peccatrici
   1814
   Responsory
   Cited as a chant whose verse (*Esto placabilis*) is sung by different
   singers in different ways. Compare John, *De musica*, pp. 111–12,
   making the same point and with musical example; HGJ, p. 134 (with
   transcription).

Genuit [puerpera regem]
   1552
   [Antiphon]
   II
   Compare John, *De musica*, p. 170 (Tonary); HGJ, p. 168.
   AM 240, **AR** 264, **AS** 52–3, **LA** 37, **LU** 396, **WA** 31

Germinavit [radix Iesse]
   1793
   Antiphon
   I, IV and VIII
   Cited as a chant that is ended in different ways by different singers.
   Compare John, *De musica*, p. 103; HGJ, p. 128.
   AM 272, **AR** 295, **AS** 79, **LA** 65, **LU** 443, **WA** 50 (all mode I)

Gloriosi principes

1807–8; 2001

Antiphon

VI and VIII

Cited as a chant that is either of mode VI or of mode VIII according to whether it begins and ends on *F* or *G*, but which is better assigned to mode VI. Compare John, *De musica*, pp. 107 and 111; HGJ, pp. 132 and 134.

AM 958, **AS** 448, **WA** 325 (all beginning on *F* and mode VI); **LA** 418 (beginning on *G* but mode III)

Hec est que nescivit

1506

[Antiphon]

III

Cited as a chant that begins on *E*, thus illustrating an initial note of its mode. Compare John, *De musica*, p. 172 (Tonary); HGJ, p. 170.

AM 679, **AR** 88, **AS** 666, **LA** 347, **LU** 1211, **WA** 353

Hodie scietis

1524; 1571

Introit

VI

Cited as a chant that begins on *D*, thus illustrating an initial note of its mode.

GR 38, **SYG** 13

In odore

2002

Antiphon

Cited as a chant that is begun the same but ended differently by different singers. Compare John, *De musica*, p. 106, cited as mode IV; HGJ, p. 131 (with transcription of **LU** 1233).

AM 687 and 1014, **AR** 820, **AS** 499, **LA** 448, **LU** 1233, **WA** 358. Of these, only **LA** 448 ends on the mode IV final *E*; all the other sources cited end on *a*.

Iste puer
>   2002
>   Antiphon
>   Cited as a chant that is begun the same but ended differently by
>   different singers. Compare John, *De musica*, p. 106; HGJ, p. 131
>   (with transcription of **WA** 323).
>   Compare **AM** 921 (mode VIII) and **WA** 323 (ending on the *viceclavis*
>   of mode I)

Letetur omne seculum
>   1491; 1549
>   Responsory
>   I
>   Cited as a chant that descends to *A re* at the beginning, thus
>   illustrating the capacity of this mode to descend a fourth below the
>   final. Also cited for its ascent to *g* at the words *eternus amor*, which is
>   delectable but regarded as irregular by some.
>   **AS** 458 (with the descent to *A*, but without the ascent to *g*)

Libera me domine
>   2137
>   Responsory
>   Cited as a chant that matches its *materia tristis* with a *cantus humilis et
>   depressus*. Could be either *Libera me domine de morte eterna* or *Libera me
>   domine de viis inferni*.
>   **AR** 174, **AS** 583, **LA** 557, **LU** 1767, **WA** 438 (*Libera me domine de morte
>   eterna*); **AR** 173, **LU** 1798–9 (*Libera me domine de viis inferni*)

Magnum hereditatis mysterium
>   1424
>   Antiphon
>   II
>   Cited as a chant that is compelled by necessity to end on the
>   *viceclavis* of its mode, *a la mi re*. Compare John, *De musica*, p. 102;
>   HGJ, p. 128 (with transcription of **AM** 275).
>   **AM** 275 and 716, **AR** 297, **AS** 79, **LA** 66, **LU** 444, **WA** 51

Miserere mihi domine [quoniam conculcavit me]
> 2253
> Introit
> Cited as a chant which has a useless repetition of the same interval.
> **GB** 99, **GR** 156, **GS** 73, **SYG** 111

Example 6. Source: **GS** 73.

mi - se - re-re   mi-hi   do-mi - ne

Miserere [mihi domine quoniam infirmus sum]
> 1539–40; 1584
> Gradual
> VIII
> Cited as an illustration of how its mode can ascend to *a superardua* at
> the words *omnia ossa*.
> **GB** 85v, **GS** 58, **SYG** 96

Misit
> 2083
> See *Misit dominus.*

Misit dominus
> 1532; 1577; ?2083
> [Antiphon]
> VII
> Cited as a chant that begins on ♮, thus illustrating an initial note of
> its mode. Also cited because some poor singers begin it on *G*.
> Compare John, *De musica*, p. 191 (Tonary); HGJ, p. 182. Could be
> either *Misit dominus...de manu* or *Misit dominus...de medio*.
> **AM** 935 and 990, **AR** 751 and 800, **AS** 470, **PM** 173, **LU** 1515 and
> 1577–8 (*Misit dominus...de manu*); **AM** 1006, **AR** 814, **AS** 486, **LA** 336
> and 441, **LU** 1597, **WA** 350 (*Misit dominus...de medio*)

Natalis
>1554
>II
>Unidentified.

Natus
>1554
>II
>Unidentified.

Nemo te condemnavit mulier
>1810–11
>Antiphon
>VI and VIII but better VIII
>Cited as a chant which is of mode VI if begun and finished on *F*, but of mode VIII if begun and finished on *G*.
>**LA** 156 (beginning and ending on *G*)

Nisi [ego abiero]
>1730
>[Antiphon]
>I
>Cited as a chant whose manner of closure indicates an authentic mode, despite previous indications. Compare *Circumdantes, Reges Tharsis* and *Volo pater*.
>**AS** 274, **LA** 247, **WA** 150

Nos qui vivimus
>1923
>Antiphon
>Cited with reference to the *tonus peregrinus*. Compare John, *De musica*, p. 154; HGJ, p. 158.
>**AM** 132 and 133, **AS** 109

O
>1552
>See *O sapientia*.

O

1561
See *O gloriosum.*

O admirable [commercium]

1524
[Antiphon]
VI
Cited as a chant that begins on *F*, thus illustrating an inital note of
its mode.
AM 271, **LU** 442–3

O decus, O Libie regnum

2139
A Latin *lai.* Item 100 in the *Carmina Burana* (without notation).
Neumed source: Munich, Staatsbibliothek, Clm. 4598, f. 61r–v. See
frontispiece.

O gloriosum

1506; 1561
[Antiphon]
III
Cited as a chant that begins on *F*, thus illustrating an initial note of
its mode. Compare John, *De musica*, p. 124 (with musical example),
also HGJ, p. 143 and Appendix pp. 196–7 (transcription from
Zagreb University Library MS MR 8).

[O] magnum mysterium

1508
Responsory
III
Cited as an illustration of how its mode only descends to *C.*
LA 35, **LR** 61, **LU** 382, **WA** 28 (all at the word *meruerunt*)

O sapientia
>797–8; 1499; 1552
>
>Antiphon
>
>II
>
>Cited as a chant that descends to *A re*, and which begins on *D*, thus illustrating an initial note of its mode.
>
>**AS** 41 (with descent to *A* at the words *nos viam*)

Omnes sitientes
>1533–5; 1577; 1579
>
>Antiphon
>
>VII
>
>Cited as a chant that begins on *d*, thus illustrating an initial note of its mode; also cited for its ascent to *g* at the word *querite*.
>
>**AM** 188, **AR** 214, **AS** 13, **LA** 6, **LU** 324

Omnis
>1559
>
>See *Omnis pulchritudo.*

Omnis pulchritudo
>1503; 1559
>
>Responsory
>
>II
>
>Cited as a chant that ascends to *d*, thus illustrating the capacity of its mode to ascend seven notes above the final.
>
>**AS** 268, **LA** 245, **LR** 97, **PM** 85–6, **WA** 147 (all ascending to *d* at the words *est super*)

Paganorum multitudo
>1516
>
>[Antiphon]
>
>V
>
>Cited as a chant that begins on *F*, thus illustrating an initial note of its mode. Compare John, *De musica*, p. 121; HGJ, p. 142 (with transcription of opening of **AR** 626).
>
>**AM** 809, **AR** 626, **AS** 411–12, **LA** 364, **WA** 276

Pauli

    1561
    III
    Possibly to be identified with *Pauli diem Pauli fidem*
    (Stäblein, *Hymnen*, melody 505).

Populus Syon

    1532; 1577
    Introit
    VII
    Cited as a chant that begins on *c*, thus illustrating an initial note of
    its mode. Compare John, *De musica*, p. 193 (Tonary).
    GB 2v, **GS** 2, **SYG** 3

Post excessum beatissimi

    1485–6
    Antiphon
    I
    Cited as a chant that begins on *C*, thus illustrating an initial note of
    its mode.
    AS 596, **WA** 403

Post partum virgo

    1512
    [Antiphon]
    IV
    Cited as a chant that begins on *G*, thus illustrating an initial note of
    its mode.
    None of the sources consulted begins on *G*

Preparate corda vestra domino

    1771
    Responsory
    I (beginning), III (end)
    Cited for moving from mode I to mode III. Compare John, *De
    musica*, p. 83; HGJ, p. 118.
    WA 166

Principes persecuti sunt me
2023; 2238–9
Communion
At the word *concupivit* bad singers sing as *b molle* what they should raise to *c*; also cited as a chant that is badly constructed because its modal character is mixed.
GB 229v, **GS** 230–1

Probasti domine
2025
Gradual
At the words *igne me* bad singers begin on *F* what they should sing on *c* above. Compare John, *De musica*, p. 105; HGJ, p. 130.
GB 217v, **GR** 579, **GS** 194, **LU** 1594–5, **SYG** 213

Propter insuperabilem
2149
[Antiphon]
Cited as a chant that matches the joyful subject matter of its text with leaps.
AS 63 and 429, **LA** 49, **WA** 38 (all at different pitch levels)

Quando natus es
2035–6
Antiphon
III
Compare John, *De musica*, pp. 107–8; HGJ, p. 132.
AM 271, **AR** 294, **AS** 79, **LA** 64, **LU** 443, **WA** 50

Qui cum audissent
1518; 2256–7
Responsory
V
Cited to illustrate the capacity of its mode to ascend to *g in linea*, and because at the word *clemenciam* there is a pleasing melodic repetition. Compare John, *De musica*, p. 119; HGJ, pp. 138–9.
AS 357–8, **WA** 240

Example 7. Source: **WA** 240.

cle–   men–

ci - am.

Qui de terra est
> 2035
> Antiphon
> III
> Compare John, *De musica*, pp. 107–8; HGJ, p. 132.
> **AS** 75–6, **LA** 63, **WA** 49

Qui habitat
> 2252
> Tract
> Cited because at the words *refugium meum deus meus* there is a
> needless repetition of the same interval. Compare John, *De musica*,
> p. 119; HGJ, p. 138 (with transcription of the relevant passage from
> **LA** 533).
> **GB** 65, **GR** 95, **SYG** 73 (all with the repetition in its most emphatic
> form), **GS** 35, **LA** 533 (with some reduction of the repetition)

Qui sedes domine
> 2021
> Gradual
> Bad singers descend too far at the words *super cherubim.* Compare
> John, *De musica*, pp. 104–5; HGJ, p. 130.
> **GB** 5v, **GR** 7, **GS** 4, **LA** 335, **SYG** 6

Quodcumque ligaveris
> 1538
> [Antiphon]
> VIII
> Cited as a chant that begins on *a*, thus illustrating an initial note of
> its mode.
> **AM** 825, 937 and 991, **AR** 600 and 753, **AS** 414 and 448, **LA** 420, **LU**
> 1517, **WA** 277

Quod dico vobis in tenebris
> 1444
> Communion
> Deuterus
> Cited as a chant which does not observe the proper course of the
> Deuterus.
> **GB** 231, **GR** 3, **GS** 220, **LU** 1173

Reges Tharsis
> 1687
> Antiphon
> I
> Cited as a chant that is of mode I, despite other indications, because
> it proceeds to its final *curialiter et paulatim*, as authentic modes do.
> Compare *Circumdantes [circumdederunt me]*, *Nisi [ego abiero]* and *Volo*
> *pater.* Compare John, *De musica*, p. 166 (Tonary); HGJ, p. 165.
> **AS** 85, **LA** 67, **LR** 70, **WA** 53

Repleti sunt omnes
    1538
    [Antiphon]
    VIII
    Cited as a chant that begins on *G*, thus indicating an initial note of its mode.
    AM 521, **LA** 254 and 261, **LU** 884, **WA** 63 and 153

Rex [seculorum quem laudat]
    2200
    [Antiphon]
    VI
    WA 301

Sancta et immaculata es virgo
    1441
    Responsory
    Protus
    Cited as a chant that ends on *a*, one of the *viceclaves* of its mode.

Sanctus, sanctus, sanctus
    1517
    V
    Cited as a chant that begins on *c in linea*, thus illustrating an initial note of its mode.

Sapientia clamitat
    1536–7; 1541; 1584
    Antiphon
    VIII
    Cited as a chant that begins on *c*, thus illustrating an initial note of its mode, which is also the lowest note of its mode. Compare John, *De musica*, p. 196 (Tonary); HGJ, p. 185.
    AM 581, **AR** 545, **AS** 307–8, **LA** 281, **LU** 990–91, **WA** 168

Solvite templum hoc
> 1516
> [Antiphon]
> V
> Cited as a chant that begins on *a*, thus illustrating an initial note of its mode.
> **AM** 376, **AR** 401, **AS** 188, **LA** 164, **LU** 1094, **WA** 104

Spiritus domini [replevit orbem]
> 1537
> [Antiphon]
> VIII
> Cited as a chant that begins on *D*, thus illustrating an initial note of its mode.
> **AM** 520 and 1076, **LU** 884 and 1677

Sub trono dei
> 2002
> Antiphon
> Cited as a chant that is begun in the same way by various singers, but ended differently.
> **AM** 261, **AR** 284, **AS** 71, **LA** 61, **LU** 431, **WA** 46 (showing considerable variation)

Tanto tempore
> 1513
> Responsory
> IV
> Cited as a chant that descends to *B*, thus illustrating the capacity of its mode to do so.
> **PM** 151 (at the words *vobiscum sum*)

Te
> 1561
> See *Te semper idem.*

Te semper idem
>   1506–7; 1561
>   [Antiphon]
>   III
>   Cited as a chant that begins on *G*, thus illustrating an initial note of
>   its mode. Compare John, *De musica*, p. 173 (Tonary); HGJ, p. 143.
>   **AS** 288, **WA** 158

Terribilis [est locus iste]
>   2029
>   [Responsory]
>   What bad singers sing among the *acuti* at the words *et porta celi* they
>   should sing at a lower pitch. Compare John, *De musica*, pp. 105–6;
>   HGJ, p. 130 (with transcription of **LR** 235).
>   **AS** p–q, **LR** 235, **WA** 317

Ter terni
>   1240
>   The didactic song attributed to Hermannus Contractus. Compare
>   John, *De musica*, pp. 70, 71 and 96; HGJ, p. 112, n. 6.

Testes
>   1571
>   VI
>   Cited as one of several chants of the plagal Tritus that take either *D*
>   or *F* as their initial note.
>   Unidentified.

Tota pulchra [es amica mea]
>   1512
>   [Antiphon]
>   IV
>   Cited as a chant that begins on *F*, thus illustrating an initial note of
>   its mode.
>   **AS** 490–91, **PM** 274, **VP** 54, **WA** 360

Tua sunt hec Christe
    1446
    Responsory
    V/VI
    Cited as a chant that takes *c,* not *F,* as its final.
    The sources display mode I

Tuam domine
    1511
    [Antiphon]
    IV
    Cited as a chant that begins on *D,* thus illustrating an initial note of
    its mode.
    The sources begin on *G*

Tu puer propheta
    1692
    Communion
    Cited as a chant that moves to its close *cadendo sive precipitando,* as
    plagals do.
    GB 200v, **GR** 25, **GS** m, **LU** 1502, **SYG** 199

Venit
    1547
    See *Venit lumen.*

Venit lumen
    1487; 1547
    [Antiphon]
    I
    Cited as a chant that begins on *F,* thus illustrating an initial note of
    its mode.
    AM 290, **AR** 312, **AS** 89, **LA** 73, **LU** 463, **WA** 56

Verbum dei deo natum

1522

Sequence

VI

Cited as a chant which illustrates the capacity of its mode to touch *d*
peracuta and then to end on the *viceclavis c.*

AH 55:211–14 (listing numerous manuscripts and prints)

Veterem hominem

2148

[Antiphon]

Cited as a chant that matches the joyful subject matter of its text
with leaps. Compare John, *De musica*, p. 79; HGJ, p. 116.

AS 95, **LA** 78, **VP** 95, **WA** 58

Vigilate animo

1511–12

[Antiphon]

IV

Cited as a chant that begins on *E*, thus illustrating an initial note of
its mode.

AM 223, **AR** 248, **AS** 35, **LA** 25, **WA** 20

Virtute magna

1509

Responsory

III

Illustrates the capacity of its mode to ascend to *g acutus.*

LA 210, **LR** 87, **PM** 217–18, **WA** 133 and 305 (all, with the possible
exception of **LA**, only ascending to *f* at the cited point, the word
testimonium)

Volo pater
>   1687
>   Antiphon
>   I
>   Cited as a chant that is of mode I, despite other indications, because
>   it proceeds to its final *curialiter et paulatim*. Compare *Circumdantes
>   [cirumdederunt me]*, *Nisi [ego abiero]* and *Reges Tharsis*. Compare John,
>   *De musica*, p. 166 (Tonary); HGJ, p. 165.
>   **AM** 641, **AR** 16, **AS** 640, **LA** 441 and 527, **LU** 1126, **WA** 419

Vox exultantis
>   2200
>   VI
>   Unidentified.

Index auctorum